KV-030-559

REGIONAL ORGANIZATIONS AND THEIR RESPONSES TO COUPS

Measures, Motives and Aims

Franziska Hohlstein

BRISTOL
UNIVERSITY
PRESS

First published in Great Britain in 2022 by

Bristol University Press
University of Bristol
1–9 Old Park Hill
Bristol
BS2 8BB
UK
t: +44 (0)117 374 6645
e: bup-info@bristol.ac.uk

Details of international sales and distribution partners are available at bristoluniversitypress.co.uk

Cover design: Andrew Corbett
Front cover image: Alamy/SIPHIWE SIBEKO
Bristol University Press use environmentally responsible print partners.
Printed by CPI Group (UK) Ltd, Croydon, CR0 4YY

Contents

List of Figures and Tables

Figures

Tables

List of Abbreviations

AC	Arctic Council
ACC	Arab Cooperation Council
ACD	Asia Cooperation Dialogue
ACS	Association of Caribbean States
ACTO	Amazon Cooperation Treaty Organization
AIC	Akaike Information Criterion
AL	Arab League
ALADI	Latin American Integration Association
ALBA	Bolivarian Alliance for the Peoples of Our Americas
AMU	Arab Maghreb Union
ANDEAN	Andean Community
APEC	Asia-Pacific Economic Cooperation
ASEAN	Association of Southeast Asian Nations
AU	African Union
BEU	Benelux Economic Union
BIC	Bayesian Information Criterion
BIMSTEC	Bay of Bengal Initiative for Multi-Sectoral Technical and Economic Cooperation
BSEC	Black Sea Economic Cooperation
CACM	Central American Common Market
CAEU	Council of Arab Economic Unity
CALC	Cumbre de América Latina y el Caribe sobre Integración y Desarollo
CAREC	Central Asia Regional Economic Cooperation
CARICOM	Caribbean Community
CBSS	Council of Baltic Sea States
CCTS	Cooperation Council of Turkic Speaking States
CDP	Congress for Democracy and Progress
CDS	Democratic and Social Convention
CE	Conseil de l'Entente
CEEAC	Economic Community of Central African States
CEFTA	Central European Free Trade Association
CELAC	Community of Latin American and Caribbean States

CEMAC	Communauté économique et monétaire de l'Afrique centrale
CENI	National Independent Election Commission
CENSAD	Community of Sahel-Saharan States
CEPGL	Economic Community of the Great Lakes Countries
CIS	Commonwealth of Independent States
CNT	National Transition Council
CoE	Council of Europe
COMESA	Common Market for Eastern and Southern Africa
CPLP	Community of Portuguese Language Countries
CSRD	Supreme Council for the Restoration of Democracy
CSTO	Collective Security Treaty (Organization)
EAC	East African Community
EAEU	Eurasian Economic Union
ECO	Economic Cooperation Organization
ECOWAS	Economic Community of West African States
EEA	European Economic Area
EFTA	European Free Trade Association
EISA	Electoral Institute for Sustainable Democracy in Africa
EIU	Economist Intelligent Unit
EU	European Union
G5S	G5 du Sahel
GCC	Gulf Cooperation Council
GDP	gross domestic product
GGC	Gulf of Guinea Commission
GUAM	Organization for Democracy and Economic Development
GISAT-BF	International Follow-up and Support Group for the Transition in Burkina Faso
HAT	High Authority of the Transition
ICG	International Crisis Group
ICGLR	International Conference on the Great Lakes Region
ICG-M	International Contact Group on Madagascar
IGAD	Intergovernmental Authority on Development
IMF	International Monetary Fund
IO	international organization
IOC	Indean Ocean Commission
IORA	Indian Ocean Rim Association
IRI	International Republican Institute
LCBC	Lake Chad Basin Commission
MDC	Movement for Democratic Change
Mercosur	Mercado Commun del Sur
MGC	Mekong-Garga Cooperation

MNSD	National Movement for a Society of Development
MRC	Mekong River Commission
MRU	Manu River Union
MSG	Melanesian Spearhead Group
N	number of observations
NAFTA	North American Free Trade Agreement
NATO	North Atlantic Treaty Organization
NC	Nordic Council
NDI	National Democratic Institute
NGO	non–governmental organization
OAS	Organization of American States
OECS	Organization of Eastern Caribbean States
OIC	Organization of Islamic Cooperation
OIF	Organisation Internationale de la Francophonie
OSCE	Organization for Security and Cooperation in Europe
PA	Pacific Alliance
PIF	Pacific Islands Forum
RO	regional organization
RSP	Régiment de sécurité présidentielle
SAARC	South Asian Association for Regional Cooperation
SACU	Southern African Customs Union
SADC	Southern African Development Community
SCO	Shanghai Cooperation Organization
SELA	Latin American Economic System
SICA	Central American Integration System
SPC	Pacific Community
SPECA	Special Programme for the Economies of Central Asia
TIM	Tiako-I-Madagasikara
UEMOA	West African Economic and Monetary Union
UN	United Nations
UNASUR	Union of South American Nations
WTO	Warsaw Treaty Organization
ZANU-PF	Zimbabwe Africa National Union – Patriotic Front
ZAPU	Zimbabwe African People's Union
ZEC	Zimbabwe Electoral Commission
ZiOP model	Zero-inflated Ordered Probit

Acknowledgements

The research this book is based on was conducted during my PhD at the University of Freiburg. I thank Prof Dr Diana Panke and Prof Dr Sandra Destradi for their very engaged and thoughtful supervision and advice. I am especially grateful for the encouragement to publish this book.

A special thank you goes to my former colleagues Simone Ahrens, Dr Julia Gurol, Ingo Henneberg, Dr Stefan Lang, Gurur Polat, Anna Starkmann, Dr Sören Stapel and Anke Wiedemann, for supporting my research and this book, yet also for way more.

Finally, I want to thank my absolutely amazing family. Your trust and support at all times keeps me going.

1

Introduction

The empirical puzzle: regional organizations and coups d'état

> We reaffirm that coups are sad and unacceptable developments in our Continent, coming at a time when our people have committed themselves to respect of the rule of law based on peoples will expressed through the ballot and not the bullet. (OAU: Lomé Declaration, 2000)

During its summit in Harare in 1997, the Organization of African Unity (OAU) for the first time took a coherent and clear position vis-à-vis a coup d'état. In its final communiqué, the organization 'strongly and unequivocally condemn[ed], the coup d'etat which took place in Sierra Leone on 25 May, 1997; and call[ed] for the immediate restoration of constitutional order' (OAU, 1997).

Three years later, in 2000, the OAU agreed on the Lomé Declaration, an official and legally binding document which did not only include the fierce condemnation of unconstitutional changes of government cited above, but, importantly, also an unequivocal definition of which events are subsumed under this term and a list of potential measures and sanctions to be imposed against coup plotters (Lomé Declaration, 2000). In 2007, the organization's successor, the African Union (AU), confirmed and fortified this position in the African Charter on Democracy, Elections and Governance (African Charter on Democracy, Elections and Governance, 2007). Through all these steps, coups d'état or simply coups, defined as coercive and illegal attempts by parts of a country's elites to grab executive power from the ruling government, became shunned as reprehensible acts on the African continent. This general condemnation of coups did not only cover successful takeovers, but also failed coups.

This development was remarkable in more than one sense. To begin with, at the point of agreeing on the Lomé Declaration, the OAU was far from being a democratic organization. In the year 2000, only 10 out of the then 53 OAU member states qualified as democracies.[1] Ironically, a noticeable number of the heads of state and government signing the Lomé Declaration had themselves claimed power by violent and unconstitutional means. Yet, despite the very diverging degrees of democracy in the member states, the RO came up with this strong democratic norm. Furthermore, it was noteworthy that the OAU, an organization which had so far held the principles of national sovereignty and non-interference in the domestic politics of its member states sacrosanct, suddenly agreed on judging and condemning a political phenomenon clearly situated in the domestic realm (Coe, 2015). Finally, it was surprising that by signing the Harare communiqué, and later the Lomé Declaration and the African Charter on Democracy, Elections and Governance the OAU and its successor, the AU, exceeded the attempts of any other regional grouping and established the most far-reaching anti-coup regime (Souaré, 2018).

So was the establishment of stern anti-coup provisions and the increasingly active role of the OAU/AU after coups a remarkable, yet exceptional development? This book will illustrate that this is not the case. To the contrary, the development within the OAU/AU is not a unique and isolated process. For a long time, coups have been a worrisome, yet pervasive political phenomenon in many world regions (Powell & Thyne, 2011). Particularly in Africa, though also in Latin America and Asia, coups used to happen frequently. While some of them arouse considerable international attention, concern and sometimes also criticism, many of them were ignored or even welcomed. A prominent example is the 1973 coup in Chile against President Allende and the (alleged) support of the US for the Pinochet regime. Accordingly, international responses to coups have been described as muted, arbitrary and contradictory (Shannon et al, 2015; Thyne & Hitch, 2020).

In principle, three sorts of international actors can respond to coups: international organizations (IOs) on a global level, in particular the United Nations (UN), IOs on a regional level and third-country states. Responses by third-country states to coups are remarkably diverse and can come from a multitude of actors. On the one hand, Western states, especially former colonial powers and important donors, often respond to and criticize coups. On the other hand, neighbour states and regional allies of ousted governments frequently respond to coups, as they are often the ones most directly affected by coups. Although the actions of third-country states can play a powerful role in certain cases, they also bear their own problems. Uncoordinated unilateral action is often less effective to exert pressure on countries than a concerted approach (Bapat et al, 2013). Besides, multilateral action is also often perceived as more legitimate, as it limits the risk that single interveners exploit the weakness of target states for their own interests (Finnemore, 1996). Furthermore, external criticism and negative responses by Western states are often perceived as inappropriate interference in national affairs by states in the Global South (Acharya, 2011).

As an alternative to single states, the UN can tackle domestic conflicts and democratic flaws. Yet the record of the UN in dealing with violations against democratic norms is not particularly strong (Donno, 2013). The UN has increasingly highlighted democratic governance as an important goal of the organization (Newman & Rich, 2004), but attempts to push for a coherent and far-reaching UN position on democracy have often been impeded by autocratic members of the organization (Rushton, 2006). As a result, it has also proved difficult to establish a far-reaching anti-coup norm at the UN level (Tansey, 2018). While the UN has become involved in the aftermath of several coups in the past – for example after the takeovers in Ecuador in 2000 and Fiji in 2006 – many other cases were neglected or the UN could not agree on a common position.

This inconsistent approach of the UN opened doors for other actors. Regional organizations (ROs) combine the benefit of institutional legitimacy with a deep and inclusive knowledge about region-specific issues and dynamics, qualifying them as ideal candidates to deal with unconstitutional leader changes in their region. For the purpose of this book, ROs are defined as institutions in which at least three states cooperate on more than one single issue and in which membership is not universally open, but based on geographical, cultural or linguistic criteria, which all states have in common.[2] Due to their regional character, ROs are often directly affected by coups and have a strong rationale to grant stability and peace in their member states. As a result, ROs have sometimes been more effective in promoting peace, democratic governance and stability norms than other actors (Ackermann, 2003; Donno, 2013). Many authors have emphasized that ROs play a crucial role in not only fostering peace and stability, but also democracy and constitutionality in their member states as well as in other countries in their respective regions (Nguyen, 2002; Pevehouse, 2002b).

The member states of ROs delegate inter alia competencies in the realms of democracy and security policy to these organizations, which give them an actor-like quality to address such challenges. Some ROs have founded special bodies for this purpose, such as, for instance, the Peace and Security Council of the AU (Barbarinde, 2011). Of course, the extent of such delegation varies. While some ROs enjoy a considerable amount of autonomy, actorness and supranational power, many other ROs function in a rather intergovernmental way, with the interests and demands of the member states playing an important role (Börzel et al, 2012). Finding compromises and common positions under such conditions can be a big challenge for ROs, especially when the standpoints of different member states are diametrically opposed. Yet even in such cases, ROs have become the central institutions through which member states discuss, organize and align their responses to coups. While single states may act unilaterally after coups, the vast majority of states coordinate their responses with and do not deviate from the respective official RO position vis-à-vis a coup. Since the 1990s, ROs around the globe have begun to take strong action against coups. Many of these non-global IOs have adopted strict anti-coup policies and have become the common channels through which their member states coordinate and align their responses to coups. They have established a global consensus that coups constitute an unacceptable method of changing political leaders, which should lead to international condemnation and rejection (Legler & Tieku, 2010).

While the AU is one of the most prominent examples, many other ROs play an important role therein. When establishing its anti-coup and democracy regime, the AU was inspired by the anti-coup provisions of another large continental grouping, the Organization of American States (OAS). Seeking to impede and fight unconstitutional leader changes in the Americas, the OAS had likewise established a sophisticated anti-coup framework, equipped with an array of diplomatic and punitive measures to respond to coups (Arceneaux & Pion-Berli, 2007; Legler & Tieku, 2010). Furthermore, the European Union (EU) upholds strict expectations with regard to democratic and constitutional standards in its external partner countries, enshrined in a series of cooperation agreements, which do not tolerate coups (Santiso, 2002).

Inspired by the example of the OAS, AU and EU, a number of other ROs, have adopted anti-coup provisions and have taken action against states violating these provisions. These organizations include, inter alia, the Pacific Islands Forum (PIF), the Caribbean Community (CARICOM), the Andean Community (ANDEAN), the Economic Community of West African States (ECOWAS) and the Southern African Development Community (SADC). In Asia, the Association of Southeast Asian Nations (ASEAN) upheld for a long time a strict policy of not interfering in the internal affairs of its member states and usually responded hesitantly to coups. Yet this position noticeably changed after the coup in Myanmar in 2021, when ASEAN sought to mediate in the crisis and finally declined to invite the junta's representative General Hlaing to the ASEAN's October 2021 summit. The parallel development of anti-coup provisions in ROs all over the globe hints at a growing consensus that coups are not acceptable any longer and must be addressed by regional actors. In other words, ROs have emerged as the promoters and defenders of a global anti-coup norm.

The emergence of the anti-coup norm and particularly the strong role that ROs have played in establishing and enforcing this norm is indisputably an impressive achievement. The anti-coup norm addresses one of the major menaces to democratic and lawful rule and thereby advances democratic and constitutional principles in ROs and their member states (Leininger, 2014). Yet a thorough and complete evaluation of the role of ROs in the context of coups requires a nuanced perspective on the issue. ROs are extremely diverse with regard to their membership, norms and commitments. It is important to note that by far not all ROs pursue the promotion of democracy and constitutionality as an inherent goal. On the contrary, a considerable number of ROs worldwide, for example the Arab League (AL), the Eurasian Economic Union (EAEU), the Gulf Cooperation Council (GCC) and the Shanghai Cooperation Organization (SCO) mainly consist of autocratic or at best semi-democratic states. Recent research indicates that such autocratic ROs and their member states rarely have an interest in promoting democracy and rather seek to consolidate autocratic practices and norms (Ambrosio, 2008; Collins, 2009; Melnykovska et al, 2012; Odinius & Kuntz, 2015). The role of such organizations after coups is mainly neglected in the existing literature, as case studies on RO responses to coups usually focus on the 'positive cases' of ROs with strong democratic provisions and anti-coup norms, such as the AU or the OAS.

This raises the question of which role ROs really can and want to play after coups. Scholarly opinion on the issue is mixed. While some authors euphorically laud the accomplishments of ROs to exert the anti-coup norm and to address the issue of coups (for example Arceneaux & Pion-Berli, 2007; Souaré, 2014; Leininger, 2015), critics call into question that the anti-coup norm actually constitutes a strong global norm, leading to inconsistent and weak responses of ROs to coups (Ikome, 2007; Tansey, 2017; Wet, 2019). A glance at the empirical evidence indicates that responses of ROs to coups are remarkably diverse. In general, ROs have become considerably more active after coups over time (see Figure 1.1).

Since the end of the Cold War, when the first ROs committed themselves to the anti-coup norm and established respective anti-coup provisions, the number of coups has declined. At the same time, the average number of RO responses to each coup has significantly increased. The risk of facing a coup is not evenly distributed. More than two-thirds of the coups since the 1990s took place in Africa (68.14 per cent), followed by Asia (15.56 per cent) and the Americas (11.85 per cent), while only few coups were staged in Oceania (3.70 per cent) and Europe (0.74 per cent). This distribution is only partially mirrored by the level of activity of ROs. The RO which most frequently responded to coups since the 1990s is the EU (62 times), followed by the AU (45), ECOWAS (23) and the OAS (12). In contrast, RO responses to coups in Asia are comparatively rare. Generally, one can observe that on all continents there are organizations which actively and frequently address the coups occurring in their region and others which have never responded to a single coup.

A closer look at the measures taken by ROs shows that they cover a large variety of policy instruments. RO responses to coups range from rhetorical concern statements and condemnations, over diplomatic measures (for

Figure 1.1: Global number of coups and RO responses to them, 1990–2019

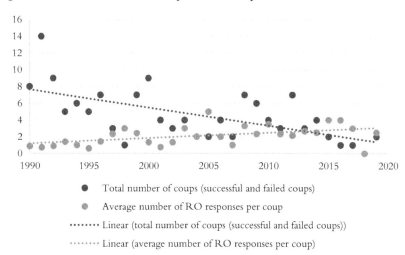

Source: Author's depiction, based on the data collected for this book

example mediation attempts and the suspension from RO decision-making bodies) to economic sanctions and culminate in the potential use of military force against coup plotters. ROs vary in their use of these instruments, with some organizations restraining themselves to the use of less severe instruments (for example rhetorical criticism) and others using stronger penalties such as economic sanctions. Yet often also one and the same RO imposes instruments of completely diverging strength to different coups. This apparent inconsistency in the way ROs respond to different unconstitutional takeovers indicates that the role of ROs in this context is more complex than being an unforgiving, penalizing authority.

Finally, ROs do not only vary with regard to the measures they apply and their strength, but also regarding the political solutions they pursue through these measures. Following coups, ROs can work towards different post-coup solutions, which include the reinstatement of the former government, the holding of new elections, a power-sharing agreement between rival parties and the acceptance of the coup plotters as new rulers. The choice of one of these solutions varies between cases. For example, ROs succeeded in restoring constitutional order in São Tomé und Príncipe in 2003 and the ousted President de Menezes was reinstated. In 2019, the coup against President al-Bashir in Sudan evoked strong external pressure from the AU and EU on the coup plotters to concede to a joint interim government with the protesters. In contrast, after the coup in Thailand in 2014, the military junta stayed in power.

In sum, one can say that RO responses to coups are extremely diverse, indicating that the role of ROs after coups is a complex and multidimensional one. Over the course of this book, this role of ROs is analysed by examining three specific, yet interrelated research questions:

1. First, what measures do ROs use to respond to coups?
2. Second, which factors influence the choice of stronger or weaker responses?
3. Third, which post-coup solutions do ROs pursue through their responses and why?

The first question is descriptive in nature, as it seeks to provide an overview of the responses of ROs to coups across regions and over time. In mapping the responses of ROs, reaching from neutral rhetorical statements over condemnations, mediation, diplomatic and economic sanctions to the (threat of) use of force, a global picture of the role of ROs after coups is provided. In contrast, the second and third question are explanatory in nature. The second question addresses the apparent and oftentimes deplored fact that ROs sanction some coups considerably stronger than others (Shannon et al, 2015; Wet, 2019). Through examining the factors determining the strength of RO responses after coups, the book sheds light on the rationale of ROs to respond to coups through instruments of varying intensity. The third question finally moves one step beyond the immediate responses to coups and focuses on the long-term political solutions pursued by ROs. In particular, it explores under which conditions ROs strive for differential post-coup solutions, including the reinstatement of the former government, new elections, power-sharing agreements or the acceptance of the coup plotters as new government.

So how can the variety and diversity of RO reactions to coups be explained? Existing studies pay remarkably scant attention to this question. Coups have constituted a phenomenon of scholarly interest for a long time (for example Finer, 1962; Thompson, 1974; Nordlinger, 1977; David, 1987; O'Kane, 1987) and in recent years there has been a renewed interest in the topic. However, the overwhelming majority of studies concentrates on the factors determining the risk of coups (Galetovic & Sanhueza, 2000; Collier & Hoeffler, 2005; Lindberg & Clark, 2008; Tusalem, 2010; Miller, 2012; Hiroi & Omori, 2013; Casper & Tyson, 2014; Lehoucq & Pérez-Liñán, 2014; Hiroi & Omori, 2015; Arbatli & Arbatli, 2016; Gassebner et al, 2016; Houle, 2016; Johnson & Thyne, 2016; Kim, 2016; Marcum & Brown, 2016; Piplani & Talmadge, 2016; Powell & Chacha, 2016; Wig & Rød, 2016; Bell & Sudduth, 2017; Gerling, 2017; Houle & Bodea, 2017; Pérez-Liñán & Polga-Hecimovich, 2017; Powell et al, 2018; Rabinowitz & Jargowsky, 2018; Sudduth & Bell, 2018; Böhmelt et al, 2019; Rozenas & Zeigler, 2019; Schiel, 2019; Schiel et al, 2020).

Other frequently examined issues are coup-proofing strategies of state leaders who seek to prevent coups (Belkin & Schofer, 2003; Roessler, 2011; Pilster & Böhmelt, 2012; Powell, 2014b; Albrecht, 2015; Böhmelt & Pilster,

2015; Brown et al, 2015; de Bruin, 2018, 2020; Powell, 2019; Escribà-Folch et al, 2020; Reiter, 2020) and the domestic consequences of unconstitutional takeovers (Fosu, 2002; Miller, 2011; Marinov & Goemans, 2014; Gong & Rao, 2016; Thyne & Powell, 2016; Chacha & Powell, 2017; Thyne, 2017; Bjørnskov et al, 2018; Easton & Siverson, 2018; Nugraha, 2018; Powell et al, 2019; Curtice & Arnon, 2020; Lachapelle, 2020).

In contrast, the literature on the international responses to coups is comparatively scarce. There are a number of insightful qualitative (comparative) case studies on the responses of a particular RO to several coups (Cooper & Legler, 2005; Arceneaux & Pion-Berli, 2007; Barracca, 2007; Ikome, 2007; Engel, 2010; Omorogbe, 2011; Trithart, 2013; Webber & Gordon, 2013; Grauvogel, 2015; Nathan, 2016c). But the existing body of literature on the responses of ROs to coups is characterized by a significant selection bias. The vast majority of studies on RO responses to coups focuses on a small number of very prominent and active ROs, including the AU, ECOWAS or the OAS. Notwithstanding the attractiveness of these ROs as objects of study, the strong focus on them has led to the situation that researchers know a lot about the strategies of the AU to fight unconstitutional takeovers, while knowledge on how and why most smaller ROs respond to coups is practically non-existent. This lack of systematic data across ROs is highly problematic, as it impedes a comprehensive and valid evaluation of the global picture of responses of ROs to coups. Besides, the focus of many existing studies concentrates on whether ROs apply the anti-coup norm in a consistent manner or not. As a consequence, they often find that RO responses do vary in their stance towards different coups but put little attention on the question why this is the case. In an insightful quantitative study, Shannon et al (2015) seek to explain why some coups draw more international attention than others. However, the authors primarily focus on explaining the number of responses and not accounting for the diverse forms such RO reactions may take or potential post-coup solutions pursued by them.

This book intends to fill these gaps in the existing scholarship and to contribute to a better understanding of the empirical puzzle of diverse, apparently inconsistent and oftentimes contradictory responses of ROs to coups. In the following, an argument which exceeds the existing theoretical approaches and accounts for the complex role of ROs in the context of coups is developed.

The argument

So how can one understand the role of ROs in the context of coups? How do ROs respond to coups and what is their rationale for doing so? A temptingly simple answer would be that ROs condemn and sanction coups because the anti-coup norm requires them to do so. The anti-coup norm condemns all coups alike as deplorable, intolerable acts (Varol, 2012). Since the 1990s, the norm has not only gained considerably in strength, but safeguarded a particularly prominent position in ROs. Thereby, the norm constitutes an essential guiding principle for the generally adverse position of ROs to coups. The deep commitment of many ROs to the anti-coup norm is mirrored in numerous explicit and extensive anti-coup provisions in ROs (Wobig, 2015). Equipped with, yet also bound to such provisions, it is no surprise that ROs regularly follow them.

Obviously, this is an unsatisfactory, partial answer at best. Arguing that ROs oppose coups because the anti-coup norm requests them to do so bluntly ignores the agency of ROs in the development of the norm. ROs constitute the key actors who established, fortified and promoted the anti-coup norm in the past and they continue to do so in the present. While states have been hesitant to constrain their own policies towards countries hit by coups through established and binding rules and the UN has been paralysed by the diverging interests of the major powers in the security council, ROs have taken the lead in the fight against coups (Tansey, 2017). They have taken a conscious decision to address the issue of coups in their member states and to establish a strong international norm against them. Yet which motives drive this step? Why do ROs oppose coups, particularly in their member states?

Coups are a tangible, yet nonetheless complex political phenomenon. On the one hand, they constitute a clear violation of democratic norms and principles. Taking power by force is an obvious and blatant breach of any idea of peaceful and ordered democratic procedures of leadership change (d'Aspremont, 2010). On the other hand, coups constitute a form of violent domestic conflict, as powerful elites compete with an incumbent for power by violent means. As such, coups also threaten the stability of affected states and the surrounding region. Hence, for truly understanding the role of ROs after coups, two perspectives are paramount.

The first and generally more prominent perspective in the literature is the concern about and commitment to basic democratic principles of many ROs. Obviously, understandings and definitions of democracy as well as the extent of commitment to democracy vary tremendously between regions and across different organizations (Sousa Santos, 2005; McMahon & Baker, 2006). Yet the act of staging a coup is hardly compatible with any conception of democracy. To the contrary, staging a coup constitutes a profoundly undemocratic act. In a coup, a small group of actors takes power from the incumbent government by force (Powell & Thyne, 2011). This does not only run counter to democratic standards which denounce such use of violence as a political measure. It also grossly violates against the very basic idea of representative democracy that leaders of a political entity must be legitimized by a mandate of the people (Coppedge, 2012). Moreover, coups can seriously undermine the confidence of the population in democratic processes per se. In particular, the occurrence of several subsequent unconstitutional takeovers carries the risk of detrimentally changing the political culture of a country and impairing the citizens' confidence in its political institutions (Farrelly, 2013). Countries such as Haiti, Venezuela, Burundi, Sudan and Thailand have all faced more than ten successful and failed coups in the past, making unconstitutional takeovers a common way of leader change.

In short, coups can be described as very blunt and open challenges to basic democratic norms. As a consequence, the opposition of ROs to coups is often framed as part and parcel of their general commitment to democracy and rule of law in their region. In the course of subsequent waves of democratization and an increased emphasis on democracy promotion, a rising number of ROs have committed themselves to democratic norms. They have emerged as key actors to promote and protect democratic standards in their member states (Pevehouse, 2002a, 2002b, 2005; McMahon & Baker, 2006). In the democracy regimes of many ROs, the anti-coup norm and the respective provisions against coups form an essential cornerstone (Legler & Tieku, 2010). Coups constitute a direct, massive and clearly identifiable threat to democracy. Therefore, it is easier to reach intra-organizational consensus on this issue than on more ambiguous topics such as the separation of powers or civil rights (McCoy, 2006). For many ROs, the anti-coup norm is a basic, unequivocal democratic standard all member states can agree on – even if other questions about democracy are disputed among those states. From this perspective, ROs with at least a basic democratic commitment address coups because they cannot tolerate that their essential democratic norms are grossly violated against by rebelling armed elites.

Concerns about democracy undoubtedly played an essential role in establishing the anti-coup norm in ROs. Yet perceiving coups exclusively as a form of violation of democratic principles falls short of completely grasping the complexity of the phenomenon. Undeniably, coups violate democratic principles. But they also constitute a non-negligible risk to the stability of a state. Countries such as Myanmar, Sudan and Mali, which have been hit by coups in recent years, suffer from significant ongoing political instability and a high level of violence. Therefore, the second crucial perspective to understand the role of ROs after coups is through a stability-oriented perspective.

The ousting of a sitting government through violent means is always a critical, not to say dangerous, moment for a state. But coups differ in their extent of violence and the number of casualties they claim (de Bruin, 2019). Some coups are swiftly conducted, meet little resistance and therefore result in a comparatively limited death toll. In some cases, even the credible threat to apply force can suffice to coerce state leaders to step down (Powell &

Thyne, 2011). For instance, when soldiers in Honduras arrested and exiled President Zelaya in 2009, they did not meet any noticeable resistance and the coup proceeded without causing any deaths or injuries (Webber & Gordon, 2013). But on other occasions coups have triggered intense and violent fighting between supporters of the incumbent regime and the coup plotters. For example, the successful coup in the Central African Republic in 2003 claimed 300 casualties (Marshall & Marshall, 2019).

Regardless of the precise extent of violence, due to the very nature of coups as leader changes via force, they constitute a form of civil conflict. As such, the responses of regional actors cannot only be looked upon from a democracy, but also from a stability perspective. There is abundant comparative literature on the security governance of ROs (Kirchner & Dominguez, 2011; Söderbaum & Tavares, 2011; Tavares, 2011; Boulden, 2013; Ahmed, 2016; Koga, 2016; Worrall, 2017). Generally speaking, ROs have a strong rationale to preserve regional stability and to address violent conflicts in their area. The security interests of the member states are a key driver for RO action. On the one hand, the idea of mutual assistance and solidarity requires member states of a RO to come to the help of their peers in case of danger. On the other hand, RO member states also have a strong self-interest to resolve or if not possible to at least contain conflicts in their neighbour states. If they fail to do so, spillover effects of conflict and political instability through the smuggling of arms, refugee flows and cross-border ethnic ties may occur (Salehyan & Gleditsch, 2006; Black, 2013; Cederman et al, 2013). A successful coup in one country can likewise fuel hopes and ambitions of dissatisfied elites in neighbour countries and therefore constitutes a source of concern for state leaders of those countries (Miller et al, 2018).

As a consequence, irrespective of the presence or absence of democratic commitments, ROs have a natural interest to condemn and sanction coups for stability reasons. Cynically, one could describe the anti-coup norm as a useful instrument to protect state leaders united in a RO from challengers to their rule, regardless of whether they are democratically elected or not. Yet this notion falls short of comprehensively understanding the relevance of stability aspects in the context of coups. When mediating in the aftermath of coups, ROs pay not only attention to the issue of democratization in a country, but also are concerned with finding compromise between fierce political rivals, preventing further violence and providing security for the population (Nathan, 2016c). Hence, apart from the common framing as democratic exercise, the responses of ROs to coups can alternatively been labelled as 'peacemaking enterprise' (Dersso, 2017).

Thus, for understanding when, how and why ROs respond to coups, it is important to take democracy as well as stability-related considerations into account. A combination of arguments from both explanatory approaches is well-suited to explain the complex pattern of RO responses to coups. In the course of the emergence of the anti-coup norm, many ROs established firm anti-coup provisions which denounce any coup as an intolerable act. However, such an undifferentiated rejection of any unconstitutional takeover is incapable of accounting for the diversity and complexity of coups. Coups are tremendously diverse with regard to their causes, circumstances and consequences (Hiroi & Omori, 2013; Thyne & Powell, 2016; de Bruin, 2019). Whereas coups against democratically legitimized leaders can have devastating consequences for the state of democracy in a country, the fall of long-lasting autocrats through coups can under certain circumstances open a window of opportunity for democratization (Powell, 2014a; Thyne & Powell, 2016). While some coups result in chaos, violence and refugee flows which destabilize the region, others are conducted in a swift and bloodless manner, significantly reducing the risk of regional instability (Miller et al, 2018).

When deciding whether and how to respond to a particular coup, ROs do not turn a blind eye to such issues. Instead, within the general framework of the anti-coup norm, they weigh the democracy- and stability-related aspects of a coup and try to assess the expected consequences of a coup on the state of democracy and security in the affected country. These assessments of ROs are naturally influenced by the characteristics of the ROs and their member states. But there is a common pattern: The more detrimental the effect of a coup on the state of democracy of a country is, the higher the likelihood that ROs will impose strong sanctions. Likewise, the higher the security risks associated with a coup are, the more likely it becomes that the coup plotters will face strong punitive measures by ROs. In a similar manner, democracy- and stability-related aspects also shape the choice of possible post-coup solutions by ROs. When deciding on which post-coup solution to pursue, the enthusiasm of ROs to back ousted incumbents as well as the willingness to make concessions to coup plotters depend on the impact of a coup on democracy and stability in the affected state. The democratic legitimacy of the ousted incumbent and the chances of democratization under the leadership of the new rulers are essential democracy-related considerations in this regard. In contrast, the domestic power constellation constitutes an influential stability-related factor.

To summarize, ROs do not treat all coups alike. The anti-coup norm serves as an important guiding principle for a general rejection of coups. Yet within the framework of the anti-coup norm, ROs enjoy discretion on how precisely to respond to a coup. When faced with a coup, ROs do not automatically impose the same set of measures and voice demands for a particular post-coup solution. Instead, they make a careful assessment of the circumstances of the case at hand, on the basis of which they take their decision. The presence and strength of RO responses to coups as well as the choice of differential post-coup solutions depend on the democracy- and stability-related implications of the coup for the affected country and the surrounding region.

Research design

For theoretically situating and grounding the research questions, the book makes use of norm theoretical elements. Based on the research on international norms, the anti-coup norm is first introduced as the central normative framework guiding the responses of ROs to coups. Building thereon, it is subsequently explored how the general goals of ROs to promote democracy and to grant stability have contributed to the emergence of the norm and continue to shape the role of ROs after coups. In a first step, the author conceptualizes which measures ROs use to respond to coups (research question 1). On this basis, expectations on the factors determining the choice of stronger or weaker responses are developed (research question 2). Finally, expectations about which post-coup solutions ROs pursue through their responses and why they do so are formulated (research question 3). In laying out the theoretical framework, a differentiated perspective on the complex role of ROs after coups is taken, which incorporates RO-specific factors, democracy-related arguments, as well as security-based considerations of the respective ROs.

In order to answer the research questions and to examine the plausibility of the theoretically derived expectations on a sound empirical basis, a mixed-methods approach is applied. Mixed methods can be defined as 'research that involves collecting, analysing, and interpreting quantitative and qualitative data in a single study or in a series of studies that investigate the same underlying phenomenon' (Leech & Onwuegbuzie, 2009). The term comprises a set of attempts by political scientists to combine different methodological approaches to achieve more thorough and reliable results (Timans et al, 2019). In the present case, the use of mixed-methods techniques is particularly advisable. Given the varying methodological requirements of the different research questions, quantitative techniques alone would fall short of providing satisfactory insights into the role of ROs in the context of coups. The same applies for purely qualitative techniques. A combination of quantitative and qualitative approaches enables the researcher to gain insights from different sources and methodologies: on the one hand, the use of quantitative data to examine the first and second research questions allows for a systematic comparison and evaluation of the behaviour of many ROs across cases and thereby grants a high degree of generalizability. On the other hand, the choice of qualitative case studies for the answering the third research question provides the opportunity to investigate in greater detail which role ROs played in particular cases.

The first research question asks what measures ROs use to respond to coups. Based on an extensive media analysis, RO responses to coups from 1990 until 2019 are coded in a systematic and comparable manner. Subsequently, descriptive statistics are used to map the data along several dimensions including variation over time, between continents and ROs, choice of instruments and RO strategies to illustrate the most important patterns in the data.

The second research question investigates which factors influence the choice of stronger or weaker RO responses to coups. Using the data from the first part of the analysis, a continuum of RO responses of increasing strength is developed. This measure is then used in a quantitative analysis to explore which explanatory factors account for the varying strength of RO responses across cases. As ROs face a dual decision of first whether to and second how strongly to respond to coups, zero-inflated ordered probit models are used in the analysis, which account for this dual-decision methodologically.

Finally, the third question examines what post-coup solutions ROs pursue through their responses and why. In contrast to the previous two research questions, this one is extremely challenging to explore in a large-N design. The conditions leading ROs to favour one post-coup solution over another are often complex and highly case-specific. Therefore, in the last part of the book, a small-N comparative case study design is adopted, examining the post-coup situation in the four cases of Madagascar (2009), Niger (2010), Burkina Faso (2015) and Zimbabwe (2017).

As such, the final qualitative part adds essential supplementary insights to the results of the quantitative parts. The descriptive analysis in the first part of the analysis outlines the general pattern of RO responses to coups. The explanatory statistics in the second part examine the factors accounting for the presence and strength of RO responses. While the first two parts already provide important insights how and why ROs respond to coups, the qualitative part enriches the overall analysis in two ways. First, by shifting the research focus from the instruments applied to the post-coup solution pursued by ROs, the qualitative part raises the important question of the intentions behind the decision to impose certain policy instruments. Second, by investigating a small number of cases in greater detail, the case studies allow us to shed light on some potentially important factors which are hard to quantify in a large-N study.

Findings and contributions

In short, the most essential findings stemming from this book can be summarized as follows: the first descriptive part shows that as over time more and more ROs received a mandate to respond to coups, the number of RO responses to coups has considerably increased. Yet these responses are characterized by a tremendously high degree of variation and no clear trend towards the use of stronger instruments is visible. Instead, regional differences catch the eye. In Africa and America, coups are more frequently condemned and sanctioned than in Asia and Oceania. Some ROs, like the AU, the OAS or the EU, are quite active after coups, while many smaller organizations have only taken action in a very limited number of cases. There is not only cross-regional and cross-organizational variation. Likewise, the responses by one and the same RO to different coups often vary. While some takeovers are only mildly criticized or even completely ignored by a RO, others are followed by harsh diplomatic, economic or even military sanctions. Hence, there is no common blueprint for ROs on how to respond to a coup. Instead, the pattern of RO responses to coups is remarkably diverse.

So which factors determine whether a RO shows a stronger or weaker response to a coup? The results of the quantitative examination in the second part of the analysis imply that ROs with binding democratic commitments are relatively consistent in their decision to respond to successful coups in their member states. The strength of these responses greatly depends on the characteristics of the RO and its member states and normative concerns about democracy-related consequences of coups, yet also on stability-oriented considerations. In responding to coups, ROs do not act arbitrarily. Instead, they follow a selective pattern, seeking to reconcile the principles of the anti-coup norm with other norms and interests held by their member states.

Finally, the insights from the last part of the analysis cast doubts on the willingness of ROs to always enforce the principles of the anti-coup norm in the aftermath of coups. The comparative case study of four coups – in Madagascar (2009), Niger (2010), Burkina Faso (2015) and Zimbabwe (2017) – shows that depending on the context, ROs pursue very different post-coup solutions through their measures, out of which some are not compatible with the anti-coup norm. The reasons for doing so lie within contradictions of the anti-coup norm with alternative concerns about the democratic situation in particular countries, yet also in pragmatic considerations about the domestic power constellation. For instance, ROs have repeatedly favoured and pushed towards post-coup solutions in which coup plotters played an ongoing and influential role.

Presenting this analysis contributes to the research on ROs and coups in three important ways. The first contribution concerns conceptual and theoretical aspects. The phenomenon of coups and the international responses towards them have attracted a lot of scholarly attention in recent years (Johnson & Thyne, 2016; Masaki, 2016; Piplani & Talmadge, 2016; Pérez-Liñán & Polga-Hecimovich, 2017; Varol, 2017; Powell et al, 2018; Tansey, 2018; Rozenas & Zeigler, 2019; Witt, 2020). Yet many studies take an overly narrow perspective on coups, either reducing them to strategic moves in a fight for power with severe security implications (Casper & Tyson, 2014; Singh, 2014; Böhmelt & Pilster, 2015; Böhmelt et al, 2019; de Bruin, 2019) or portraying them exclusively as violations of democratic norms (Engel, 2010; Leininger, 2014; Tansey, 2016b). In fact, coups are both. In order to appropriately account for the multi-dimensionality of coups, stability- and democracy-oriented theoretical arguments are combined and reconciled in this book. Thereby, the ground for thoroughly theorizing and understanding the complex decision-making mechanisms which underlie RO responses to coups is provided. In essence, the study seeks to explore the potential of ROs in two domains: first, to resolve violent intra-state conflicts in their member states and to avert resulting risks to the stability of the affected state and the region as a whole, and second, to act as promoters of democratic norms and values and to successfully assert such central norms in their sphere of influence.

In the light of this duality, a critical look at the anti-coup norm is taken, examining its potentials, yet also its limitations in shaping RO responses to coups. Previous studies have often portrayed the anti-coup norm as a narrowly defined directive for ROs of how to respond to coups, whose 'consistent' application is the subject of many studies (Ikome, 2007; Shannon et al, 2015; Nathan, 2016c). Yet outlining the argument and testing it empirically shows that for understanding the responses of ROs to coups, it is more insightful to perceive the anti-coup norm as a broadly defined guiding principle, within which ROs enjoy the leeway to weigh the implications of a coup for the regional democracy and security situation. The anti-coup norm is no isolated, intangible principle. Instead, it influences and is influenced by other norms and interests of ROs and their member states. In taking such a perspective, the book makes an important contribution to the emerging literature on the interaction and mutual influence of diverse norms (Nathan, 2016b; Fehl, 2018; Lantis & Wunderlich, 2018), as well as the interplay of norms with interests (Shannon, 2000; Cortell & Davis, 2005). In addition to formulating a theoretical account of why ROs respond to coups, the book also conceptualizes the instruments ROs use to do so. Based on insights from the literature on foreign policy instruments and intervention mechanisms, a systematic conceptualization of RO responses to coups is developed, accounting for the underlying logics, mechanisms and strength of different policy instruments. Such a conceptualization is very helpful for systematically and objectively capturing, comparing and analysing the responses of different ROs to coups.

The second contribution of the book relates to methodological aspects. In using a mixed-methods design, the assets of a systematic quantitative analysis across a high number of coups are meaningfully combined with the deeper insights drawn from the qualitative study of a small number of carefully selected cases. While research on coups and the international responses to them has increased, the vast majority of studies in the realm are qualitative in nature. Single case studies or comparisons between a small number of cases make up the bulk of the literature. They provide invaluable insights into the reasons and consequences of, as well as the responses to coups. Yet the caveat is that the vast majority of studies focus on few prominent ROs, such as the AU or the OAS. By contrast, very little is known about the role of smaller, less prominent and active ROs. The present book fills this gap by systematically collecting and comparing the responses of all ROs in a large-N design.

Notwithstanding, a purely quantitative analysis of the role of ROs after coups would face certain problems. Much of the existing literature points towards the fact that RO responses to coups are often strongly context-dependent, in the sense that country-specific factors, character traits of the protagonists and personal ties play an important role (Cooper & Legler, 2005; Hartmann, 2017). As such factors are hard to grasp for a large number of cases, the best solution is combining the quantitative and qualitative techniques in a mixed-methods design. Taken together, the quantitative and qualitative parts of the analysis add up and provide novel insights.

The third and final contribution is an empirical one. Despite the renewed interest in the phenomenon of coups, systematic and comparable data on responses to coups across ROs are missing so far. The present book makes an important empirical contribution in this regard by creating the first encompassing and global dataset on RO responses to coups. In examining the responses of ROs to coups, the book makes use of a multitude of quantitative and qualitative data from different sources. The systematic and comprehensive data collection process in the first part of the analysis resulted in a novel and innovative dataset of RO responses to coups. These data do not only constitute a solid foundation for the analysis in the quantitative parts of the book but can also be used to explore a series of future research questions related to the causes and consequences of regional responses to coups.

In addition, the materials collected for the case studies provide rewarding insights into the issue of post-coup solutions. While the immediate responses of ROs to coups are often well documented and researched, the question of the long-term post-coup development and role of ROs in the aftermath of coups often evades scholarly attention (Grewal & Kureshi, 2019). Therefore, the compiled qualitative information on the four cases of Madagascar (2009), Niger (2010), Burkina Faso (2015) and Zimbabwe (2017) provides an interesting starting point for future research on this issue.

Plan of the book

Having briefly described these essential points, the structure of the book and the content of the subsequent chapters are outlined in the following. The book is divided into six chapters. As a first step, the research interest of the book, the role of ROs in the context of coups, was introduced in the present chapter. The relevance of this topic was emphasized and three specific research questions were formulated and discussed. Additionally, the theoretical framework, the methodological approach as well as the findings and contributions of the study were briefly summarized.

As the next step, the theoretical framework of the book is presented in Chapter 2. Inspired by the model of the norm life cycle (Finnemore & Sikkink, 1998), it illustrates how the anti-coup norm emerged and developed since the 1990s and changed the position of ROs vis-à-vis coups and led to the adoption of formal anti-coup provisions and mandates. Next, the implications of the anti-coup norm for the role of ROs in the context of coups are discussed. It is first conceptualized what measures ROs use to respond to coups (research question 1). Subsequently, potential explanations on which factors influence the choice of stronger or weaker RO responses (research question 2) and which post-coup solutions ROs pursue through their responses and why they do so are derived (research question 3).

In Chapter 3, the first research question on what measures do ROs use to respond to coups is brought to the fore. The chapter starts by introducing the dataset, providing details on the selection of coups and ROs, the data collection and coding process. Subsequently, the most important trends in the data are presented in a comprehensive descriptive analysis. In particular, the declining prevalence of coups since the 1990s and the simultaneous increase in the level of RO activity is described. Comparisons over time and across continents are drawn with particular attention to the choice of diverse instruments of different strength by ROs.

In Chapter 4, the second research question on which factors influence the choice of stronger or weaker responses is analysed and the potential explanations of this issue explored in Chapter 2 are subjected to an empirical test. As a start, the measurement of the dependent and independent variables and the statistical models used in the analysis are briefly described. Subsequently, the empirical findings of a series of different model configurations in the statistical analysis are reported. The findings show that several democracy- as well as stability-related factors exert an important influence on the choice of policy instruments by ROs. The chapter concludes by visually illustrating the most important effects and discussing their implications on the role of ROs after coups.

Chapter 5 focuses on the third and final research question: which post-coup solutions do ROs pursue through their responses and why? The theoretical expectations formulated in Chapter 2 with regard to when and how ROs should be more likely to insist on a complete return to constitutional order and democratic principles after coups or when ROs might be more likely to compromise the anti-coup norm are examined. In doing so, the research design of the comparative case studies is first briefly sketched. Based on the comparison of four carefully selected cases, the choice of different post-coup solutions in the cases of Madagascar (2009), Niger (2010), Burkina Faso

(2015) and Zimbabwe (2017) is described. The author discusses to which extent the post-coup solutions chosen by ROs are compatible with the strict refusal of coups enshrined in the anti-coup norm and illustrates why ROs chose the respective options and reflect on the implications for the role of ROs in the context of coups.

The book concludes with Chapter 6, in which the main results of the analysis are summarized. Based on the findings of the evaluation of the three research questions, a final assessment of the role of ROs in the context of coups is made. Subsequently, the implications of the findings for the academic study of coups as well as for practitioners are elaborated on and several avenues for future research are pointed out.

2

Theorizing the Role of ROs after Coups

In this chapter, a theoretical framework which accounts for the complex role of ROs after coups is introduced. This framework provides to opportunity to conceptualize and explain the responses of ROs to coups, to derive theoretical expectations on the research questions and guides the empirical analysis. The central element of the theoretical framework is the anti-coup norm. In the existing literature on coups, the emergence of the anti-coup norm is an essential and recurring theme (Boniface, 2002; Leininger, 2015; Powell et al, 2016). In short, the anti-coup norm comprises a rising global consensus that coups constitute unacceptable violations of democratic and constitutional principles, which should be opposed by the international community (Tansey, 2018). A noteworthy element of the anti-coup norm is its double character and audience. The first component of the norm is directed towards potential coup plotters, thus powerful and dissatisfied elites on the domestic level and interdicts them to pursue political change through violent means. In contrast, the second component addresses international actors and requests them to address and condemn such events. Hence, the anti-coup norm includes two components – a ban of coups and a call for punitive action against them (see Figure 2.1).

As illustrated, the two components are not isolated and independent of each other. The first component forms the basis for the second, as the requirement to sanction coups is contingent on their incidence in the first place. The second component also affects the first, as the prospect of decisive and strong punitive measures by ROs after coups influences the decision making of potential coup plotters whether to stage a coup or not. International responses to norm violations play a decisive role for many norms (Cardenas, 2004; Deitelhoff & Zimmermann, 2019), but usually such responses are not an integral part of the norm itself. Through explicitly formulating the responsibility of ROs to intervene in the case of a coup, the anti-coup norm has a distinctly dual character. In this regard, the anti-coup

Figure 2.1: Components of the anti-coup norm

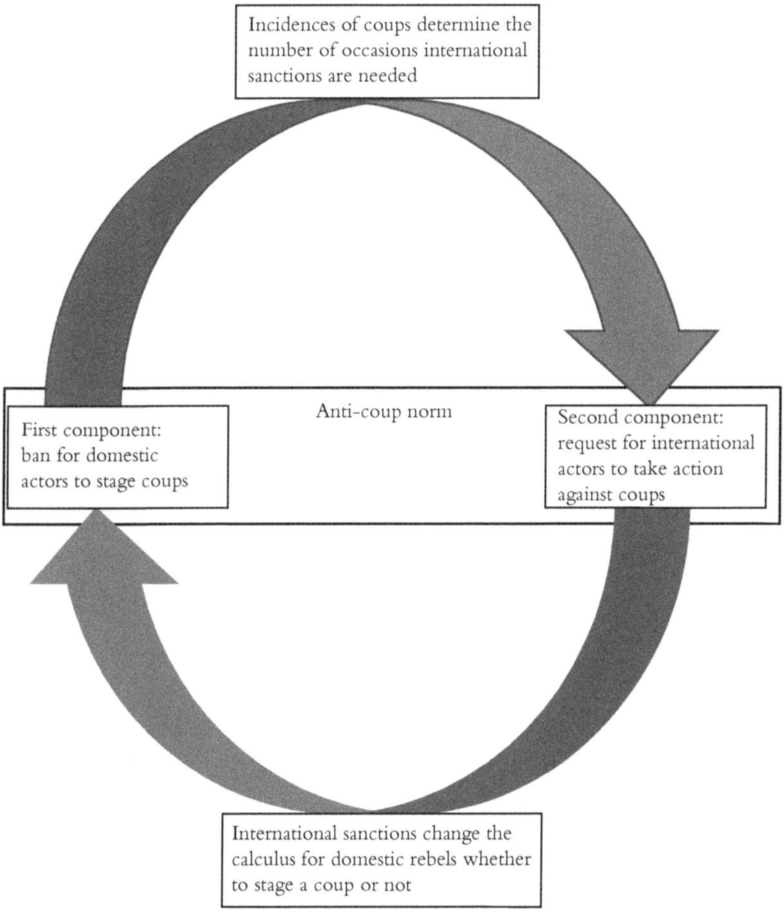

Incidences of coups determine the number of occasions international sanctions are needed

First component: ban for domestic actors to stage coups

Anti-coup norm

Second component: request for international actors to take action against coups

International sanctions change the calculus for domestic rebels whether to stage a coup or not

norm resembles the R2P (responsibility to protect) norm, which in a similar manner first requires state leaders to protect their populations and second demands the international community to step in case state leaders are unable or unwilling to do so (Welsh, 2019).

The emergence of the anti-coup norm has fundamentally changed the position of ROs vis-à-vis coups. In earlier times, responses to coups were usually contingent on pragmatic calculations concerning whether the new regime constituted a more promising ally than the old one or vice versa (Thyne, 2010). Yet with the emergence of the anti-coup norm, coups became reprehensible acts, calling automatically for condemnation and sanctions by regional actors (Souaré, 2014). Hence, the anti-coup norm constitutes a universal normative guideline that coups should be opposed. This is not to say that ROs have completely abandoned the practice of strategically evaluating the case-specific consequences of coups. On the contrary, ROs do care about which implications a particular coup has for the state of democracy and stability in a country as well as for the neighbour states and they adjust their responses accordingly. Thus, the anti-coup norm is not an isolated and intangible principle. Instead, the anti-coup norm forms the framework within which a constant weighing of democracy- and stability-related considerations of ROs takes place. The result of this weighing process finally shapes the role of the respective regional actors.

In this chapter, this weighing process is modelled and the importance of the anti-coup norm for the role of ROs after coups is discussed. In doing so, elements from the rich body of literature on international norms are used. In a first step, the emergence and development of the anti-coup norm in ROs is described and its consequences are illustrated. On this basis, the implications of the anti-coup norm for the three research questions are elaborated on. The author conceptualizes which measures ROs use to respond to coups (research question 1), accounts for the choice of RO responses of varying strength (research question 2) and discusses which post-coup solutions do ROs pursue through their responses and why they do so (research question 3). The chapter concludes with a short summary of the most important aspects and the implications for the analysis.

The development of the anti-coup norm in ROs

Many scholars examining the international responses to coups attempts make reference to the presence of an emerging and increasingly influential anti-coup norm (Ikome, 2007; Legler & Tieku, 2010; Omorogbe, 2011; Trithart, 2013; Hartmann & Striebinger, 2015; Nathan, 2016c; Powell et al, 2016; Thyne et al, 2018). ROs have emerged as the most active and influential actors when it comes to responding to coups, exceeding by far the efforts of the UN and single states (Tansey, 2018). This observation is in itself surprising. Many ROs put strong emphasis on the sovereignty of their member states and have traditionally been hesitant to interfere in their internal conflicts (Coe, 2015). Hence, how did it happen that many ROs committed themselves to the anti-coup norm, adopted respective anti-coup provisions and started to take action against states hit by coups?

Norm emergence: the birth of a global anti-coup norm in ROs

Despite the resulting political instability, one could argue that the consequences of coups are less destructive than those of other forms of domestic conflict. For instance, civil wars are often characterized by long and recurring periods of fighting (Balch-Lindsay & Enterline, 2000; Cunningham et al, 2009), severe destruction of vital infrastructure (Kang & Meernik,

2005), the looting of valuable natural resources (Findley & Marineau, 2015; Bove et al, 2016), high numbers of casualties and major grievances for the civilian population (Ghobarah et al, 2003; Humphreys & Weinstein, 2006; Wood, 2014; Krcmaric, 2018).

In comparison, the immediate consequences of coups are considerably less harmful. A characteristic feature of coups is that they are quickly and unexpectedly conducted and explicitly targeted towards the state leader (Powell & Thyne, 2011). Normally, this results in a very short period of actual fighting, comparatively low numbers of casualties, particularly among the civilian population, and negligible immediate economic damage for a state. In some cases, there is not even a spark of combat, as already the threat of the use of force suffices to coerce state leaders to step down (de Bruin, 2019). For instance, the coup in Thailand in 2014 claimed not a single casualty. Some scholars have argued that coups are not only less harmful than other forms of domestic conflict, but even bear the potential to change the situation in some states for the better. They suggest that coups in autocratic states can increase the chances of democratization (Powell, 2014a), regardless of whether they are successful or not (Thyne & Powell, 2016). For instance, Marinov and Goemans (2014) argue that the majority of coups have been followed by competitive elections, making them a window of opportunity for democratization processes.

As a result, coups were perceived as a deplorable, yet not unusual political phenomenon for a long time. Prior to and during the Cold War, coups constituted a common rather than an exceptional way of leader change. In particular, Africa and Latin America were highly prone to coups (Powell & Chacha, 2019). Between 1950 and 1990, they experienced 135 (Latin America) and 129 (Africa) coups, on average more than three coups per year (Powell & Thyne, 2019). Domestic elites staging coups against their government had relatively little reason to worry about the international response to their actions. The vast majority of these incidents did not evoke much international attention and definitely no serious external pressure on the coup plotters. Until the end of the Cold War, many IOs, in particular the UN, were paralysed by the East–West divide. In fact, the major powers assessed coups according to the alignment of the ousted government and the successive coup plotters and were even sometimes actively involved in the ousting of disliked governments (Thyne, 2010).

Yet with the end of the Cold War, the international attitude towards coup plotters slowly, but inexorably, changed. Indeed, from 1990 onwards, a notion emerged that coups are not an acceptable way of changing the government of a country and should consequently be condemned and sanctioned by the international community (Tansey, 2017). One obvious reason for this development was that notwithstanding the validity of the aforementioned arguments, coups bear major problems. A coup is an incisive event with far-reaching consequences. The forceful removal of a state leader concusses a state. Even when coups fail, they constitute an alarming sign of political instability and affect the political culture of a country.

Many countries have faced several subsequent coups. For instance, Guinea-Bissau has faced no fewer than 11 coups since 1990. If coups have turned out to be a viable way to take power in the past, they are seen as an attractive option for future potential rebels and thus destabilize the political system and culture. In this case, the involvement of military forces into the political decision-making of states becomes a deeply entrenched custom, making coups a regular and tolerated event (Heiduk, 2011). For example, Farrelly (2013) illustrates that the persistent occurrence of coups in Thailand has created a 'coup culture' that justifies military interference in political affairs in the eyes of the population. In some cases, coups can also lead to so-called 'counter coups', meaning that leaders who have been ousted by a coup seek to regain control by using military force themselves (Hiroi & Omori, 2013). For instance, in June 1995 the emir of Qatar, Khalifa bin Hamad al-Thani, was ousted by his own son. While the international community quickly recognized the new government, al-Thani attempted to retake control of Qatar in a counter-coup in February 1996 (Kamrava, 2009).

The fact that coups are fairly common in some countries by no means implies that they are beneficial. The use of military force to take power undermines the principles of constitutionality and democracy in politics and subverts the supremacy of civilian rule over the armed forces (Kuehn, 2017). Besides, previous studies indicate that coups can have additional major negative consequences for states. Coups tend to have an adverse effect on the economic development of affected states, as the prospect of political instability deters domestic as well as foreign investments (Fosu, 2002; Gong & Rao, 2016). Coups are also often followed by violations of civil rights (Curtice & Arnon, 2020; Lachapelle, 2020). The recent coup in Myanmar is a good example. The ousting of the democratically elected government of Aung San Suu Kyi sparked massive popular resistance against the military junta. Estimates indicate that the coup plotters' repression of the opposition led to the death of approximately 1,500 civilians in 2021, including some who were summarily executed or tortured to death in interrogation centres. Nearly 9,000 additional persons were arrested, charged or jailed (ICG, 2022).

Despite the fact that coup plotters often promise to initiate a democratization process in order to gain international recognition, the chances that they actually conduct meaningful democratic reforms are often limited (Miller, 2011; Derpanopoulos et al, 2016). For instance, after the coup in Sudan in 2019, a carefully negotiated agreement stated that a joint interim government of civilian members of the opposition and representatives of the military junta were to implement a democratic transition in the country. However, another coup in October 2021 illustrated the military's fear of losing influence under a civilian leadership and its will to consolidate their grip on power (ICG, 2021). These findings imply that coups rarely improve the economic and political situation of a state and that few coup plotters prove to be capable rulers. Thus, while the immediate consequences of coups are often less harmful than those of other forms of domestic conflict, coups constitute a clear risk to the political and economic stability of the affected countries. Although coups may under certain conditions open up avenues for democratization and progress, more frequently, they lead to a deterioration of the political and economic situation.

As a consequence, from the 1990s onwards, an international consensus emerged to reject coups. This 'anti-coup norm' was impressively demonstrated by the resolute and hostile echo of the international community to the coups in Haiti and the Soviet Union in 1991 (Franck, 1992). In both cases, international actors vocally protested against the undemocratic character of the events and exerted considerable pressure on the respective coup plotters. The successful reversal of the coup in the Soviet Union and the final reinstatement of President Aristide in Haiti were interpreted as important catalysts for the anti-coup norm (Tansey, 2017).

From the very beginning, ROs played a crucial role in the emergence and promotion of the anti-coup norm (Tansey, 2017). Apart from the EU, which started to take a resolute stance against coup plotters shortly after the end of the Cold War, in particular the continental ROs in Africa and America, the OAS and the AU took a very clear and fierce position against coups (Legler & Tieku, 2010). It is telling that both these ROs have adopted automatic and decisive anti-coup mechanisms, a step which has still not been taken by the UN (van Sickle & Sandholtz, 2009). Within ROs, the anti-coup norm was vividly promoted by a number of 'norm entrepreneurs', actors who committed themselves to a clear and non-negotiable rejection of coups as a means of political change at an early stage. These did not only comprise state leaders hoping to establish more democratic structures in their regions but also influential actors in RO bureaucracies, secretariats and executive bodies (Souaré, 2018).

The subsequent rapid rise of the anti-coup norm within ROs can be attributed to the construction of a successful cognitive frame. According to Finnemore and Sikkink (1998), the successful adoption of new norms is often facilitated by the linkage and fit with existing established norms. Clusters of related norms are more resilient to challenges than isolated single norms and thus have a higher potential to shape the behaviour of the respective actors (Lantis & Wunderlich, 2018). In the case of the anti-coup norm, the new norm was closely linked to the powerful cluster of democratic norms. From the 1990s onward, democracy promotion became an increasingly important aim, not only for Western states in their foreign relations with other countries, but also for regional actors (Legler & Tieku,

2010). By framing coups as one of the major challenges to democracy, norm entrepreneurs succeeded in tying the anti-coup norm to a central theme of international politics and made it a crucial topic for many ROs.

Indisputably, concerns about democracy are an important reason why ROs have promoted and adopted the anti-coup norm. In fact, many ROs explicitly refer to the aim of protecting democracy against coups in their charters (Shannon et al, 2015). But the assumption that the main goal of the anti-coup norm is to protect democratic standards is not unchallenged (Omorogbe, 2011). Apart from a genuine commitment to protect democratic standards, ROs also have very practical benefits from supporting the anti-coup norm. In its efforts to promote democratic values worldwide, the EU has encouraged and also financially supported other ROs to adopt democratic provisions in their statutes (Grugel, 2004). Thus, the adoption of the anti-coup norm in ROs can also follow an instrumental logic. ROs may adopt the norm to prove to Western donors their commitment to democratic norms and receive financial support for their activities in return. For instance, for the AU the high dependence of the organization on external finance played an important role for the adoption of anti-coup norm (Leininger, 2014).

Besides, ROs have also an evident stability-related interest to combat coups. For decades, coups have been one of the major risks and most frequent ways for state leaders to lose power (McGowan, 2003). For democratic state leaders, coups are among the most severe forms of illegal interruption of their rule, but also the majority of autocratic breakdowns results from coups (Bove & Rivera, 2015). State leaders who lose power through non-constitutional means often face bleak prospects. In countries without regularized succession procedures, a loss of power often entails further punishment than being replaced. Instead, state leaders are often imprisoned, sentenced or exiled (Escribà-Folch, 2013). In addition, coups severely threaten the political and economic stability of a state and carry the risk of leading to further political turmoil and violence not only in the affected state but potentially also in the wider region.

Hence, by branding coups as unacceptable acts, which call for the intervention of regional actors, the anti-coup norm does not only protect democratic standards. Instead, the norm also protects incumbents in the member states of ROs from one of their major risk of losing power. In a very revealing study on the Union of South American Nations (UNASUR) and Mercosur, Closa and Palestini (2018) illustrate that particularly weaker and more fragile states seek the 'tutelage' of stronger and more stable RO members. This protection is not directly dependent of their own degree of democratic legitimacy. Accordingly, if a RO adopts the anti-coup norm, the state leaders of its member states secure the support of the other RO members in a potential future challenge to their rule (d'Aspremont, 2010). Thus, a priori, the member states of any RO would profit from committing themselves to the anti-coup norm. The aim of preserving regional stability is a guiding motive apparent in the stance of ROs towards coups (Nathan, 2016b). Hence, apart from the desire to promote and protect democratic standards, concerns about the risks to stability associated with the fall of state leaders are an essential factor explaining the emergence of the anti-coup norm in ROs.

Norm cascade: the spread of the anti-coup norm across ROs

After the emergence of the anti-coup norm, several ROs adopted the norm in a gradual process. Apart from establishing a regular praxis of denouncing coups as reprehensible violations of democratic principles, ROs started to institutionalize the anti-coup norm in specific sets of rules. International norms vary considerably regarding how explicitly and officially they are formulated. Many norms with a claim of global validity become codified and anchored in international law or in the statutes of IOs at some point in time (Hawkins & Shaw, 2008). Other norms remain less official, yet nevertheless constitute valid and important guiding principles of international interactions (Percy, 2007). With regard to codification, the anti-coup norm is a particularly interesting case. On the global level, the codification of the norm is still rather weak. The UN approach towards coups can most aptly be described as inconsistent and selective. Over time, the UN has ensured that operational coordination of the responses to coups of its different actors has improved, including the UN Security Council, the UN General Assembly and the Secretary General, and to streamline its internal procedures. Yet attempts to push for a more consistent and binding political anti-coup strategy have largely failed (Tansey, 2018).

As a result of the lack of a globally valid codification of the anti-coup norm, several influential ROs moved ahead to formulate and enshrine their own versions in their statutes. It certainly helped that with the EU, the OAS and the AU three of the largest and most powerful organizations from three different continents embraced the anti-coup norm relatively early and decisively: the most well-known RO voicing its strict rejection of unconstitutional leader changes is the EU. Coups are very rare events in Europe and no coup has ever happened in any EU member state at the time of writing (Marshall & Marshall, 2019; Powell & Thyne, 2019).

Nevertheless, the EU is an important actor regarding the international responses to coups. As the EU actively promotes and requests democratic standards in its partner countries all over the world, the organization has often taken a clearly hostile position against coups. The EU is not only an active, but also an influential actor. In particular via the transfer of foreign aid, the EU has a strong leverage to foster constitutionality and democracy in other countries and to deter and punish coup plotters by the very same means (Molenaers et al, 2015). In a range of its international agreements with third-country states, such as for instance the Cotonou Agreement, the EU has insisted on binding democratic requirements and commitments excluding inter alia coups (Natens, 2018).

Second, in the Americas the OAS was the pioneer norm entrepreneurs promoting the anti-coup norm. The organization was among the first ROs to name democratic stability as a core goal on its security agenda (Chanona, 2011: 110). With the signing of the Santiago Commitment to Democracy in 1991, the organization also for the first time formulated concrete procedures on how to respond to interruptions of democratic processes in one of its member states. In subsequent years, these procedures were confirmed in the Washington Protocol (OAS, 1992) and the Inter-American Democratic Charter (OAS, 2001) and supplemented by the possibility to suspend member states which are affected by major democratic setbacks (Weiffen, 2017).

Finally, on the African continent, the AU and its predecessor, the OAU, turned out to be among the most influential actors in the spread of the anti-coup norm. In the Lomé Declaration, the AU explicitly declared that 'Governments which shall come to power through unconstitutional means shall not be allowed to participate in the activities of the Union' (Lomé Declaration, 2000). This clear rejection of coups was further strengthened and confirmed in the African Charter on Democracy, Elections and Governance, which provides an explicit definition of which incidents are considered as unconstitutional leader changes by the AU and a list of punitive measures to impose in such cases (African Charter on Democracy, Elections and Governance, 2007). As a consequence, the AU is nowadays one of the most prominent and strongest advocates of the anti-coup norm (Leininger, 2015).

The fact that three influential ROs with a large membership decisively embraced the anti-coup norm gave a strong momentum to the norm. These front-runner ROs not only fought coups themselves, but also effectively pushed for a spread of the anti-coup to a wider community. In the sequel, a number of other sub-regional ROs followed the examples of the EU, the OAS and the AU and adopted the anti-coup norm (Souaré, 2018). Among others, the Latin American organization Mercosur, despite being mainly concerned with trade and economic issues, has enshrined a democratic membership clause and emphasized its rejection of coups (Pirzer, 2012). Also the then-relatively young and now-defunct UNASUR committed itself to the protection of democratic principles and a clear rejection of coups in its Georgetown Protocol in 2010 (Weiffen et al, 2013; Closa & Palestini, 2018; Nolte, 2018). Similarly, in Africa, ECOWAS expressed its strong commitment to liberal democracy standards in the Protocol on Democracy and Good Governance from 2001 and has taken a clear stance against coups in its member states (Hartmann & Striebinger, 2015). Likewise, the member states of the PIF committed themselves in the Biketawa Declaration of 2000 to '[u]pholding democratic processes and institutions which reflect national and local circumstances, including the peaceful transfer of power...' (Biketawa Declaration, 2000).

Whereas a significant number of ROs have adopted anti-coup provisions, other important ROs have not officially done so. To gain a comprehensive and nuanced picture of the role of ROs after coups, it is important to pay attention not only to prominent supporters of the anti-coup norm, but also to more hesitant or even opposed organizations. A number of sub-regional ROs in Africa and Latin America have not enshrined an explicit anti-coup norm in their statutes. The fact that ROs have not individually codified the anti-coup norm does not automatically imply that they reject or ignore it. Also without a formal endorsement in their statutes, some ROs refer to and apply the anti-coup norm when they are confronted with coups in their member states or neighbourhood. For example, CARICOM has not included any official anti-coup provisions in its statutes, yet the RO has taken a decisive stance against coups and has condemned a number of coups in Latin America (Smith, 2005). Most of these organizations legitimize their responses to coups with their general mandate to protect democratic and constitutional standards in their member states (Closa, 2013).

Especially in Asia and the Middle East, some ROs have been more hesitant to commit themselves to binding anti-coup provisions and to take any measures against coup plotters. Some organizations, which mainly consist of autocratic states, for instance the GCC, have shown no interest at all in taking a consistent and decisive position towards unconstitutional leader changes (Tansey, 2017). Other ROs have taken a less adverse, yet hesitant approach. For instance, in 2007, the member states of ASEAN agreed that one of the organization's purposes is 'to strengthen democracy, enhance good governance and the rule of law, and to promote and protect human rights and fundamental freedoms' (Charter of the Association of Southeast Asian Nations, 2007). The predominance of a very strong norm of non-interference in the internal affairs of the organization's member states has for a long time hindered the emergence of stronger common security and democracy norms (Acharya, 2004; Foot, 2012; Davies, 2018). Yet the most recent coup in Myanmar in 2021 changed this position and evoked not only mediation attempts, but also diplomatic sanctions from ASEAN.

Table 2.1 provides an overview of the anti-coup provisions adopted by ROs. The first column details ROs with explicit provisions against unconstitutional leader changes and ruptures of democratic order. The second column includes ROs with a more general democratic commitment which coups would violate. The third column includes ROs which do not include formal anti-coup provisions or a democratic commitment in

Table 2.1: Overview of anti-coup and democracy provisions in ROs

ROs with explicit provisions against unconstitutional leader changes and disruptions of democratic order	ROs with general democracy clauses	ROs without provisions against coups or democracy clauses
ANDEAN Mercosur	ASEAN COMESA	AC EFTA
AU OAS	CALC EAC	ACC G5S
CELAC OIF	CARICOM ICGLR	ACD GCC
CPLP PIF	CBSS MSG	ACS GGC
ECOWAS SADC	CE OSCE	ACTO GUAM
EU UNASUR	CEEAC PA	AL IGAD
	CENSAD SICA	ALADI IOC
	CoE Commonwealth	ALBA IORA
		AMU LCBC
		APEC MGC
		BEU MRC
		BIMSTEC MRU
		BSEC NAFTA
		CACM NATO
		CAEU NC
		CAREC OECS
		CCTS OIC
		CEFTA SAARC
		CEMAC SACU
		CEPGL SCO
		CIS SELA
		CSTO SPC
		EAEU SPECA
		ECO UEMOA
		EEA WTO

their statutes. This does not automatically mean that these are autocratic ROs: there are a number of ROs with a dominantly autocratic membership (for example the EAEU, the GGC and the SCO). Yet the table shows that the group of ROs in the third column is very diverse: many ROs therein have a narrow focus on other policy issues, such as economic cooperation (for example the European Free Trade Area/EFTA, the North American Free Trade Agreement/NAFTA, the Southern African Customs Union/SACU) or environmental protection (such as the Arctic Council/AC, the Amazon Cooperation Treaty Organization/ACTO, the Mekong River Commission/MRC). Others comprise only established democracies as members for which coups were never an issue (for example the Benelux Economic Union/BEU, the European Economic Area/EEA, the Nordic Council/NC). Yet the table also illustrates that a considerable number of

ROs has either an explicit mandate to address coups or a more general democratic commitment covering such action. The ROs listed in the first two columns comprise classical geographical yet also cultural-based ROs; they come from all continents and include larger as well as smaller ROs.

The anti-coup provisions adopted by ROs are of high importance for their responses to coups. While national constitutions prohibit coups, making the actions of coup plotters illegal, there is no international law which obliges ROs to take action against coups (d'Aspremont, 2010). Besides, due to the lack of codification in international law or an internationally accepted convention against coups, globally accepted reference points on what constitutes a coup and what measures should be taken against them are missing (Tansey, 2018). Although a multitude of academic definitions of coups exist (see Powell & Thyne, 2011), they often differ in important aspects and are hardly ever referred to by practitioners. As a consequence, the provisions of the different ROs themselves constitute their key guidelines for implementing the anti-coup norm.

Yet as Table 2.1 shows, these provisions vary considerably regarding their degree of precision. Sometimes, they only include relatively vaguely formulated mandates to protect democracy in the member states. In other cases, they also specify the policy instruments a RO is allowed to or even supposed to apply against coup plotters. For instance, Mercosur specifies in its Montevideo Protocol in detail that in the case of an interruption or danger of democratic order, the organization may inter alia use the instruments of

a. *suspension of the rights to participate in particular organs of the organization;*
b. *partially or completely closing the borders, suspending or limiting trade, air and sea traffic, communications, energy, service and delivery provisions;*
c. *suspension of the affected state from the rights and benefits of the integration agreement;*
d. *promotion of the suspension of the affected state from other regional and international organizations;*
e. *supporting regional and international efforts to find a peaceful solution in the affected state;*
f. *adopting political and diplomatic sanctions.*
(Protocolo de Montevideo sobre Compromiso con la Democracia en el Mercosur (Ushuaia II), 2011, emphasis original)

However, none of these measures is explicitly requested to be taken after a coup. Very few organizations have automatic and mandatory procedures after coups. One of the rare examples is the OAS, which is obliged to automatically call an emergency meeting in the event of any 'sudden or irregular interruption' of democratic rule to decide on legal instruments to apply against the regime (Tansey, 2017). Likewise, the provisions in the

African Charter on Democracy, Elections and Governance require the AU to suspend every member state in which a coup took place:

> When the Peace and Security Council observes that there has been an unconstitutional change of government in a State Party, and that diplomatic initiatives have failed, it shall suspend the said State Party from the exercise of its right to participate in the activities of the Union in accordance with the provisions of articles 30 of the Constitutive Act and 7 (g) of the Protocol. The suspension shall take effect immediately. (African Charter on Democracy, Elections and Governance, 2007)

However, the implementation of this rule has proved difficult in the past and the AU has quite some discretion with regard to the question of which additional measures the organization may take against coup plotters and which steps a country must take for the suspension being lifted (Ikome, 2007).

Internalization: global acceptance of the anti-coup norm in ROs

Indisputably, the anti-coup norm has undergone an impressive development; indeed since 1990, the norm has been officially adopted by many important ROs encompassing a vast majority of countries worldwide. The unequivocal and strong positions of three of the largest and most influential ROs, the EU, the AU and the OAS, grant a hedged position of the norm. Moreover, even many ROs who have not included explicitly formulated anti-coup provisions nevertheless have democracy clauses in their statutes against which coups obviously violate.

Yet it is not only important to assess the scope of the anti-coup norm, but also its depth. According to Finnemore and Sikkink (1998), the life cycle of a norm does not only include the stages of norm emergence and norm cascade. In a final internalization stage, relevant actors genuinely adopt and internalize a norm until it has become an integral part of their identity. Following the definition of Finnemore and Sikkink (1998), completely internalized norms 'may become so widely accepted that they are internalized by actors and achieve a "taken-for-granted" quality that makes conformance with the norm almost automatic'.

Has the anti-coup norm reached a stage of internalization, practically dictating the behaviour of ROs? Interestingly, scholars vary tremendously in their evaluation of the influence of the anti-coup norm on the responses of ROs. Some authors take a rather optimistic view, praising the achievements of the norm. For instance, Leininger (2015) calls it in the African context 'a legally binding norm that holds national governments of AU member states responsible for a stable and democratic regime within their countries'. Several authors point out that since the adoption of the anti-coup norm by

ROs, the number of coups has decreased and that ROs have predominantly been successful in responding to coups (Legler & Tieku, 2010; Souaré, 2014; Manirakiza, 2016). A further indication of the significance of the anti-coup norm for ROs is that RO actors frequently make reference to their anti-coup provisions when confronted with coups. Nevertheless, the anti-coup norm has also received strong scepticism. Some authors acknowledge the existence of an anti-coup norm in ROs, but deplore inconsistencies and difficulties in its application (Ikome, 2007; Omorogbe, 2011; Nathan, 2016c). Yet the anti-coup norm has also faced more profound critique, arguing that regional responses to coups are best described as inconsistent and that no globally accepted anti-coup norm in ROs exists (Shannon et al, 2015; Tansey, 2017, 2018).

These apparently contradicting evaluations of the relevance of the anti-coup norm for ROs raise the question which role ROs actually play in the context of coups and how the anti-coup norm shapes their actions. This book builds upon the notion that despite the successful rise of the anti-coup norm, the nature of the norm itself provides ample opportunity for interpretation and discretion by the ROs which have adopted it. Previous research has established that regional actors are no passive recipients of global norms. On the contrary, regional actors actively shape global norms and adjust them so that they fit with exiting regional norms, beliefs and interests (Acharya, 2004, 2011). Such processes can lead to considerable differences in how a global norm is perceived and applied in different world regions (Barqueiro et al, 2016). In the following, it is illustrated which discretions ROs enjoy within the framework of the anti-coup norm and how they make use of it. Democracy- and stability-related factors are deeply entrenched within the framework of the anti-coup norm and shape the role of ROs after coups in decisive ways. Based upon this notion, the next section conceptualizes what measures ROs use to respond to coups (research question 1). Subsequently, the factors influencing the choice of stronger or weaker RO responses are discussed (research question 2) and finally the question which post-coup solutions ROs pursue through their responses and why they do so is elaborated on (research question 3).

Conceptualizing RO responses to coups

As illustrated in Figure 2.1, the anti-coup norm includes two components. While the first component entails a direct ban of coups, the second component requires ROs to take action against coup plotters. The first research question focuses on how this second component of the anti-coup norm is put into practice and examines what measures ROs use to respond to coups. Unfortunately, the second component of the anti-coup norm only prescribes that ROs should take action against coups without specifying which forms that action shall take. Hence, there is no globally accepted blueprint of how an appropriate response to a coup should look like (d'Aspremont, 2010). The only guideline provided by the anti-coup norm itself is the general opposition to coups, resulting in a call for adverse responses. As mentioned before, many ROs have listed possible measures in their anti-coup provisions. But the choice of one or several of these adverse responses is at the discretion of the respective RO. Several ways to communicate the criticism of ROs and to penalize coup plotters are conceivable. After a coup, ROs can apply four key sorts of instruments: rhetorical, diplomatic, economic and military.

The use of rhetorical instruments is the least intrusive and cost-intensive form of response. Following a coup, ROs can make an official statement commenting on the events. Such statements can easily be done by every RO, as they require very few preconditions apart from a basic agreement on a common RO position. Rhetorical responses are comparatively lenient in nature, as they impose few direct costs on the coup plotters or the affected state. As such, they often also constitute a feasible compromise for ROs when some RO members opt of sanctioning a coup, yet others are opposed to imposing punitive measures. Notwithstanding, they can have an important effect. The principle of 'naming and shaming', in other words clearly identifying and criticizing norm violations by certain actors, is an important mechanism for ROs to establish and exert international norms (Ruggeri & Burgoon, 2012; Esarey & DeMeritt, 2017; Terechshenko et al, 2019). If a RO criticizes the behaviour of the coup plotters, this undermines their legitimacy on the international as well as on the domestic level (Thyne et al, 2018). Furthermore, rhetorical responses can also be read as indications which position a RO takes vis-à-vis a coup and which further instruments it may be willing to impose.

Rhetorical instruments can be structured into three categories. The first comprises relatively neutrally formulated statements of concern about the respective situation of the respective RO. As ROs do not directly take sides in such statements, they are the most lenient possible responses to the coups. As such, neutral statements after coups are a measure which ROs without comprehensive anti-coup provisions or democracy clauses in their statutes also regularly use. However, the fact that a RO feels obliged to express its concern indicates a level of alertness hinting towards a critical assessment of the events and the situation in a state. The second category includes statements which express the support of the RO with the ousted government. With such statements, ROs *do* directly take side, buttressing the legitimacy of the incumbent. The third category comprises all statements which explicitly and directly criticize the coup plotters and condemn their actions.

Following rhetorical responses, diplomatic instruments are the next intense measures ROs may take. Many ROs have established provisions through which they can mediate in political crises and domestic conflicts in their member states (Nathan, 2016c; Herz et al, 2017; Witt, 2017). In such cases, representatives of ROs conduct and oversee talks between the ousted government and the coup plotters with the aim of finding a political solution to the crisis. ROs may also take a less conciliatory approach towards coup plotters. In addition to mediation, ROs have other diplomatic tools at hand to exert pressure on coup plotters. Minor forms of diplomatic sanctions can comprise the cancelling of visits, consultations or the calling of ambassadors. If such tools prove to be ineffective, ROs may also impose more severe diplomatic instruments. The most prominent and commonly used in the context of coups is the suspension of the affected state from the decision-making bodies of the RO. While the state formally remains a member of the RO, it is deprived of its membership rights (particularly its voting rights), equating not only to a strategic disadvantage but also to a major reputational loss.

If rhetorical and diplomatic instruments fail to lead to a satisfactory outcome, ROs can also make use of economic instruments to exert pressure on the affected state. Economic sanctions are a commonly used instrument to penalize states for norm violations and to induce a change in behaviour (Hufbauer et al, 1990; Bapat et al, 2013). They are stronger instruments than rhetoric and diplomatic means, as economic sanctions usually entail considerable costs for the target as well as for the sender states (Hovi et al, 2005). Imposing effective economic sanctions usually requires a strong consensus among the RO member states. If due to diverging political and/or economic sanctions some member states decide not to implement or secretly to circumvent sanctions, the effectiveness of the measure is normally undermined.

ROs may impose different sorts of economic sanctions on states hit by coups. One of the most frequently used ones is the partial or complete reduction of funding in the form of development cooperation or regional funding programmes. In addition, ROs may also impose export or import embargoes or pursue the coup plotters via targeted sanctions in the form of travel bans or asset freezes. The literature on sanctions emphasizes that it is important to distinguish between sanction threats and actually imposed sanctions (Nooruddin, 2002; Clifton et al, 2014). By no means in all cases will actors who threaten sanctions proceed to actually imposing them. Sometimes the target state already gives in once sanctions are threatened and in other instances sender states hesitate to put their threats into practice. Therefore, it makes sense to conceptually distinguish between the threatening and the actual use of economic sanctions.

As a last resort, ROs may also rely on military measures to respond to coups. The use of force is the most intrusive, dangerous and costly form of RO responses to coups, which requires even stronger consensus among the RO member states than diplomatic and economic sanctions. The announcement to militarily intervene in a country after a coup has major implications and requires considerable financial, logistic and military resources. As ROs normally do not have their own military forces, one or several member states have to contribute soldiers, weapons and other military equipment. For instance, the military intervention of ECOWAS after the coup in Sierra Leone in 1997 would not have been possible without Nigeria taking the leading role and contributing most soldiers to the ECOMOG force (Francis, 2010). Consequently, the use of military measures is usually only chosen as the last available option after other instruments like diplomatic or economic measures have failed. As with economic sanctions, it makes sense to distinguish between the threat to intervene militarily and the actual deployment of troops to a state hit by a coup.

These different instruments to respond to a coup can be conceived as a continuum ranging from mild forms of criticism to severe punishment of the coup plotters (see Figure 2.2). Obviously, the order of the responses is not immune to criticism. For instance, economic sanctions can be of rather symbolic nature and might have in practice less consequences for a country than a suspension from a RO. Similarly, in some mediation attempts ROs might sound more conciliatory than in rhetorical condemnations. However, the conceptualization is well suited to illustrate the increasing severity and the rising costs of the four groups of instruments for ROs. Besides, it captures the logic and temporal order in which the instruments are usually applied.

These different options vary greatly with regard to their expected impact. In general, severe measures against coup plotters are often assumed to be more effective in exerting pressure, yet, they are also associated with higher costs. On the one hand, each form of action an organization takes to tackle a crisis bears some cost for the organization – be it of a military, financial, economic, diplomatic or reputational nature (Beardsley & Schmidt, 2012), b ut there are considerable differences. Condemning a coup rhetorically is comparatively easy and inexpensive for a RO, whereas the imposition of economic sanctions or even the employment of military troops is associated with considerable costs (Regan, 1996; Hovi et al, 2005; Bapat & Kwon, 2015). On the other hand, non-action can bear its own costs. If a RO does not respond to a coup, this can be interpreted as a sign of weakness, encouraging dissatisfied political elites in other states to stage coups in the future. Besides, without the support of regional actors the situation in a coup country might also further deteriorate, potentially leading to major chaos. For instance, the coup against the government of president Ndadaye in Burundi in 1993 resulted in large-scale eruptions of ethnic violence between Hutus and Tutsis in the country, claiming an estimated 150,000 casualties (Grauvogel, 2015). Thus, active responses as well as passiveness after coups are associated with certain risks for ROs.

Figure 2.2: Instruments to respond to coups

concern statements | support for incumbent | condemnation | mediation | minor diplomatic sanctions | major diplomatic sanctions | economic sanctions threat | economic sanctions imposed | military intervention threats | military interventions imposed

Since the 1990s, many ROs have subsequently strengthened the role of the anti-coup norm within their organization. They have increased the degree of legal obligation of the norm within their statutes, for example by establishing automatic mechanisms and procedures to be followed after coups (Bamidele & Ayodele, 2018). Besides, many ROs have agreed on new and more severe instruments to be applied against coup plotters, including suspensions, mediation and economic sanctions (Souaré, 2014). Hence, whereas in earlier times ROs had a limited range of instruments at hand to respond to coups, in recent times more ROs have gained competencies to impose stronger measures against coup plotters. Obviously, the mere availability of policy instruments does not automatically grant that they are used. Scarce resources within ROs, diverging interests of member states and difficulties to reach compromises constitute challenges for ROs when addressing coups. Therefore, Chapter 3 examines empirically which instruments ROs actually use to respond to coups.

Explaining the strength of RO responses to coups

The previous section illustrated that ROs have a plethora of instruments to respond to coups at hand. The anti-coup norm requires ROs to generally disapprove coups, yet ROs enjoy considerable leeway over how they do so. Some critics oppose the differential responses of ROs to coups, claiming that ROs react in an inconsequential and arbitrary manner. They criticize that ROs sanction some coups more severely than others, while staying silent on some incidents altogether (Ikome, 2007). It is evidently true that ROs vary in this regard. ROs differ in their decisions on when and how often they get active after coups in the first place and once they decide to respond to a particular coup, their responses vary considerably in strength (Shannon et al, 2015). Yet to thoroughly evaluate the role of ROs and their implementation of the anti-coup norm, it is not sufficient to show that RO responses to coups vary. It is also essential to explain why they do so. Teasing out the factors which shape the decisions of ROs over whether and how to respond to coups in particular ways provides invaluable insights into the priorities, considerations and motives of the respective ROs. Therefore, the next section theorizes the effect of several potential explanatory factors and develops respective expectations.

RO decision to respond to coups

The first essential question in this regard is when and why ROs decide to get active after a coup. Non-reactions can be perceived as the weakest form of response to a coup. Ignoring a coup and waiting to see how the situation develops can be an attractive option for ROs. By far not all coups have evoked attention by regional actors in the past and ROs differ considerably with regard to the number of coups they have responded to. An obvious explanation of the different approaches of ROs to coups is the great diversity between different regional groupings. Accordingly, the first two expectations discuss RO-related characteristics which shape the responses of ROs to coups.

The first aspect determining whether a RO responds to a coup is the presence of an official mandate to do so. The anti-coup norm is not backed up by binding international law against coups (Tansey, 2018). Hence, there is no legal obligation to respond to coups on the global level (d'Aspremont, 2010). While democratic governance has been described as an 'emerging right' on the global level (Franck, 1992), attempts to anchor democracy as a key UN principle with global validity have been cumbersome (Rushton, 2006). But since the end of the Cold War, many ROs have adopted democratic provisions for membership (Closa, 2013), hence, ROs usually derive their mandate to address coups from RO-specific democratic commitments. Coups constitute clear violations of such provisions and therefore require ROs to address them. In cases in which some member states of a RO favour an intervention, while others are opposed to it, an official mandate to respond to coups is a strong argument for action.

As a result, the presence of binding democratic provisions within the statutes of ROs is a crucial factor determining whether a RO feels obliged to respond to a coup. Since the 1950s, the number of ROs has significantly increased and the universe of ROs worldwide is characterized by strong diversity in terms of the policy mandates and legal competencies (Panke & Starkmann, 2018). Some ROs, such as the OAS or the AU, have adopted sophisticated, detailed and formalized democratic provisions (Cooper & Legler, 2001; Leininger, 2015). Some of these protocols and treaties even explicitly mention coups as one form of violation of democratic principles. Other ROs have less official and obligatory democratic provisions or lack them at all. The presence of official democracy provisions is no necessary condition for ROs to take action against a coup. As discussed, ROs might also oppose coups out of concerns about regional stability and security. In this case, ROs can refer to their more general competencies in the realm of foreign and security policies. But the presence of explicit democratic provisions in the statutes of a RO fortifies the obligation to take action against unconstitutional leader changes and thereby increases the chances that a RO responds to a coup, as formulated in the first theoretical expectation:

E1a: *If a RO has official democratic provisions codified in its statutes, it is more likely to respond to a coup.*

A second crucial issue is the sphere of influence and responsibility of ROs. Generally, ROs are characterized by a strong focus of their activities on issues within their own region. In recent years, ROs have increasingly engaged in building partnerships and networks with other ROs. However, these ties usually focus on partnership, the exchange of knowledge and mutual learning (Söderbaum & van Langenhove, 2005). While many ROs have subsequently reached more and more competencies to resolve problems within their member states, the vast majority of ROs are very hesitant to interfere in the affairs of other regional groupings and do not engage in conflict resolution or democracy promotion outside their boundaries. One noteworthy exception to this pattern is the EU, whose foreign policies in all world regions are geared towards conflict resolution and the promotion of democratic and liberal values (Santiso, 2003; Schimmelfennig & Scholtz, 2008; Freyburg et al, 2009; Kotzian et al, 2011). Also some other ROs have, on selected occasions, responded to coups in countries not (yet) belonging to their organization, for example ASEAN after the coup in Cambodia in 1997, which was at the time an accession candidate for the Asian RO. Yet in general, ROs concentrate their activities after coups on their own member states.

In the case of the anti-coup norm, this focus of ROs on issues within their own member states implies a clear division of labour. When observing a coup in Latin America, it is not plausible to assume that ASEAN or the AU will respond to it. Instead, the likely candidates to respond are the OAS and sub-regional Latin American ROs such as ANDEAN or Mercosur. Most states do not belong to one single RO, but are simultaneously members in several regional groupings (Panke & Stapel, 2018). Due to this phenomenon of 'overlapping regionalism', usually not one but several ROs are directly affected by a coup. Of course, the membership in a RO is not a perfect predictor of whether a RO will take action or not. Under no circumstances do ROs respond to all coups in their member states. Besides, some ROs, in particular the EU, also respond to coups outside their territory. Nevertheless, the strong focus of most ROs on issues within their boundaries suggests that ROs are more likely to respond to coups in their own member states than to takeovers in external countries.

E1b: *If a coup happens in a member state of a RO, the RO is more likely to respond to the coup.*

Importantly, the decision whether a RO responds to a coup does not only depend on the RO, but also on the incident in question. One central criterion influencing the chances that a coup is addressed by ROs is the outcome of the attempt. Although attempts to oust governments take place on a regular basis, by far not all coups are successful. On the contrary, more than half of the coups recorded since 1950 have failed (Powell & Thyne, 2011) and approximately the same ratio of failed coups is apparent in the present data (see Chapter 3). It is important to note that the failure of a coup does not automatically rule out responses by external actors. For instance, the failed coup in Turkey in 2016 evoked a massive amount of international attention and reaction (Esen & Gumuscu, 2017).

Failed and successful coups alike constitute a sign of severe political unrest and instability. Therefore, ROs do not only respond to successful but also to failed takeovers. Yet the decision over whether to respond to successful and failed coups is completely different. Confronted with a failed coup, ROs do not face much pressure to respond. ROs may, however, respond to the incident to underline their general disapproval of coups and to strengthen the position of the incumbent. Yet they have no significant pressure to take such action, as the immediate danger of the coup is already averted. In contrast, after successful coups, ROs face a direct challenge to a central democratic norm and to regional stability. In such situations, ROs not only have to defend their position as credible norm enforcers, but also have to address a severe political crisis in one of their member states, with potential risks for the whole region. Consequently, the pressure on ROs is much higher and it is expected that successful coups have a higher probability to lead to responses by ROs than failed ones.

E1c: Successful coups are more likely to lead to RO responses than failed ones.

Strength of responses

The role of ROs in the context of coups cannot be boiled down to the question of whether or not ROs respond to a coup. Instead, RO responses differ considerably in strength: some coups only face mild rhetorical criticism, while others are followed by costly diplomatic, economic or even military penalties. This variety of RO responses raises the question why ROs decide to use strong instruments after some coups, yet not after others. In the following, some potential explanations for this diversity are presented and respective theoretical expectations are formulated.

RO characteristics

The previous section argued that the nature of the RO at hand influences the likelihood of a RO taking action in a particular case. Additionally, it is assumed that the identity and capacity of a RO also plays an important role in determining the strength of RO responses. One particularly important aspect is the level of democracy in the member states. Existing research shows that ROs can be influential actors in promoting, protecting and consolidating democratic values in their member states (Pevehouse, 2002a, 2002b; McMahon & Baker, 2006; Pirzer, 2012; Closa, 2013; Poast & Urpelainen,

2015). Yet by far not all ROs can be described as democratic. A number of ROs dominantly consist of autocratic member states. International cooperation of states in such 'autocratic clubs' has been shown to be an important tool for authoritarian leaders to legitimize and stabilize their rule (Ambrosio, 2008; Collins, 2009; Dimitrova & Dragneva, 2009; Obydenkova & Libman, 2019).

The composition of dominantly democratic or autocratic member states is expected to play an important role once a RO has to decide whether and how to respond to a coup. Autocracies do not necessarily approve coups and occasionally support other autocratic regimes against violent challenges to their rule. However, their approach can be described as less reliable and driven more strongly by strategic self-interest (Odinius & Kuntz, 2015). Hence, autocratic member states have tendency not to support or even to impede strong RO action against coup plotters. Lacking a values-based democratic commitment, ROs with a dominantly autocratic membership have hence fewer incentives to clearly oppose coup plotters. The situation is different for ROs with a dominantly democratic membership. The ousting of a government via a coup leads by definition to an undemocratic form of government (von Soest & Wahman, 2015). In ROs in which the majority of states is democratic, this is expected to lead to a vocal and strong response, as coups violate a key norm and criteria for membership in their group. Accordingly, it is expected that a more democratic membership of ROs should lead to stronger responses after coups.

E2a: *The more democratic the member states of a RO are, the stronger are the responses to a coup.*

When confronted with a coup, ROs often face considerable pressure to do something regarding the issue. Responding to coups is not just about proving the credibility of the organization's anti-coup commitments or deterring potential future coup plotters. Often, member states bordering the affected country also urge the RO to solve the crisis and ousted governments themselves have called for help from their fellow RO members on many occasions. Notwithstanding this apparent pressure to get active, a key question is what ROs can realistically hope to achieve.

Not all ROs have sufficient resources at their disposal to effectively address coups. For example, the PIF expressed its strong condemnation and disapproval of the coup in Fiji in 2006. However, due to the lack of regional institutional capacity and the extremely limited financial and military resources, the PIF had few options to exert additional pressure (Tavares, 2010). Similarly, CARICOM has enshrined democracy and the rule of law as key values in their guiding principles, yet the constant shortage of resources has impeded a more robust response towards the coups in Haiti (1991,

2000) and Trinidad & Tobago (1990) (Byron, 2011). Many smaller African ROs face similar problems of underdeveloped security mechanisms and scarce resources. Whereas the AU and ECOWAS have more developed and at least adequately funded security institutions (Barbarinde, 2011; Hartmann & Striebinger, 2015), smaller ROs such as the intergovernmental Authority on Development (IGAD), SADC and the Economic Community of Central African States (CEEAC) suffer from a constant shortage of institutional and financial resources (Meyer, 2011; Murithi, 2011; Schoeman & Muller, 2011).

Yet even the more well-endowed and powerful ROs are dependent on the financial and military contributions of their member states and their budgets for conflict interventions are usually quite limited (Hentz et al, 2009; Engel & Mattheis, 2020; Stapel & Söderbaum, 2020). Regional hegemons, like Nigeria in ECOWAS or South Africa in SADC, hold a pivotal role in this regard, as stronger RO measures after coups are not possible without their contributions. Given these financial constraints, international actors are known to carefully assess the expected chances of success of their foreign policy measures (Aydin, 2010). Consequently, ROs adjust their responses to coups according to the feasibility of successfully exerting pressure on the coup plotters. In general, smaller and poorer countries have less capacity to counter external pressure and are therefore attractive targets for ROs to demonstrate their resoluteness and strength. For instance, one of the key factors leading to the decisive ECOWAS intervention in Gambia in 2017 was the fact that the small Gambian army was perceived as incapable to offer any noteworthy resistance to the ECOWAS forces (Hartmann, 2017). In contrast, ROs are often wary of directly confronting their powerful member states and regional hegemons. For example, after the coup in Egypt in 2013, the AU officially suspended the country, but refrained from exerting any further pressure, as it is one of the five financially strongest AU members (EIU, 2013). Resulting from these observations, one can assume that the more power a RO has in relation to the state affected by a coup, the stronger are the responses by the respective RO.

E2b: *The more leverage a RO has vis-à-vis a state affected by a coup, the stronger are the responses by ROs.*

To conclude, the diversity of ROs plays an important role in explaining why they respond differently to coups. However, not only inter-organizational, but also a considerable amount of intra-organizational variation exists. For instance, the AU does not only respond differently to coups than ECOWAS, but the AU also does not uniformly respond to all coups in its sphere of influence. This implies that the anti-coup norm is frequently interpreted and applied differently by one and the same RO on different instances. The interesting question, then, is which factors guide the interpretation of the anti-coup norm by ROs? Which considerations shape the decisions of regional actors to only mildly criticize one coup yet to impose severe instruments after another?

Obviously, by adopting the anti-coup norm, ROs signal their clear opposition to coups. Yet this does not explain why they respond to one coup more strongly than another. An evident idea is that ROs and their member states take the reasons, circumstances and effects of a coup into account when deciding on appropriate responses. These aspects can be assessed from two perspectives: on the one hand from a value-guided perspective, evaluating the expected effects of a coup on the democratic and humanitarian situation in a country, and on the other hand from a more pragmatic angle, assessing the economic consequences and security risks of a coup for the other RO members.

Democracy-related criteria to assess coups

As democracy-related arguments have always featured more prominently in the global discourse on coups than security interests, the former are discussed first. The starting point is the premise that (at least many) ROs reject and oppose coups, since they perceive coups as a violation of democratic and constitutional standards, which the RO upholds. Yet if the anti-coup norm and the resulting opposition of ROs to coups is grounded on concerns regarding a deterioration of democratic and constitutional standards in their member states, ROs should pay particular attention to the record and prospects of the very same in the country affected by a coup. Apparently, coups constitute an undeniable challenge to central democratic principles of many ROs. Yet not all coups are the same. Coups can have a multitude of different underlying reasons and countries facing a coup can take very diverse post-coup trajectories (Striebinger, 2015). Consequently, one would not expect ROs to treat every coup alike. Instead, one would assume that ROs assess the situation of a country prior to a coup, the impact of the takeover and its potential to induce changes to the better or to the worse.

A central aspect in these considerations is the level of democracy in a country. As mentioned before, the ousting of a government by the use of force is obviously a highly undemocratic political act. Democratic standards denounce the use of violence as a political measure and therefore condemn coups as profoundly undemocratic (von Soest & Wahman, 2015). Yet the relationship between coups, democracy and constitutionality is not unidimensional. From a procedural perspective, coups are definitely undemocratic. But from an outcome-centred perspective, this is not necessarily the case. In order to assess whether coups improve or weaken the level of democracy in a country, one has to take the baseline situation in a country into account. As a matter of fact, the majority of coups do not take place in model democracies, but in autocracies and semi-democratic countries (Marshall & Marshall, 2019; Powell & Thyne, 2019). Thus, it is often not the case that a coup leads to the fall of a legitimate and democratically elected government. In fact, in most instances a coup simply replaces one undemocratic regime with another.

In recent years, a vivid debate about the effects of coups on democracy has emerged (Tansey, 2016b). While there is a consensus that the violent ousting of democratically elected governments lessens the state of democracy, opinions on the effects of coups in autocracies diverge. Some authors argue that coups in highly autocratic countries can serve as triggers for democratization processes and can increase the level of democracy (Varol, 2012; Marinov & Goemans, 2014; Powell, 2014a; Varol, 2017). Following a successful takeover, coup plotters face higher pressure to democratize in order to secure domestic and international support for their rule (Thyne et al, 2018). Besides, failed coups also increase the pressure on incumbents to introduce reforms to decrease the risk of further coups (Thyne & Powell, 2016). Other authors contradict this standpoint, arguing that the majority of post-coup elections are far from being fair and free. They further claim that the democratic transitions following a coup are consequently often superficial and shallow (Tansey, 2016b) and that most coup-plotters have not governed any better than the previous regimes (Ikome, 2007; Miller, 2011; Lachapelle, 2020).

Without resolving the debate regarding the democratization potential of coups, a central conclusion can be drawn from it: the level of democracy prior to a coup is a crucial factor for assessing the consequences of a coup. When deciding on appropriate measures after a coup, ROs tend to take the democratic legitimacy of the ousted government into account (Shannon et al, 2015). The ousting of a respected democratic government almost inevitably leads to a decline in democratic and constitutional standards in the affected country. In contrast, a coup against a semi-democratic or autocratic regime bears at least the chance to increase the level of democracy in a country (Derpanopoulos et al, 2016). Accordingly, the member states of a RO have much more reason to oppose coups in democratic states than takeovers in autocracies. Thus, the ousting of a democratically elected government is expected to evoke stronger regional responses than a coup against an autocratic regime.

E3a: *The more democratic an ousted government has been, the stronger are the responses of ROs to the coup.*

The democratic legitimacy of a government cannot be reduced to the formal political institutions of a country. As well as the institutional level of democracy, also the perceived support of the population for the incumbent or a leader change play a role. The motivations of coup plotters to oust a government cover a broad range. In some instances, dissatisfied military officials or other elite members have ousted governments in order to receive higher revenues, attain more political influence or guard their privileges. For example, Burkina Faso's elite Régiment de sécurité présidentielle (RSP) ousted the interim government of the country in 2015, for fears of the dissolution of the regiment and its close political alignment with the former President Blaise Compaoré (EIU, 2016b). However, in many cases coups do not only result from the personal aims of ambitious elites; they are at least accompanied or preceded by massive discontent and suffering of the population. Large-scale domestic protests against a regime have been shown to considerably increase the risk that coups take place (Johnson & Thyne, 2016; Gerling, 2017). If considerable public discontent with the current regime exists, coups might be assessed favourably by the domestic population. For instance, the successful coup against President Maaouya Ould Sidí Ahmed Taya in Mauritania in 2005 was overwhelmingly welcomed by the domestic population, which appreciated it as the end of a despotic and repressive regime (EIU, 2005).

Obviously, matters are not always as simple as they appear in these two ideal-type examples. It would be naïve to think that coup plotters can be separated along a dichotomy of selfish power seekers and selfless guardians of the people. On many occasions, multiple motivations to oust a regime coincide and overlap. For instance, ambitious elites can make use of popular discontent with a prior regime to pursue their own strivings for power. Nevertheless, ROs are likely to take the position and opinion of the domestic population towards a coup into account when deciding on their responses to it: if there have been signs of major discontent of a country's population with its prior regime, ROs should be more inclined to show understanding and leniency towards coup plotters. In contrast, coups against popular and domestically supported governments are expected to face stronger responses by ROs.

E3b: *If the ousted regime has been challenged by popular protests prior to the coup, ROs show weaker responses.*

Finally, not only the characteristics of the prior regime are important for the responses of ROs, but also the identity of the coup plotters matters. A central feature of coups is that they are perpetrated by actors belonging to a country's elite. This particularity distinguishes coups from other forms of domestic conflict such as popular revolutions and civil wars, which are characterized by the involvement of larger parts of the domestic population. Besides, as coups by definition include the (threat of) the use of force, usually (parts of) the armed forces are involved in a coup. However, the main actors behind a coup do not have to be military leaders, they can also be civilian elites (Powell & Thyne, 2011).

Consequently, coups can be distinguished as military or civilian in nature. In military coups, all important leaders of the coup stem from the military and civilian actors have no or very little influence in the process. In contrast, in civilian coups civilian political adversaries of the incumbent regime play an active role (Kinney, 2019). The identity of the coup plotters matters for ROs and their member states for several reasons. First, the supremacy of civilian political actors over the military forces is a central prerequisite for successful democratic governance of a country (Croissant, 2004; Foster, 2005; Croissant et al, 2010). Accordingly, ROs who seek to foster democratic values in their member states have taken a particularly sceptical stance against military juntas. Thus, even for a new regime which has come to power by means of a coup, civilian political leaders still provide it with a veneer of legitimacy that exclusively military regimes lack (Barracca, 2007). Second, many ROs do not only oppose exclusively military juntas due to their identity and lack of popular support, but also due to their failure to improve the situations in affected states. Most military governments have a disastrous track record of effective and successful governance (Miller, 2011), thus, ROs are often sceptical about the capabilities of military regimes to act as a reliable and competent partner within their organization. Consequently, one would expect that ROs distinguish between military and civilian coups when deciding on their responses and respond more harshly to military coups.

E3c: *If a coup is exclusively conducted by military actors, ROs should show stronger responses.*

Stability-related criteria to assess coups

Undoubtedly, all points outlined are important aspects for ROs, which are concerned about democratic and constitutional principles in their member states. Yet as this chapter has established, stability-related aspects also played a strong role for ROs when adopting the anti-coup norm. Consequently, the member states in ROs will also consider the likely consequences of a coup on the stability of a region and adjust their responses accordingly. From a democracy-oriented perspective, a coup violates ideas of choice of government by the people and the non-violent transfer of power. Yet from a stability-oriented perspective, a coup constitutes primarily a violent conflict in a member state which might or might not be addressed by the RO. The decision whether and how a RO actually responds to such a crisis is contingent on three stability-related aspects: the success of the coup, the level of violence and the respective risk of spillover and adverse effects on the regional economy.

According to Expectation 1c, the chances that ROs respond to a coup are higher for successful coups. The success of a coup is not only expected to increase the likelihood of RO responses to a coup, but also the strength of these responses. Confronted with a failed coup, ROs may criticize the attempt in order to emphasize their general disapproval of coups and to fortify the position of the incumbent against his or her challengers. However, as the immediate risk of a leader change will have already vanished, ROs generally have few incentives to show more severe and costly responses than rhetorical action. For instance, more severe instruments like economic sanctions or the suspension of the country from regional bodies are not necessary and would actually hurt the incumbent more than the coup plotters.

In contrast, the successful ousting of a government constitutes a completely different situation. Whereas failed coups and resulting purges may deter dissatisfied elites in neighbouring countries from staging coups, successful coups are likely to encourage imitators. As such, the governments of the other member states have a strong impetus to push for decisive RO action after successful coups. Moreover, as a consequence of a successful coup, the government of a state at least temporarily changes, with all risks and uncertainties associated to it. Generally, ROs do not know how the new regime will act, whether it will succeed in upholding at least a minimum degree of peace and stability and whether it will respect and comply with regional arrangements and treaties. As such, successful coups constitute a considerably larger risk to regional stability than failed ones. Therefore, they are more likely to evoke stronger responses.

E4a: *If a coup is successful, ROs should show stronger responses than to a failed coup.*

While the situation in a coup country itself is an important issue for ROs, most of their member states are often also predominantly concerned about the external effects of a coup on the broader region. Recent studies indicate that (especially autocratic) regimes are mainly concerned with regional stability and the potential negative consequences for their own rule when confronted with sudden political transitions in their neighbourhood (Bader et al, 2010; Odinius & Kuntz, 2015). Coups are distinct from other sorts of political violence, for example, revolutions and civil wars, in the sense that they often proceed very quickly and claim only few casualties. These characteristics make coups generally less likely to spread to surrounding countries than large-scale forms of political violence like civil wars or revolutions (Black, 2013; Miller et al, 2018).

Nevertheless, all coups carry an inherent risk of diffusion and spillover effects of political volatility into the broader region (Tansey, 2016a). Interestingly, not all coups have the same potential to spill over into neighbouring countries and therefore alarm regional actors. While coups generally claim fewer casualties than other forms of political unrest, there are noticeable differences between cases (de Bruin, 2019). On some occasions, coups do not lead to fatalities at all, as the threat of the use of violence by the military or police forces suffices to coerce incumbents to step down (Powell & Thyne, 2011). Other coups claim a very limited number of casualties, out of which the majority belong to the ousted regime, their personal guardsmen or the coup plotters. However, sometimes fighting also spreads to the streets, resulting in a higher death toll among the population.

The extent of violence related to a coup is a central factor for the spillover risk of coups. The more people are killed in a coup, the more likely it becomes that fighting and violent opposition to the new regime will continue after the takeover. Previous studies have shown that such lasting intra-state conflict can significantly increase the risk of civil conflict in the region (e. g. Hegre & Sambanis, 2006). Additionally, if a coup results in major clashes and high numbers of casualties, parts of the domestic population might be forced to flee the country and seek refuge in neighbouring countries, which also increases the risk of conflict in the latter (Salehyan & Gleditsch, 2006). Hence, member states in close proximity to the country hit by a coup have a strong rationale to demand strong RO responses after violent coups.

E4b: The higher the number of casualties in a coup, the stronger the responses shown by ROs.

A comprehensive understanding of regional stability does not only include the absence of civil conflict and political violence, but also economic aspects. If a coup and the resulting political turmoil is expected to have a major detrimental impact on the regional economy, ROs are more likely to address the issue. The existing literature on civil conflicts indicates that the probability of external interventions into domestic conflicts is shaped by the existence and density of trade relations of the affected state. For instance, Stojek and Chacha (2015) show that states are more likely to intervene in civil wars to protect their close trading partners against domestic threats. This logic can easily be transferred to coups. When coups lead to the ousting of a government, the existing trade relations between the respective country and its trading partners are at risk. Coup plotters do not necessarily cut down trade relations, yet after a coup considerable uncertainty about the future policies and strategies of coup plotters exists. Accordingly, close trading partners of a state facing a coup have strong incentives to become active to protect their existing economic relations with the respective state.

This argument is particularly important for regional actors. The economic ties between neighbour states are particularly strong and dense (Reyes et al, 2014), hence, regional actors are usually most affected by the economic consequences of coups and have therefore the strongest incentives to become involved after coups. Of course, not all states are equally well integrated and important for regional trade networks. Logically, one would expect that the more important the role of a state within a regional trade network is, the more other member states will favour a decisive intervention by the RO. Accordingly, the chances that a RO shows a severe and resolute response to the coup increase.

E4c: *The more important a state is for a regional trade network, the stronger the responses shown by ROs.*

Interaction effects

So far, three sets of potential explanations have been formulated. Responses of ROs to coups are expected to depend on the nature of the RO, a desire to protect democratic and constitutional standards in their member states, as well as concerns about the potential risks of a coup to regional stability. It is important to state that the latter two motivations are not mutually exclusive. ROs do not reject coups because they either perceive them as violations of democratic principles or because they fear a deterioration of stability in the region. In many cases, both considerations play an (equally) important role. Accordingly, the two sets of expectations should not be perceived as competing, but as complementary explanatory approaches.

Notwithstanding this, not all of the expectations might be similarly applicable to all ROs. As illustrated, ROs are very diverse with regard to their membership, capacities and normative orientation. The three expectations linked to the democracy-related concerns should hold stronger explanatory power for ROs with a membership of predominantly democratic states which hold a clear normative commitment to democratic and humanitarian standards. Hence, it is expected that ROs with a democratic membership should put more focus on the democracy-based criteria (democracy level of the ousted regime, public protests and civil identity of coup plotters). In contrast, the stability-oriented considerations about the consequences of a coup (success, risk of spillover, feasibility) apply for all ROs alike, as their effect is basically the same for autocratic and democratic ROs. Accordingly, one can formulate the additional following expectations regarding the strength of the explanatory factors for different ROs:

E5a: *The positive effect of the democracy level of the ousted government on the strength of RO responses should be more accentuated for ROs with a democratic membership.*

E5b: *The negative effect of prior popular protests on the strength of RO responses should be more accentuated for ROs with a democratic membership.*

E5c: The positive effect of exclusively military coups on the strength of RO responses should be more accentuated for ROs with a democratic membership.

To conclude, a series of factors influencing the presence and strength of RO responses to coups were discussed in this section. The respective expectations are summarized in Table 2.2.

Table 2.2: Expectations on research question 2

Aspects	Expectations
RO activity	E1a: If a RO has official democratic provisions codified in its statutes, it is more likely to respond to a coup.
	E1b: If a coup happens in a member state of a RO, the RO is more likely to respond to the coup.
	E1c: Successful coups are more likely to lead to RO responses than failed ones.
Strength of responses: RO characteristics	E2a: The more democratic the member states of a RO are, the stronger are the responses to a coup.
	E2b: The more leverage a RO has vis-à-vis a state affected by a coup, the stronger are the responses by ROs.
Strength of responses: democracy-related factors	E3a: The more democratic an ousted government has been, the stronger are the responses of ROs to the coup.
	E3b: If the ousted regime has been challenged by popular protests prior to the coup, ROs show weaker responses.
	E3c: If a coup is exclusively conducted by military actors, ROs should show stronger responses.
Strength of responses: stability-related factors	E4a: If a coup is successful, ROs should show stronger responses than to a failed coup.
	E4b: The higher the number of casualties in a coup, the stronger the responses shown by ROs.
	E4c: The more important a state is for a regional trade network, the stronger the responses shown by ROs.
Strength of responses: Interaction effects	E5a: The positive effect of the democracy level of the ousted government on the strength of RO responses should be more accentuated for ROs with a democratic membership.
	E5b: The negative effect of prior popular protests on the strength of RO responses should be more accentuated for ROs with a democratic membership.
	E5c: The positive effect of exclusively military coups on the strength of RO responses should be more accentuated for ROs with a democratic membership.

Explaining the choice of differential post-coup solutions

The previous section elaborated on the question which factors drive the presence and strength of RO responses to coups. Yet a frequently voiced reproach is that these activities are just a flash in the pan. Critics claim that while ROs do speak up and take action against coups immediately after the event, such efforts are often fruitless and rather symbolic, as ROs fall short in effectively insisting on democratic transitions in the long run. Instead, ROs have frequently been shown to lift sanctions or to readmit countries in which coups had taken place after coup plotters made vague and often shallow promises to initiate democratization processes (Omorogbe, 2011). This critique addresses another central aspect of the role of ROs in the context of coups: the choice of differential post-coup solutions in the aftermath of coups.

In fact, the situation of ROs in the aftermaths of coups is a complex and challenging one. On the one hand, a strict interpretation of the anti-coup norm would request ROs to take a very fierce and adverse position against any country in which a coup has taken place and to uphold this position until the coup is reversed. On the other hand, the fact that many coups happen for a reason (for example, poor and autocratic governance of the prior regime, attempts of incumbents to stretch their ruling terms against the constitution) and the volatile situation in post-coup settings leads many ROs to take a more conciliatory position after coups. Therefore, in the present section it is illustrated why ROs strive for differential post-coup solutions in different cases. The aim of it is to explain under which circumstances ROs insist on the reinstatement of the ousted government, push for a power-sharing agreement or new elections or accept the coup plotters as new rulers. The argument is that in addition to the framing of the coup itself, particularly democracy- and stability-related arguments are decisive in this regard.

Importantly, this question is not necessarily temporarily distinguished from the responses of ROs to coups described in the previous section. Instead, the two issues are connected through a causal link. Once a coup takes place, ROs may show responses of differing strength. As previously discussed, a series of factors can influence this strength of responses, yet responses to coups are not shown by ROs for their own sake. Instead, by showing particular responses, ROs seek to achieve certain solutions to the volatile situations created through coups. The question of what these solutions look like and which conditions shape the decision of ROs to pursue differential post-coup solutions in different cases is of great interest, yet is still largely under-researched.

The present section seeks to answer this question and to develop potential explanations on it. In a first step, the situation in the aftermath of a coup is briefly discussed and it is illustrated which possible post-coup solutions exist. Subsequently, the role of ROs in this situation and their potential to shape post-coup trajectories is reflected on. Next, four conditions influencing which post-coup solutions ROs strive for are discussed (unequivocal applicability of the anti-coup norm, democratic record of the incumbent, chances of democratization under the new rulers and domestic power constellation). Based on these considerations, respective theoretical expectations are derived. The chapter closes with a short summary of the most important points.

The aftermath of coups and the role of ROs

The period starting from the moment when coup plotters have successfully taken power until the point when a stable political order is restored is defined as post-coup trajectory or aftermath of a coup.[1] Post-coup trajectories can result in different outcomes. In the case of unsuccessful coups, the solution is almost always predetermined: The incumbent successfully averts the threat to his rule and consolidates his claim to power, as it was for instance the case after the failed military coup in Turkey in 2016 (Esen & Gumuscu, 2017). In contrast, successful coups result in the fall of the previous leader and coup plotters take over control of a state. Due to the swift nature of coups, this is usually achieved within hours or at the maximum within a couple of days. Yet this does not mean that coup plotters have then secured a stable hold on power and the necessary extent of external and internal legitimacy. Instead, post-coup situations are characterized by a high degree of volatility and political instability and can result in different outcomes (Chacha & Powell, 2017). The question of how such volatile situations can be resolved is of high importance for affected ROs. Lasting instability in one member state is likely to lead to negative externalities, which have an adverse effect on the other members. Consequently, ROs have an interest in promoting stable post-coup solutions.

Although a coup is primarily a domestic form of conflict between a government and dissatisfied elites, ROs have the potential to exert a decisive impact on post-coup trajectories. In the volatile setting following a coup, the stance of external actors, in particular the position of regional partners is of utmost importance. A number of studies show that regional actors hold a pivotal position in shaping post-coup trajectories (Seibert, 2003; Collins & Fraenkel, 2012; Trithart, 2013; Souaré, 2014; Nathan, 2016c). The proponents of the argument that coups can open up an avenue towards democratization in autocratic contexts emphasize the importance and high leverage of external actors for post-coup development. Following coups, most coup plotters do not only seek to win domestic support from the population, but also attempt to receive international recognition. Both aspects are crucial prerequisites to secure the political survival of coup plotters (Thyne et al, 2018).

Hence, international actors and in particular ROs can exert considerable influence in the aftermath of coups. For instance, Marinov and Goemans (2014) show that international actors have the potential to successfully press coup plotters to hold elections and to democratize. According to Chacha and Powell (2017), the chances of democratization increase with closer ties between the country hit by the coup and the international community. ROs play an especially important role in this regard. If a post-coup regime gains the formal recognition of the respective regional grouping, this is not only a crucial step to rebuild political and economic connections with its neighbours, but also an important signal to the wider international community. The signal that the respective regional groupings acknowledge and cooperate with the new coup-born regime can help tremendously in restoring its international reputation. Consequently, the anti-coup norm in ROs and the position of ROs towards takeovers is of paramount importance not only immediately after coups, but also for the long-term post-coup trajectory. The fact that ROs apparently play an important role for the post-coup trajectories of affected countries raises the question of how ROs fill this role. Evidently, the anti-coup norm is a key factor to answer this question, yet, as is illustrated in the following, not the only one.

The choice of differential post-coup solutions by ROs

As previously described, ROs have an obvious interest to reach stable post-coup situations in their member states. Yet what does such a solution look like? In a simplified model, a coup can be described as a conflict about power between an incumbent government and rivalling elites, which finally try to overthrow the incumbent. Following a successful coup, these rival elites manage to take power – at least temporarily. Yet their hold on power is still fragile and the question of who will rule the country is not finally resolved through a coup. Both the ousted government as well as the coup plotters are potential candidates to do so. Resulting from this, four options for post-coup solutions emerge (see Figure 2.3). The upper right and the lower left quadrant of the matrix include the two options when one of the two factions emerges as a clear winner. On the one hand, a 'reversal' of the coup and a reinstatement of the ousted government can restore the pre-coup rule of the incumbent (upper right quadrant). On the other hand, coup plotters may also consolidate their claim to power and become permanent rulers (lower left quadrant). Besides, there are two 'compromise solutions'. Either a negotiated solution leads to a power-sharing agreement between the coup plotters and the ousted government (upper left quadrant) or a new government under the leadership of an actor belonging neither

Figure 2.3: Potential post-coup solutions

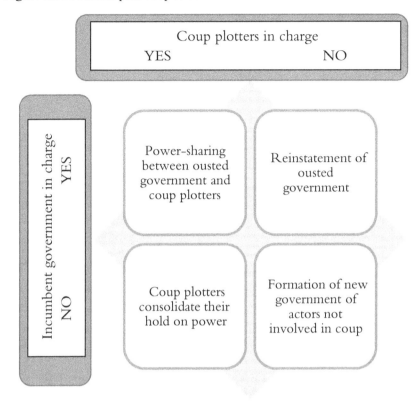

to the coup plotters nor to the ousted government can take control (lower right quadrant). All four possibilities constitute potential solutions for post-coup situations.

A first cursory glance at the empirical reality indicates that ROs have pursued all four options to resolve post-coup situations in the past. The apparent logical consequence of the anti-coup norm would be to push for a complete reversal of the coup and to insist on the reinstatement of the ousted government. Yet interestingly, this step is rarely taken. Of course, there are instances in which ROs have successfully pushed for the restoration of ousted regimes after coups. For instance, after the coup in São Tomé and Príncipe in 2003 the joint efforts of several ROs led to the return of the ousted government (Seibert, 2003). But this example is rather the exception than the rule. As Nathan (2016c) points out, only two out of 15 successful coups in Africa between 2000 and 2015 have been followed by the reinstatement of the ousted government. In other world regions, the quota is not higher.

Instead of requesting the return of the ousted government, ROs usually call more generally for the restoration of constitutional order and/or the democratization of the respective country (Nathan, 2016c). For many ROs, this does not necessarily mean the reinstatement of the ousted ruler, but rather to support a democratically elected successor (Manirakiza, 2016). Obviously, the formation of a new democratic government does not undo a coup, yet such a step rules out the possibility that coup plotters install their own long-lasting autocratic regimes. Therefore, the formation of a new government via elections has frequently been pursued by ROs in the aftermath of coups. For example after the coup in Papua New Guinea in 2012, the general elections in 2013 offered a chance to resolve the political impasse between the ousted President Somare and his challenger O'Neil (May, 2013).

As an alternative, power-sharing agreements between coup plotters and their opponents have become an increasingly popular tool to integrate divergent political forces. A very prominent recent example was the agreement reached after the coup in Sudan in 2019, which foresaw a 39-month transitional phase alternately chaired by civilian and military representatives. Surprisingly, ROs are sometimes also content to accept ongoing rule by coup plotters. For instance, after Faure Gnassingbé staged a coup in Togo in 2005, ECOWAS and the AU pushed for new elections and accepted Gnassingbé's subsequent election as president in a highly contentious electoral contest, criticized for major electoral flaws (Banjo, 2008).

A literal interpretation of the norm suggests that ROs are required to only pursue solutions situated at the right side of the matrix in Figure 2.3. The anti-coup norm contains a strict condemnation of coups and those responsible for them. Coup plotters are norm violators par excellence, accordingly ROs should not pursue a solution which allows coup plotters to stay in power. Thus, a consolidation of the rule of coup plotters runs counter to the principles of the anti-coup norm. A negotiated solution leading to power-sharing is slightly less problematic for the anti-coup norm, as coup plotters are at least forced constrain their powers and to make compromises. Yet also within this solutions coup plotters are not held responsible for their actions.

Both the formation of a new government as well as the reinstatement of the ousted government are more in line with the anti-coup norm. A strict interpretation of the anti-coup norm might suggest that a complete reversal of the coup and the reinstatement of the ousted government is the ideal solution. But also a solution in which a new government which does not contain members of the coup plotters and the ousted government is more compatible with the anti-coup norm than a power-sharing or consolidated rule of the coup plotters. To summarize, according to a literal interpretation of the anti-coup norm, ROs would be required not to favour solutions which include coup plotters as leaders or members of the new regime.

Apparently, however, this principle is not always put into practice. While the anti-coup norm provides a consensus that coups have to be condemned, no blueprint of how to resolve post-coup situations exists. This raises the question of which differential solutions ROs push in the aftermath of coups and why they do so. A promising starting point for theorizing the choice of post-coup solutions by ROs out of the described matrix is the issue of the unequivocal applicability of the anti-coup norm to a particular case. In the aftermath of coups, the question of whether the forced resignation of a government qualifies as a coup and thus as an incident calling for the application of the anti-coup norm is often highly controversial and the framing and interpretation of the events is a decisive factor (Nathan, 2016c). In principle, coups are characterized by a number of clear-cut and easily verifiable criteria (Powell & Thyne, 2011). Coups are usually clearly noticeable events attracting international attention and news coverage. Hence, at first glance it might be surprising how debates about whether a leader change constitutes a coup or not can emerge.

But at second glance, this becomes more apparent. The term coup d'état bears a major negative connotation. Through the dominant political frame, coup plotters are portrayed as ruthless rebels, denying them the legitimacy to rule a country (Thyne et al, 2018). Such a label has severe negative consequences for coup plotters. As a result, once a coup takes place, plotters often make strong efforts to justify their actions and to cast doubts on the allegation that their move actually constitutes a coup. Framing coups as 'acts of the will of the people' or 'unpleasant yet necessary steps to protect democracy against misrule of the incumbent' are widely used strategies to avoid a strict application of the anti-coup norm and have become a common practice among coup plotters (Marsteintredet & Malamud, 2019). For instance, the Sudanese coup plotter Abdel Rahman Suwar al-Dahab argued after the coup in 1985 that 'the armed forces in order to save bloodshed, secure the liberation of the country and unity of its lands, decided unilaterally to stand by the people […] to seize power and transfer it to the people after a limited transitional period' (Yukawa et al, 2019).

In some instances, attempts to deny or alleviate the fact that a coup has taken place appear far-fetched and implausible. Yet on other occasions, governments emerging from irregular leader changes have cast more credible doubts whether their behaviour can actually be categorized as a coup (Yukawa et al, 2020). In particular, when the use of violence is not directly apparent, when the involuntary nature of a former president's resignation is disputed or the constitutional provisions for the succession of a state leader are not clear, discussions can easily arise over whether a leader change actually constitutes a coup and thereby invokes the anti-coup norm. Interestingly, external actors sometimes also downplay a coup to justify leniency and passivity towards coup leaders. For instance, the US carefully avoided referring to the ousting of Egypt's President Morsi in 2013 as a coup, as this would have triggered domestic legal requirements to halt military aid to the country (Tansey, 2016a). The potential for varying interpretation of particular events is not only illustrated by the diverging wording coming from ROs and states when referring to one and the same incident. Likewise, researchers disagree on their definition and interpretation of coup events resulting in datasets which diverge in their assessment of many cases.[2]

The question of how unequivocally a case can be defined as a coup has important implications for the responses of ROs to the event. If the coup leaders succeed in casting reasonable doubts about the unconstitutionality of their actions, ROs are more inclined to agree on post-coup solutions favourable for the coup plotters (consolidation of power or sharing power with the incumbent government). In contrast, if the leader change clearly qualifies as a coup, ROs and other international actors have little room for manoeuvre to evade the provisions entailed in the anti-coup norm. Accordingly, they are more likely to push for the two post-coup solutions which are compatible with the anti-coup norm: the reinstatement of the ousted government or the formation of a new neutral government.

E6:   If the anti-coup norm is unequivocally applicable to a particular case, ROs are more likely to push for a reinstatement of the ousted government or the formation of a new government in the aftermath of coups.

Within the general framework of the anti-coup norm, democracy- and stability-related arguments play an important part in shaping the choice of ROs to pursue particular post-coup solutions. Coups violently replace one leader with another. The anti-coup norm categorically and universally condemns any such act as deplorable. Yet the question of who is actually ousted and why is an essential one for ROs. Classically, coups have been portrayed as ruthless acts by ambitious elites seeking to increase their personal benefits, powers and interests (Finer, 1962; Janowitz, 1977). However, most authors agree that elites' ambitious struggle for power and wealth is not the only – and maybe not even the dominant – reason why many coups happen. Instead, in numerous cases, coups are preceded by major deficits in the incumbent's record of governance. Apart from socio-economic grievances, many ousted rulers have been accused of an extremely autocratic leader style, repression, electoral fraud and attempts to illegally and undemocratically change constitutional provisions constraining their political powers (Marinov & Goemans, 2014). Thus, many state leaders toppled by coups are no democratic paragons.

This has an important impact on the decisions of ROs considering the aftermath of coups. Reinstating an ousted leader into office is a challenging and expensive task. Once ousted from office, and maybe detained or forced to flee the country, a state leader has demonstrated weakness and incapability to keep the security apparatus under control. Besides, requests to reinstate a disliked and unpopular ousted leader are prone to spark massive resistance from the coup plotters and all stakeholders sympathizing with their position. Thus, if ROs make the effort to reinstate a leader, he or she must be worth it, in the sense that the rule of the leader is perceived as legitimate and effective. Central elements in this regard are the question of whether a leader is democratically chosen to rule a country and whether his or her conduct of governance is perceived to be in line with constitutional and democratic standards.

Obviously, many ousted state leaders clearly fall short of meeting such criteria. The former Sudanese President Omar al-Bashir serves as a prime example. Al-Bashir took over power in 1989, ironically in a coup. During his 30 years of rule, he was accused of extremely autocratic practices, severe repression and major human rights violations. When public protests sparked against the president and the armed forces finally toppled al-Bashir, the option to reinstate him as president was not even suggested by international actors. Admittedly, not all cases are as unequivocal as Sudan. Some toppled leaders, like for instance Mamadou Tandja in Niger, came to power through legal democratic procedures, yet later abused their powers and became increasingly authoritarian (Baudais & Chauzal, 2011). In such cases, power-sharing agreements can serve as a means to force coup plotters and the former government to cooperate. Thereby, not only different political standpoints are accounted for, but the power of the ousted government is also partly restored. However, a vital prerequisite for this is that the ousted government is perceived to have a certain degree of democratic legitimization.

In a nutshell, ROs will only push for the reinstatement of a leader or his or her participation in a power-sharing agreement if he or she enjoys a sufficient level of democratic legitimacy. If this is not the case, ROs perceive coups as windows of opportunity for change. Under such conditions, they are likely to consider a new government as the more promising alternative or may even accept the continued rule of the coup plotters as the better bet.

E7:   *Democratic legitimacy of the ousted ruler increases the chance that ROs will push for a reinstatement of the ousted ruler or his participation in a power-sharing agreement.*

Apparently, ROs make their preference for certain post-coup solutions not only contingent on the democratic legitimization of the ousted incumbent. After all, the ousted incumbent is only one side of the equation. The democratic legitimization and performance of the incumbent is always weighed against the prospects of democratization under the new regime. In the first instance, this may sound odd; after all, political actors who stage a coup apparently disregard key democratic principles including the selection of state leaders by the people, the supremacy of political actors over the armed forces and the non-use of violence as a political means.

Nevertheless, many coup plotters do not frame themselves as anti-democrats. A popular concept in research on coups is the idea of so-called 'guardian coups' (Ezrow & Frantz, 2011). This concept implies that armed forces do not stage coups out of self-interest to permanently take control of a country, but to correct autocratic tendencies of the incumbent, to preserve the country from political turmoil and to get a country back on a democratic track. Admittedly, such reasons and promises may sound reasonable, honourable and reassuring; yet they have to be treated with great care. Since the emergence of the anti-coup norm, the term coup has gained a major negative connotation (Marsteintredet & Malamud, 2019). As a result, it has become an automatism for coup plotters to put forward more or less convincing justifications why their actions are excusable or even necessary (Yukawa et al, 2020). Similarly, the promise to implement democratic reforms is not a remarkable concession of coup plotters, but a common strategic move to appease the international community.

Hence, how do regional actors assess whether coup plotters are earnest about implementing a democratic transition? A central criterion is whether the coup plotters conduct democratic reforms of state institutions and set a credible and timely electoral schedule. Together with the creation of effective and impartial institutions, free and fair post-coup elections play a vital role for the prospects of democratization in the aftermath of coups (Grewal & Kureshi, 2019). They are often framed as the prime instrument to restore democratic and constitutional order and to lead the people to retake control after the political turmoil caused by a coup (Marinov & Goemans, 2014). As such, the holding of free and fair elections has become the most central request voiced by ROs in the aftermath of coups.

However, conducting democratic reforms and holding timely and democratic post-coup elections is also a challenging endeavour. While many coup plotters promise to hold elections to reassure and appease the international community, as well as the domestic population, it has become a common tactic to postpone these elections, often under questionable pretences. For instance, after the coup in Guinea-Bissau in April 2012, elections were rescheduled several times and it took two years until they could finally be held in spring 2014 (EIU, 2014). Once elections actually take place, the quality and fairness of the electoral process is often also an issue. Electoral fraud, the intimidation of voters and electoral violence are common characteristics of elections in post-coup settings. Accordingly, by far not all post-coup elections have been evaluated to be fair and free (Tansey, 2016b).

Notwithstanding these challenges, free and fair post-coup elections are an essential step towards democratization. Hence, if coup plotters show a credible and binding commitment to hold timely, fair elections, ROs tend to favour one of the two solutions situated in the lower half of the matrix in Figure 2.3: the formation of a new government emerging from the elections or the electoral endorsement of the coup plotters themselves. If democratic elections are to be expected, both solutions feature appealing advantages for ROs. Pushing for a new government, which is freely and fairly elected by the people, allows ROs to present themselves as promoters and guardians of democratic values and to make sure that coups are followed by a genuine democratization process. Besides, particularly if ROs face the dilemma of choosing between an autocratic incumbent and similarly unpromising coup plotters, elections can be a salomonic solution.

Ideally, these elections lead to a new government, democratically legitimized to rule the country. Such a solution is highly beneficial for ROs. However, even if the electoral contest leads to a victory of the coup plotters, a belated electoral endorsement of the latter makes cooperation with these actors far less prone to criticism. Put differently, in light of the anti-coup norm and wider democratic norms, ROs are often criticized when they cooperate with coup plotters. Yet once coup plotters are confirmed as government by an electoral victory, their democratic legitimization and hence their 'acceptability' increases tremendously.

E8:   *If coup plotters set up a timely and credible electoral schedule, the likelihood increases that ROs will favour the formation of a new government or the consolidation of the coup plotters' rule.*

An attentive reader may ask why ROs allow coup plotters to run as candidates in post-coup elections. To be sure, if coup plotters stand for election, the actual degree of their popular support is revealed. If the majority of the population of a country stands behind their action to oust the former regime, they may win an electoral contest and subsequently count on an important source of democratic legitimization. Yet doubts concerning the participation of coup plotters in post-coup elections remain. In the vast majority of countries affected by coups, elections are organized by understaffed, inadequately financed and often non-independent electoral commissions. Frequently, the leaders of such commissions are appointed by the current rulers, opening the door for interference and in the extreme also electoral fraud (Cheeseman & Klaas, 2018). Even if elections are held in a tolerably free and fair manner, the question persists as to why coup plotters should be rewarded for violently toppling a government by giving them the chance to run for government. The AU has taken a clear stance on this issue, stating in its Charter on Democracy, Elections and Governance, that '[t]he perpetrators of unconstitutional change of government shall not be allowed to participate in elections held to restore the democratic order or hold any position of responsibility in political institutions of their State' (African Charter on Democracy, Elections and Governance, 2007).

Yet in reality, candidatures of coup plotters in post-coup elections are common. And when coup plotters run, they also tend to win. Hence, why do ROs accept or even push for elections in which coup plotters are allowed to run and likely to achieve an electoral victory? The answer lies within the fact that not only democracy but also stability is a key consideration inseparably linked with the anti-coup norm. ROs do not only care about the consequences of a coup for democratic standards; they are also concerned about the impact a coup may have on the stability of a country.

The anti-coup norm portrays coup plotters as despicable norm violators, who should ideally be replaced, sentenced and penalized. Unfortunately, doing so proves difficult in many real cases. There are, however, instances in which the conspirators of failed coups have been severely punished. Measures can extend to large-scale purges of suspicious militaries and citizens, as recently illustrated by the failed coup in Turkey (Esen & Gumuscu, 2017; Easton & Siverson, 2018). However, successful coup plotters usually evade punishment altogether – simply because no one is capable of holding them accountable. The reality is that following a coup, plotters become influential actors. In the aftermath of a coup, they control vital state functions, posts and assets, including the security forces, ministries and financial resources.

The challenge for ROs is to come to terms with these actors without breaking the principles of the anti-coup norm. While many ROs vocally criticize the moves of coup plotters, they are also often forced to make certain compromises with them. When addressing political crises and domestic conflicts, ROs often do not focus on democracy alone. Instead, they often make concessions to powerful autocratic actors in order to create at least a basic level of stability and to constrain violence in a state (Nathan, 2016b). A central factor determining to which degree ROs must make such concessions after coups is the strength of the position of the coup plotters.

Coup plotters vary considerably regarding their domestic backing and the support they hold (Hoyle, 2019). In some cases, coups have been widely celebrated and praised by the population. Hence, some coup plotters can count on massive popularity and support from the population. Under such conditions, it is difficult for ROs to unconditionally insist on the principles of the anti-coup norm. In fact, ROs have been shown to be remarkably responsive to the domestic response to coups. For instance, following the coup in Mauritania in 2005, the AU and other international actors at first vocally and sternly condemned the event. However, when the leader change was widely celebrated by the population of the West African state, the AU quickly adjusted its strategy and accepted the timetable for constitutional reform suggested by the coup plotters (Ikome, 2007). In contrast, when President Jorge Serrano Elfas attempted a self-coup in Guatemala in 1993 he faced strong domestic opposition within the government, from the Supreme Electoral Tribunal, the Court of Constitutionality as well as Guatemalan civil society. The clear public disapproval of the coup influenced the international responses by the OAS and other regional actors, which unequivocally condemned and opposed the coup (Boniface, 2002; Levitt, 2006).

The response of the population is not the only criterion determining the robustness of the coup plotters' grip on power. Also the support of other political forces, influential businesspeople and the security apparatus is essential. After the coup in Sudan in 2019, mass demonstrations against the coup plotters taking power took place. However, the plotters' strong military means combined with their resolve to cling to power forced the AU and SADC to include the coup plotters in a power-sharing agreement. These examples illustrate that the stronger the overall position of the coup plotters is, the more likely it is that ROs will pursue a solution which reflects this strength, thus either a power-sharing agreement or a consolidation of the rule of the coup plotters.

E9:   *The stronger the domestic support of the coup plotters, the higher the likelihood that ROs will favour a power-sharing agreement or the consolidation of the coup plotters' rule.*

In sum, it is expected that four factors influence the choice of ROs to favour and pursue different post-coup solutions: the unequivocal applicability of the demands of the anti-coup norm itself to penalize coup plotters and not to accept them as new rulers, the democratic legitimacy of the ousted leader, the credibility of the promises of coup plotters to restore democratic order and the domestic power constellation. The expectations are summarized in Table 2.3.

With regard to the importance and explanatory power of the four aspects, no a priori assumptions are made. Importantly, the four aspects are not seen as isolated competing explanatory approaches. Instead, it is acknowledged that they can mutually influence each other: a clear identification of an event as being a coup might be driven by background information about the democratic record of the incumbent. The prospects of democratization are naturally judged against the performance of the prior regime. Likewise, both of these factors may influence the popularity of the two parties and thereby the domestic power constellation in a country.

A final note of caution is needed here. In the preceding paragraphs, the factors that make ROs likely to push for one out of several solutions to post-coup situations were discussed. Yet the fact that ROs prefer and work towards a certain post-coup solution does not automatically mean that this outcome will ultimately materialize. ROs have proved to be influential and decisive players after coups and in many cases ROs succeeded in bringing about their

Table 2.3: Expectations on research question 3

Aspects	Expectations
Unequivocal applicability of anti-coup norm	E6: If the anti-coup norm is unequivocally applicable to a particular case, ROs are more likely to push for a reinstatement of the ousted government or the formation of a new government in the aftermath of coups.
Democratic legitimacy of incumbent	E7: Democratic legitimacy of the ousted ruler increases the chance that ROs will push for a reinstatement of the ousted ruler or his participation in a power-sharing agreement.
Chances of post-coup democratization	E8: If coup plotters set up a timely and credible electoral schedule, the likelihood increases that ROs will favour the formation of a new government or the consolidation of the coup plotters' rule.
Domestic power constellation	E9: The stronger the domestic support of the coup plotters, the higher the likelihood that ROs will favour a power-sharing agreement or the consolidation of the coup plotters' rule.

preferred solution after coups (Legler & Tieku, 2010). Nevertheless, on some occasions coup plotters have successfully resisted significant external pressure. A telling example is the 2006 coup in Fiji. In December 2006, the army staged a coup against the government of Prime Minister Laisenia Qarase. Several ROs, including the EU, the Organisation Internationale de la Francophonie (OIF), the Commonwealth and the PIF sharply criticized the event and called for new elections and a return to democratic and constitutional order. Yet despite increasing international pressure through sharp condemnations, suspension from several ROs and economic sanctions from multiple actors, the junta led by Commander Bainimarama stood his ground for almost eight years until elections were finally held in 2104 (Ratuva, 2011; Tansey, 2016b).

The question of when and why ROs are successful in enforcing their positions in the aftermath of coups is of great interest and would definitely deserve further exploration in future studies. However, it is also beset with major challenges. The vivid debate about the effectiveness of economic sanctions pointedly illustrates the difficulties of measuring the success of international actors in pursuing political demands in other states (Hufbauer et al, 1990; Pape, 1997; Hovi et al, 2005; Bapat et al, 2013). First, there is the challenge of reliably assessing whether coup plotters really comply with demands of democratization or whether they just pretend to do so, for instance by holding elections, yet engaging in electoral fraud. Second, if the post-coup trajectory of a state actually leads towards democracy, the question is up to which degree this development was caused by the actions of ROs or by other actors and developments. Striebinger (2015) illustrates that actual post-coup trajectories are dependent on the responses of actors on different levels, including the military, the domestic as well as the international audience. Therefore, it is hardly possible to examine the impact of one of this 'layers' on post-coup trajectories in an isolated analysis.

Summary

This chapter presented the theoretical framework of the book. In a first step, the development of the anti-coup norm in ROs and the resulting implications for the role of ROs after coups were described. The argument developed builds upon the notion that the anti-coup norm is the overarching framework which requires generally adverse responses of ROs to coups but provides a certain extent of discretion for ROs how they respond to particular coups. This approach allows to account for the complexity of the norm, which touches upon democracy as well as on stability issues. It is explicitly acknowledged that ROs seek to reconcile democracy- as well as stability-related considerations in their responses.

Based upon these assumptions, theoretical expectations for the research questions were derived. For answering the first research question, what measures ROs use to respond to coups, a conceptualization of the instruments ROs can use to express their disapproval of coups and to exert pressure on the coup plotters was developed. These instruments form a continuum which ranges from rhetorical over diplomatic and economic to military measures. The second research question asks which factors influence the choice of stronger or weaker responses to coups by ROs. To answer this question, a series of expectations on factors which either make RO responses more likely or lead to stronger responses were formulated. These factors can be assigned to three groups: RO-related factors, making certain ROs more likely to show more and stronger responses than others, as well as democratic concerns and stability-oriented considerations. The third research question goes beyond the applied instruments and examines what post-coup solutions ROs pursue through their responses and why they do so. Here, it was argued that four factors shape the preferences of ROs for different post-coup solutions: the unequivocal applicability of the anti-coup norm, the democratic legitimacy of the ousted incumbent, the chances of a democratic transition under the leadership of the new rulers and the domestic power constellation. These theoretical arguments and expectations will guide the empirical analysis in the subsequent chapters of the book.

3

Mapping the Global Pattern of RO Responses to Coups

As Chapter 2 has illustrated, since the 1990s, the rise of the anti-coup norm has changed the stance of ROs vis-à-vis coups tremendously. The adoption of anti-coup provisions by a number of 'front-runners' was progressively mirrored by many other ROs leading to the rise of a global anti-coup norm within ROs. At the time of writing, 12 ROs have established explicit anti-coup provisions and an additional 16 comprise democracy clauses which serve as the basis for anti-coup measures. Yet the question is how do these provisions shape the role of ROs after coups? What impact did the rise of the anti-coup norm have on the international responses to coups? Have the emergence and increasing institutionalization of the norm led to a higher number of and more resolute responses by ROs to coups over time?

This chapter seeks to answer these questions from an empirical perspective by taking a closer look at how ROs have responded to coups since the anti-coup norm emerged. The chapter contains the first of the three parts of the analysis. The evidence presented in the chapter provides an important overview of the pattern of RO responses to coups. Thereby, it does not only answer the first of the three research questions, but also constitutes the basis for the subsequent analysis on the strength of responses and the choice of differential post-coup solutions.

Novel empirical data on the RO responses to coups in the timeframe from 1990–2019 are presented. They constitute the first comprehensive and systematic database on how ROs respond to coups. The data do not only provide an overview of the overall level of RO activity after coups, but also allow for differentiated perspectives on the issue: for instance, they allow us to compare the patterns of response between different regions, to analyse trends and dynamics over time and to zoom in to the preferred strategies of specific ROs after coups.

The chapter is organized as follows: first, the dataset is introduced and the data collection process, the operationalization and coding of the data are described. In a next step, the empirical evidence on the RO responses to coups over time, across regions and between and within particular organizations is presented. Subsequently, the implications of the findings for the role of ROs after coups are discussed. In a brief summary, the chapter is concluded by emphasizing the most important results.

RO responses to coups – a new dataset

Systematic and comparable data on the responses of external actors to coups is surprisingly scarce and to the author's knowledge no systematic database on regional and international responses to coups exists. To close this gap, a new dataset on responses of ROs to coups was created. This process and the methodological choices made are briefly described in the following.

The question of how to define the term coup d'état has occupied and troubled researchers for a long time. Coups constitute an inherently contested concept. The term is heavily normatively loaded with a notion of illegitimacy and viciousness. Yet at least the pretence of a legitimate claim to power is decisive for democratic as well as autocratic state leaders (Thyne et al, 2018). As a result, state leaders coming into office through irregular procedures have good reasons to deny that their accession to power constitutes a coup. On the other hand, actors who lost power have incentives to defame new rulers as coup plotters. For the purpose of this study, coups will be defined as coercive and illegal attempts by parts of a country's elites to grab executive power from the ruling government. Coups qualify as successful if the coup plotters manage to take over power at least temporarily. Importantly, coups can thus succeed or fail. In the following, data on both successful and failed coups are displayed. Likewise, the definition and the dataset also include so-called 'self-coups' or 'autogolpes' in which parts of the ruling government irregularly reshuffle the government to establish themselves as the single rulers.

In order to reach a comprehensive global set of coups, two of the most encompassing and widely used datasets, the Coups d'État Events Dataset by Marshall and Marshall (2019) and the Coups in the World Dataset by Powell and Thyne (2019) were merged. As the two datasets use slightly different definitions of coups, convergence of the data was checked for. Additionally, it was ensured that evidence for each incident recorded in the datasets exists and that it actually can be considered a coup according to the previously discussed definition.

In the end, 135 coups between 1990 and 2019 were included in the analysis. The scope of the analysis of RO responses to coups was restricted to this time period for three reasons. First, for coups which took place a long time ago the availability and quality of data continuously declines. Media coverage of coups, especially in small states, gets very sparse for earlier time periods, potentially inducing a significant reporting bias. Second, many studies point to the fact that the characteristics of coups and the responses towards them have changed considerably since the end of the Cold War (Marinov & Goemans, 2014: 799). The end of the deep rivalry between the West and Russia ended a pragmatic approach of judging coups according to the conflict side the ousted former and the newly installed government were aligned to. Finally, many ROs have only developed competencies to respond to internal processes in their member states comparatively recently. Most researchers pinpoint the birth of the anti-coup norm in 1991, with the vocal international response to the coups in Haiti and the Soviet Union (Franck, 1992). In the decades prior to these events, RO responses to coups were rare. Therefore, there is little reason to analyse the responses of ROs to coups for time periods in which none of these organizations had the capacity nor the mandate to do so. To sum up, the observation period was limited to the time between 1990 and 2019 for reasons of data quality, geopolitical context and intra-organizational developments.

In a next step, data on the responses of ROs to the 135 coups were collected.[1] ROs are defined as institutions in which at least three states cooperate on more than one single issue and in which membership is not universally open, but based on geographical, cultural or linguistic criteria, which all states have in common. This definition led to 78 ROs for which data were collected and analysed. When analysing RO responses to coups, an actor-like quality was assumed. ROs differ considerably in their competencies, capacities and powers, yet basically all of them can formulate their own positions and can take action in different policy fields. Many ROs provide information on their activities and decisions via social media, their website and other channels. However, the quality and scope of this information varies considerably and is vulnerable to bias. While some bigger ROs like the EU, the OAS and the AU provide relatively good and encompassing documentation of their activities, a series of smaller ROs do not even regularly update their websites. Therefore, it was decided against retrieving data directly from the ROs.

Instead, information on the responses of ROs to coups mainly stems from two sources: country reports from the EIU and newspaper articles retrieved form the search facility Lexis-Nexis. While the former includes neutral, standardized and comparable information on the economic and political situation in a given country and the actions of its most important international partners, the latter provides ample evidence of the stance of different international actors towards a coup. Obviously, the extent and depth of news coverage of coups increases over time and also varies depending on the economic and geostrategic significance of the affected country. The problem of uneven media attention between cases and the resulting differences in data quantity and quality is addressed with several measures. To reduce biases in the data, the search for articles was guided by a number of fixed search terms which were applied in the research and coding of every coup.[2]

To further alleviate potential bias and ensure the comprehensiveness of the dataset, the data were triangulated and supplemented by using qualitative case studies from academics, reports from non-governmental organizations (NGOs) and think-tanks and datasets on different forms of international foreign policy instruments like mediation, economic sanctions and military interventions.[3] This process led to very minor adjustments, yet mainly revealed that the initial coding of EIU reports and newspaper articles provides a very comprehensive and accurate picture of the pattern of international responses to coups, with very few and almost no severe responses omitted. While being aware that the data are not immune to reporting biases, one can be confident that it constitutes a sound and informative basis for analysis.

Once the data collection process was completed, a text analysis with MAXQDA software was conducted to identify the responses of international actors and in particular ROs from the retrieved material. Guided by the theoretical expectations about the differential means of ROs to respond to coups (see Chapter 2), a systematic coding scheme was created. The coding scheme includes the categories shown in Table 3.1. For the sake of transparency and replicability, detailed descriptions of the different categories are included. The categories correspond to the continuum of rhetorical, diplomatic, economic and military measures as outlined in the Chapter 2.

As shown in Table 3.1, ROs may not *only* use those four theorized forms of expressing their disapproval of a coup. In addition, ROs may also stay silent on a coup or even show signals of approval, for example congratulating coup plotters or promising them support. While such responses are not in line with the anti-coup norm, they form a small, yet non-negligible part of the empirical reality and therefore need to be included. Based on the coding scheme, all passages of the texts which contained indications on RO responses to coups were systematically coded and each response was assigned to a category. The coding scheme is fine-grained and makes important differentiations between oftentimes related steps (for example between threatening and actually imposing economic sanctions). Therefore, the material was not automatically coded, but hand coded in order to reach a higher level of accuracy. The coding resulted in a dataset containing information on the responses of 78 ROs to 135 coups between 1990 and 2019. The data can be retrieved in several formats, depending on the level of aggregation (RO, country or coup level). The most important trends and patterns in the data are illustrated in the following.

Table 3.1: Categories of responses to coups

Measure	Category	Description
	Approval of coups	Includes statements expressing approval of the coup attempt, congratulations, recognition of the coup plotters as government of the respective state, diplomatic consultations with the coup plotters and the (promise of) delivery of weapons, troops, money or other resources.
	No response	Used when no response of a particular actor was found.
Rhetorical measures	Concern	Includes statements expressing concern about the situation, requests to resolve the conflict and calls to stop violence in context with a coup. Importantly, this sort of response does not explicitly blame one side, but takes a neutral tone.
	Support for incumbent	Includes statements expressing support for the incumbent government and/or the message that coup plotters are not recognized as legitimate representatives of the coup-affected country. The focus lies on the role of the incumbent.
	Condem-nation	Includes statements of explicit and strong disapproval and rejection of the coup plotters' actions. The focus lies on the role of the coup plotters. In contrast to the former category, the criticism of the coup plotters is blunt and sharply formulated.
Diplomatic measures	Mediation	Includes offers and/or attempts to mediate in the conflict between the incumbent government and the coup plotters in an affected state, in the form of sending an envoy with a mandate to mediate and/or inviting the conflict parties to talks.
	Minor diplomatic sanctions	Includes minor diplomatic sanctions such as the calling of ambassadors, postponing diplomatic consultations, calling emergency meetings in ROs, etc.
	Major diplomatic sanctions	Includes severe diplomatic sanctions, for example the interruption of diplomatic relations, the suspension of a state from the decision-making bodies of the respective RO or delay of accession negotiations.
Economic measures	Economic sanction threats	Includes explicit threats of economic sanctions against coup plotters. Economic sanctions can take different forms, for example reduction or complete stop of foreign aid, asset freezes, travel bans, partial or total embargoes.
	Economic sanction imposition	Includes the actual imposition of economic sanctions against coup plotters. Economic sanctions can take different forms, for example reduction or complete stop of foreign aid, asset freezes, travel bans, partial or total embargoes.

Table 3.1: Categories of responses to coups (continued)

Measure	Category	Description
Military measures	Military intervention threat	Includes the explicit threats of a military intervention against coup plotters. It does not necessarily entail fighting, yet the RO threatens to send troops to the respective state.
	Military intervention imposition	Includes the actual imposition of a military intervention against coup plotters. It does not necessarily entail fighting, yet the RO sends troops to the respective state.

Mapping

Number of coups over time

For contextualizing the RO responses to coups, first a brief overview of the development of the number of coups over time and across continents is provided, before the responses of ROs towards them are shown. A glance at the datasets of Marshall and Marshall (2019) and Powell and Thyne (2019) illustrates that the number of coups has considerably declined since 1946/1950 (see Figure 3.1 and 3.2).

After the Second World War, coups took place very frequently. In the 1960s, 1970s and 1980s, several years witnessed more than ten coups. In the late1980s, the numbers slightly decline, only to reach another peak at the end of the Cold War. Subsequently, the occurrence of coups became less common. Although the numbers fluctuate, it is obvious that considerably fewer coups have occurred since the 1990s than in the preceding decades.

As already explained, the following analysis focuses on the time period from 1990 to 2019, when the anti-coup norm started to emerge and gain strength among ROs. Also within this observation period a clear downward trend in the prevalence of coups can be observed. The present dataset includes 135 confirmed coups from 1990 to 2019. Out of these 135 incidents, 65 coups happened in the first decade, 43 took place from 2000 until 2009 and only 27 coups were recorded from 2010 onwards. Yet, as Figure 3.3 shows, this trend is not a smooth one, but the number of coups fluctuates considerably. In 1991, 14 attempts to topple governments took place, the highest number of coups in a single year in the data. In subsequent years, the number of coups declined. Yet for instance in the year 2000, a sudden peak of nine coups was recorded. Whereas in the early 2000s relatively few coups happened, the numbers rose again between 2008 and 2013, but fell again to only four coups in the last three years. 2018 was the first year in the observation period for which no coup was recorded.

Apart from the overall number of coups, also their success rate is of interest. As Figure 3.3 shows, there is no clear trend with regard to the chances of

Figure 3.1: Number of coups according to Powell and Thyne (2019)

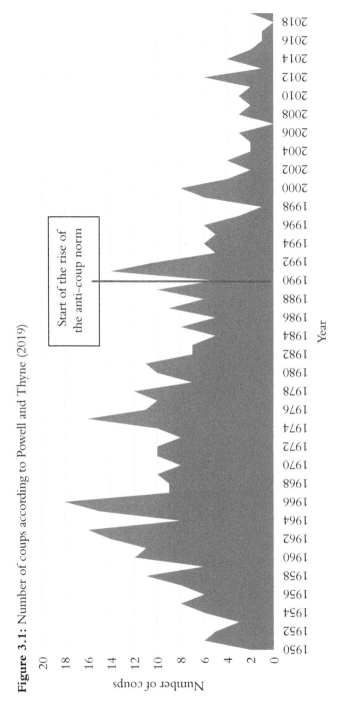

Source: Author's depiction, based on data by Powell and Thyne (2019)

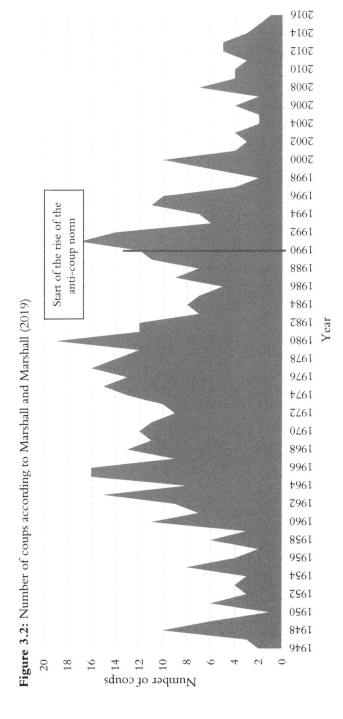

Figure 3.2: Number of coups according to Marshall and Marshall (2019)

Source: Author's depiction, based on data by Marshall and Marshall (2019)

Figure 3.3: Successful and failed coups, 1990–2019

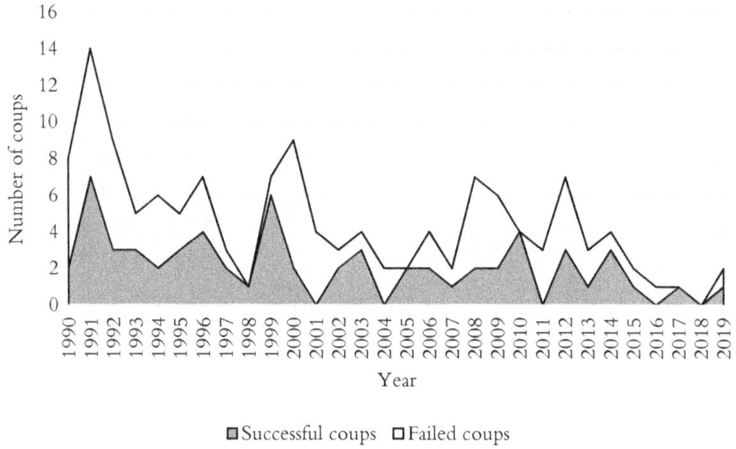

□ Successful coups □ Failed coups

Source: Author's depiction, based on the collected data

successfully ousting a government over time. Out of the 135 coups included in the data, 63 were successful, meaning that the coup plotters managed to grab executive power at least temporarily. In contrast, in 72 cases coups were immediately defeated. Apparently, the emergence of the anti-coup norm has not influenced the ratio between successful and failed coups.

Number of coups across continents

Apart from the distinction between successful and failed coups, also geography constitutes an essential aspect. It is important to note that the global distribution of coups is far from even. Instead, the risk of facing a coup varies tremendously between different world regions. Figure 3.4 clearly illustrates that most attempted and successful coups happen in Africa. Taking a look at the global geographical distribution of coups, one sees that African states have faced 92 coups between 1990 and 2019, accounting for more than two-thirds of all attempted coups in the data (68.14 per cent). Besides, Figure 3.4 also pointedly illustrates that many African states have not only faced one, but several coups in the last 30 years. Next to Africa, Asia is the continent with the second highest number of coups between 1990 and 2019 (21, 15.56 per cent), followed by 16 attempted takeovers in the Americas (11.85 per cent). In Oceania, only five coups have been recorded in the observation period (3.70 per cent). In Europe, no more coups have taken place since the attempted overthrow of President Gorbachev in the Soviet Union in August 1991 (0.74 per cent).

The global trend of a declining number of coups is visible in most continents (see Figures 3.5, 3.6 and 3.7). In Africa, the most coup-prone

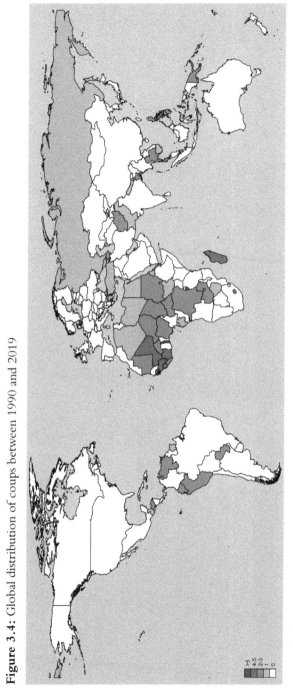

Figure 3.4: Global distribution of coups between 1990 and 2019

Source: Author's depiction, based on the collected data

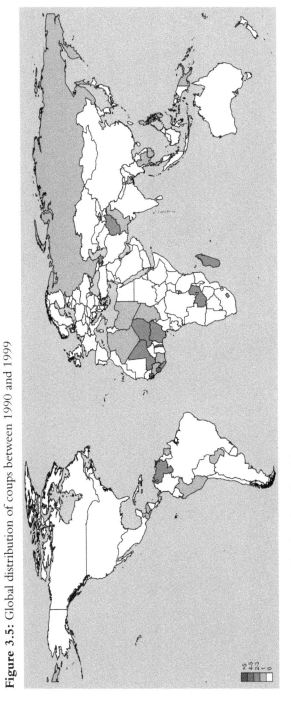

Figure 3.5: Global distribution of coups between 1990 and 1999

Source: Author's depiction, based on the collected data

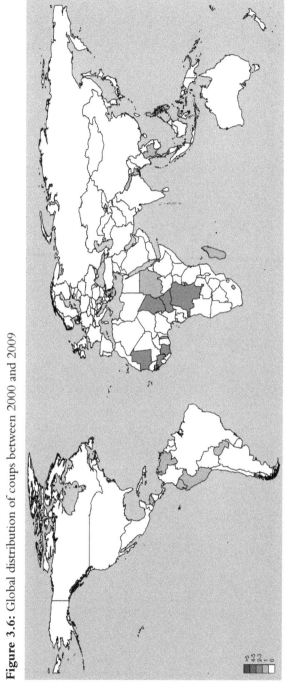

Figure 3.6: Global distribution of coups between 2000 and 2009

Source: Author's depiction, based on the collected data

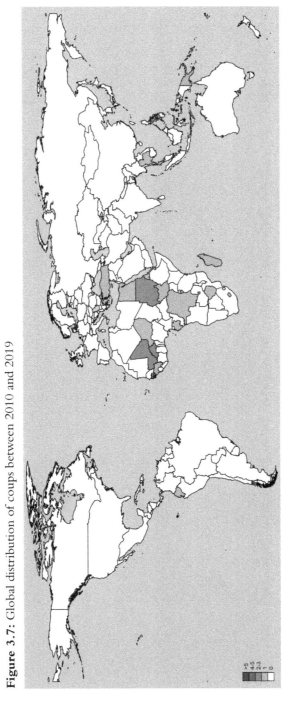

Figure 3.7: Global distribution of coups between 2010 and 2019

Source: Author's depiction, based on the collected data

continent, the number of coups declined from 41 in the 1990s to 30 in the 2000s. From 2010 to 2019, only 21 coups are recorded. In Asia, the prevalence of coups has similarly declined: in the first decade of the observation period, the continent faced 12 coups attempts, more than twice the number of coups in the subsequent decades (2000s: 6 coups; 2010s: 3 coups). In Latin America, the number of coups also halved from the 1990s to the 2000s (10 vs. 5 coups).

Noticeably, no more coups have been recorded on the continent since the attempt to oust the government of Ecuador in 2010. Only in Oceania does the trend look somewhat different: while the coup in Papua New Guinea in 1990 was the single one in the first decade of the observation period, in the 2000s three subsequent coups took place in Fiji and there was another attempted takeover in Papua New Guinea in 2012.

To conclude, since the emergence of the anti-coup norm in the 1990s, the incidence of coups has considerably declined. Yet a differentiated view on the data shows that coups have not disappeared and continue to regularly challenge the political and economic stability of states, particularly in Africa and Asia. Thus, despite the rise of the anti-coup norm, a substantial number of violations against the norm by rebels, militaries and opposition forces are still recorded. Once such incidents occur, the second component of the anti-coup norm requires ROs to take actions against coup plotters. In order to assess whether this is actually the case, it is analysed how the responses of ROs against coup plotters have developed since the emergence of the anti-coup norm in the following. First, general trends in the activities of ROs after coups are presented before zooming in on different patterns across regions and ROs.

Number of RO responses over time

From the 1990s onwards, ROs have taken a noticeably stronger interest and more active position towards coups. In total, there are 244 responses of ROs to the coups in the data. Although the level of activity of ROs fluctuates following the peaks and lows in the number of coup incidents per year, the data also clearly reveal that within the since the 1990s ROs have become more active after coups. Yet the development is different for successful and failed coups. Unsurprisingly, the former tend to attract more international attention than the latter, with 176 responses following the 63 successful coups and 68 responses occurring after the 72 failed ones. As Figure 3.8 illustrates, the average number of RO responses to successful coups has risen from less than two to almost five since the 1990s. In contrast, Figure 3.9 shows that while RO responses to failed coups have also increased in frequency, they occur only about half as often as after successful coups.

Figure 3.8: Number of successful coups and RO responses, 1990–2019

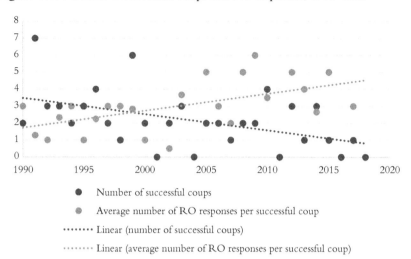

- ● Number of successful coups
- ● Average number of RO responses per successful coup
- •••••••• Linear (number of successful coups)
- •••••••• Linear (average number of RO responses per successful coup)

Source: Author's depiction, based on the collected data

Figure 3.9: Number of failed coups and RO responses, 1990–2019

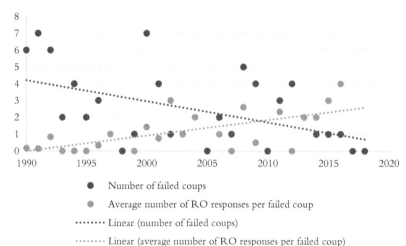

- ● Number of failed coups
- ● Average number of RO responses per failed coup
- •••••••• Linear (number of failed coups)
- •••••••• Linear (average number of RO responses per failed coup)

Source: Author's depiction, based on the collected data

Level of activity of different ROs

The general level of activity of ROs after coups has increased considerably since the emergence of the anti-coup norm. Yet does this apply to all ROs? As shown in Chapter 2, by far not all ROs have adopted anti-coup provisions. The data on RO activities after coups reveal that in total 34 ROs have shown at least one response after a coup between 1990 and 2019. Thus, apparently a broad variety of regional actors seems willing to become engaged after coups. However, these 34 ROs vary greatly with regard to their level of activity. Figure 3.10 depicts the number of instances in which ROs have shown responses after coups.[4]

In general, many ROs have only been active in a small number of cases. Yet out of the 34 ROs which have shown a response at least once there are also clear front-runners. The RO most eager to state its opinion or take actions on coups is the EU with 63 responses. This is particularly noteworthy, as the dataset contains only a single coup in Europe (the Soviet Union in 1991). Accordingly, the EU regularly addresses coups in distinct areas. In contrast to the EU, all other ROs limit their attention to coups in their member states and close geographical neighbourhood. In Africa, by far the most important ROs with regard to responses to coups are the AU (46) and ECOWAS (23). Yet also SADC (7), the Community of Sahel-Saharan States (CENSAD, 4) and COMESA (4) have taken action after coups several times. In America, the OAS (12) is the most active RO, but also CARICOM (5), Mercosur (3), ANDEAN (2) and the Bolivarian Alliance for the Peoples of Our Americas (ALBA, 2) have responded to coups.

Interestingly, the Organization of Islamic Cooperation (OIC, 11) belongs to the most active ROs, although it does not include a strong commitment to democratic values in its charter. Also the other cross-continental ROs, the Commonwealth (12), the OIF (10) and the Community of Portuguese Language Countries (CPLP, 5) comparatively frequently show responses after coups. It is worth noting that none of the Asian ROs shows a high number of responses to coups. ASEAN and the South Asian Association for Regional Cooperation (SAARC) are the most active ROs in this region, with only three and two responses respectively. The data show that the majority of responses stems from ROs, which hold a democracy-based mandate to take action after coups (Chapter 2). However, also a number of ROs without such a mandate (such as the GCC, IGAD and ALBA) have responded to coups, indicating that a formal adoption of explicit democracy or anti-coup provisions is not a necessary condition to follow the anti-coup norm.

Intra-organizational variation

Recalling that the dataset includes a total of 135 coups, the comparatively low numbers indicate that RO responses to coups are no automatism. Many ROs have only selectively responded to a small number of coups in their members while ignoring other instances. Even the most active ROs are far from responding to every coup in its sphere of influence. As Figure 3.11 shows, most ROs only respond to a fractional amount of the coups in their member states. Frontrunners like the AU or ECOWAS have only responded to approximately half the coups taking place in their member states

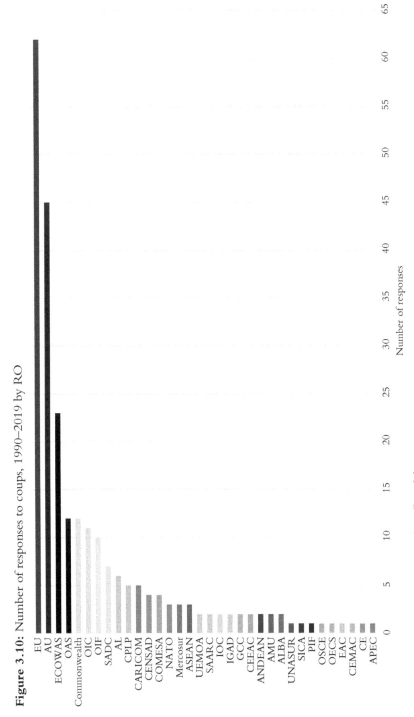

Figure 3.10: Number of responses to coups, 1990–2019 by RO

Source: Author's depiction, based on the collected data

Figure 3.11: Level of RO activity after coups in member states

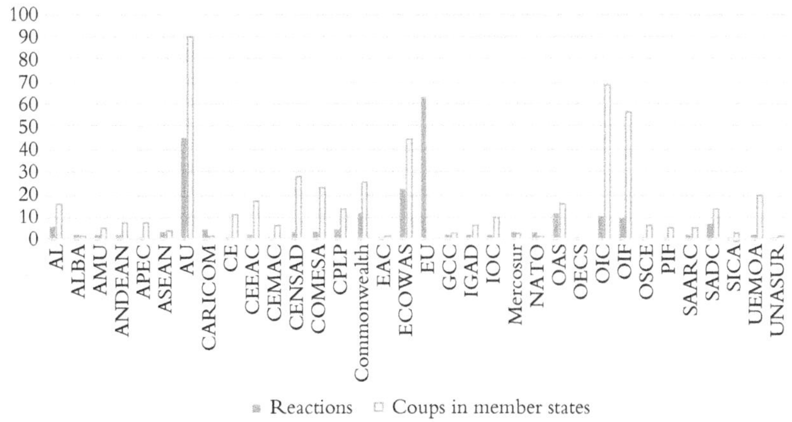

Source: Author's depiction, based on the collected data

(51.11 per cent and 52.27 per cent respectively). The non-geographical ROs also only respond to selected cases (CPLP 38.46 per cent, OIC 16.42 per cent, OIF 17.86 per cent). In contrast, some ROs with small absolute numbers of responses, such as **ALBA**, **CARICOM**, the East African Community (**EAC**), the **GCC**, Mercosur, North Atlantic Treaty Organization (**NATO**) and **UNASUR** have responded to all coups in their member states.

To conclude, the data show that ROs have in general become more active after coups since the emergence of the anti-coup norm. The number of RO responses per coup has considerably increased since the 1990s. Yet the data also indicate that not all ROs address coups. A relatively small number of ROs is responsible for the majority of responses and many ROs only rarely respond to coups. Besides, even the most active ROs have by far not responded on all potential occasions. Hence, not all ROs have become more active after coups, and even the most active ones still tend to stay silent on many occasions.

Variation in the strength of responses

Obviously, RO responses to coups cannot be reduced to their presence or absence. The sheer number of ROs responses does not necessarily correspond to the severity of responses. Confronted with domestic conflicts or democratic setbacks, external interveners can choose between a wide array of different instruments to respond to the situation (van Sickle & Sandholtz, 2009; Beardsley & Schmidt, 2012). Correspondingly, ROs have a diverse set of instruments to express their position towards a coup, exert pressure on the coup plotters and oppose the takeover. These instruments include verbal statements, economic and diplomatic measures and, as a

Table 3.2: Different responses to coups

Concern statements (neutral)	66
Support for incumbent	31
Condemnation of coup plotters	156
Mediation offers/attempts	52
Minor diplomatic sanctions	26
Major diplomatic sanctions	30
Economic sanctions threatened	28
Economic sanctions imposed	39
Military intervention threatened	7
Military intervention imposed	2

last resort, the (threat of) use of military force. These different options to respond to a coup can be conceived as a continuum ranging from rather neutrally formulated concern statements to severe punishment of the coup plotters.[5] Some of the of the instruments used by ROs after coups are much more frequently applied than others. The frequency of the occurrence of the different responses is depicted in Table 3.2.

In 66 cases, ROs expressed their concern about the situation in countries where coups have taken place but fell short of explicitly blaming one conflict party. Such statements are often accompanied by calls for restraint and mutual dialogue. In 31 cases, external actors voiced their support for the ousted government to back it against the challenge of coup plotters. The most frequent response of ROs to coups is an outright condemnation (156). Taken together, these three forms of rhetorical measures to react to coups account for 57.89 per cent of all responses. Diplomatic measures make up 24.71 per cent of all RO responses. ROs offered to mediate between the incumbent and the coup plotters in 52 instances and in 26 instances minor diplomatic sanctions were imposed, in the form of postponing consultations with the affected country, calling emergency meetings between their member states or sending fact-finding missions. Yet ROs frequently also suspended affected states from participating in the meetings and programmes of the RO, a step which can have severe ramifications for a country (30). The threatening and imposition of economic sanctions are the next steps of escalation, which were taken 28 and 39 times respectively. Hence, 15.33 per cent of all RO measures in response to coups were of an economic nature. The most popular sort of economic sanction in this context is reducing or completely ceasing to provide development cooperation to the affected country, as such a measure can be comparatively easily and promptly be implemented. Finally, in a few cases a military intervention was either threatened (7) or imposed (2). However, such extreme steps are very rare and account for only 2.06 per cent of all RO responses.

In many cases, external actors did not choose a single response, but combined several measures. For instance, ROs often very promptly condemn coups and express their concern and/or support for the incumbent and later impose more robust measures such as sanctions and military action, which usually need more time to agree on and to prepare. However, one can also observe great variation with regard to this aspect. In some cases, ROs responded remarkably fast and decisively with economic or military means, whereas in other cases even the application of weaker measures took a long time.

A rare yet puzzling phenomenon are positive RO responses towards coups. Although most ROs emphasize their strong rejection of coups, takeovers are not always opposed, but sometimes even welcomed by ROs. In 15 cases, ROs voiced their approval of the actions of coup plotters by congratulating them, meeting them in official diplomatic functions, promising or sending financial, material or military support. For instance, ASEAN was quick to resume diplomatic ties with the new Thai authorities after the coups in 1991 and 2006, clearly signalling the organization's recognition and approval of the new regime. Importantly, most but not all positive responses to coups stemmed from autocratic ROs or organizations lacking explicit anti-coup provisions. ROs are not always united in their assessment of coups. Whereas the AU rejected the coup in Egypt in 2013 and suspended the country, the Secretary General of the AL declared its support for the new regime and the member states of the GCC provided important financial support for the heavily indebted country. Sometimes, regional actors also shift from an initial hostile attitude towards coup plotters to a more conciliatory position. For instance, the ousting in 2003 of President Ange-Félix Patassé of the Central African Republic was originally condemned by many ROs, including the AU, the Communauté économique et monétaire de l'Afrique centrale (CEMAC), CENSAD and the EU. However, in the aftermath of the coup, international support for the new regime increased: the AU and the EU de facto recognized the new authorities and CEMAC and CENSAD openly declared their support for them.

Strength of responses over time

How has the use of responses of different strength changed over time? Figure 3.12 displays how often the different instruments have been applied after coups in the three decades of the observation period. In order to put the number of instruments used into relation with the prevalence of coups in the respective time period the total number of coups in the decade is also depicted. The graph illustrates several important points. First, while

Figure 3.12: Use of different instruments after coups over time

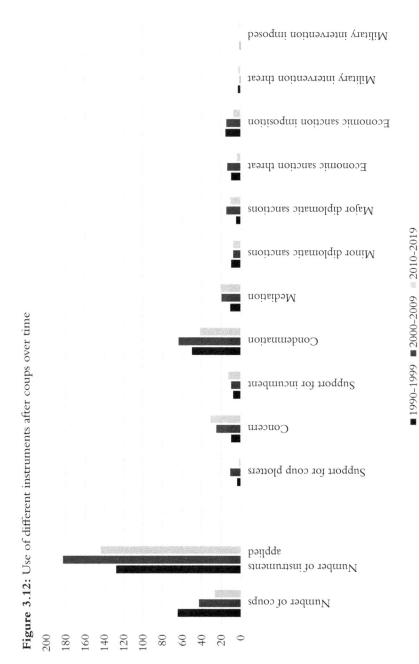

1990–1999 ■ 2000–2009 2010–2019

Source: Author's depiction, based on the collected data

the total number of coups has declined over the three decades, the number of instruments used by ROs first increases in the 2000s and then decreases again after 2010. Thus, taking into account that the number of coups is declining, a coup is nowadays on average followed by the use of significantly more measures than in the 1990s.

Second, if one focuses on single instruments, a diverse and interesting pattern emerges. The frequency of the use of some instruments, as for instance the imposition of minor diplomatic sanctions or condemnations, remain comparatively stable over time. In contrast, for other instruments, noticeable changes are visible. Over time, some instruments have become much more common. Comparing the frequency of neutral concern statements of the first and the third decade, we see that the numbers have more than tripled (10 times vs. 31 times). This implies that ROs are nowadays more willing to immediately respond to coups, even if they have not finally decided which side to take or do not have strong stakes in a conflict. Two other important instruments show an increase in usage: compared to the 1990s, ROs mediated considerably more often after coups in the 2000s and 2010s (1990s 11 times; 2000s 20 times; 2010s 21 times). Similarly, the use of major diplomatic sanctions such as the suspension of states from a RO has considerably increased (1990s 5 times; 2000s 15 times; 2010s 11 times).

In contrast, the total number of economic sanctions and sanction threats has declined in the last decade. Whether this is due to the fact that fewer coups took place since 2010 or to a conscious decision of ROs against economic statecraft as a means to exert pressure on coup plotters is hard to tell. Interestingly, the use of military means seems to have a u-shaped distribution: Whereas in the 1990s three military threats (Burundi in 1993, Sierra Leone in 1997 and Guinea-Bissau in 1998) and one actual military intervention after a coup took place (Burundi in 1993), only one military threat was recorded in the 2000s (São Tomé and Príncipe in 2003). Yet since 2010, ROs seem to have turned back to military means to exert pressure on coup plotters: after the 2012 coup in Mali, ECOWAS threatened to intervene, as well as in Guinea-Bissau in the same year. In the latter case, the RO put its words into practice. Besides, the coup also evoked a military threat from the CPLP.

Strength of responses across regions

As outlined earlier in this chapter, the risk of a country facing a coup has not only changed over time, but also varies tremendously across continents. This varying prevalence of coups across world regions has also affected the responses of the respective ROs to coups. Accordingly, the next section takes a closer look at which responses coups on different continents have received.

In the Americas, ROs have been alert to coups for a long time: in the early 1990s and 2000s, 14 coups took place on the continent, which triggered a high total number of 34 responses by ROs. In 2009 and 2010, two more coups in Honduras and Ecuador occurred, which led to clearly negative responses by six and four ROs respectively. This high number of responses can be explained by the fact that several ROs with overlapping membership and mandates in the realm of security and democracy governance exist on the continent. Not only the OAS, but also Mercosur, ANDEAN, UNASUR and Community of Latin American and Caribbean States (CELAC) are important regional actors in this regard (Weiffen, 2017). Accordingly, many different ROs have shown responses after coups. The OAS responded to the majority of coups and also the EU responded in nine instances. Apart from these major actors, also several sub-regional ROs including ALBA, ANDEAN, CARICOM, Mercosur, the Organization of Eastern Caribbean States (OECS), the Central American Integration System (SICA) and UNASUR expressed their opposition to coups. The responses to coups in Latin America have not only come from many actors but have usually also been swift and decisive. As a consequence, out of the 16 coups in the region only three did not receive any response: the attempted takeovers in Peru in 1992 and 2000 and in Honduras in 1999, which were all immediately defeated by troops loyal to the respective governments. In all remaining cases one or often several ROs showed their clear disapproval and opposition to the coup. While two coups in Trinidad and Tobago in 1990 and Haiti in 1991 only led to verbal condemnations, all other coups evoked at least minor diplomatic sanctions and three of them were followed by the imposition of economic sanctions, as for instance the coup in Honduras in 2009.

In Africa, the emerging picture is a different one. The rate of RO responses to coups was comparatively low at the start of the observation period but has significantly increased. Whereas in the 1990s 23 out of 41 coups did not receive any RO response at all, the level of activity of African ROs subsequently rose. The average number of RO responses per coup increased from 1.17 in the 1990s to over 2.24 in the 2000s and to 2.68 post-2010. These numbers indicate that since the emergence of the anti-coup norm, ROs have become considerably more active after coups in Africa. But the spectrum of responses to coups in Africa is tremendously diverse. On the one hand, more than a third of the coups on the continent (35 out of 92) did not lead to any response by ROs. On the other hand, all instances in which ROs threatened to or actually applied military means against coup plotters, the most severe form of response, have taken place in Africa. With regard to the strength of responses, there is no geographical pattern discernible. Even subsequent coups in the very same country have often led to very distinct responses by ROs.

In contrast, the rate of RO responses in Asia remained constantly low for most of the observation period. Nine out of the 21 coups did not receive any response from ROs and another seven only led to rhetorical actions. There are only four cases in Asia in which more severe instruments were applied: the coups in Cambodia (1997), in Pakistan (1999), the Maldives (2012) and in Thailand (2014), the latter featuring quite prominently in the media. Yet in the cases of Pakistan (1999) and Thailand (2014) the more severe measures were actually economic sanctions imposed by the EU. Cambodia (1997) and the Maldives (2012) are the only coups after which Asia ROs (ASEAN and SAARC respectively) have taken more than rhetorical stances.

In Oceania, only five coups took place between 1990 and 2019. The emerging picture of responses towards these events is mixed. The successful coups in Fiji (twice in 2000 and in 2006) evoked considerable action from the EU, the Commonwealth and the PIF, including mediation, diplomatic and economic sanctions. In contrast, the failed attempts in Papua New Guinea in 1990 and 2012 did not lead to any RO responses.

Patterns of the most active ROs

Apparently, a multitude of instruments are applied to express ROs' disapproval of coups. These instruments vary considerably in strength. Besides, there are tremendous regional differences in the responses to coups, How can this diversity be explained? An obvious idea is that ROs have adopted different strategies and procedures on how they deal with coups. Figure 3.13 depicts the choice of instruments of the six most active ROs (AU, Commonwealth, ECOWAS, EU, OAS, OIC).

For all these ROs, rhetorical condemnations are one of the most important and frequently applied instruments. However, with regard to the choice of other more severe measures, they vary considerably: the AU has frequently engaged in mediation after coups and has suspended member states in which a coup took place. In relative terms, ECOWAS puts even more emphasis on mediation. However, the organization is also the most active one with regard to the threat and imposition of military intervention. The OAS takes a consistently negative position towards coups, issuing not a single neutral concern statement, but clear condemnations instead. Additionally, the RO has an established practice of calling emergency meetings whenever a coup takes place in one of the organization's member states and of mediating in the format of intra-elite dialogue roundtables or 'Mesas', as in the cases of Peru (2000) and Venezuela (2002–2004) (Cooper & Legler, 2005). The EU in turn has never faced a coup in one of its member states, but exclusively responds to coups in external countries. Consequently, the EU lacks the possibility to suspend coup countries or impose other intra-organizational diplomatic sanctions. Instead, one of its main strategies to exert pressure on coup plotters are economic sanctions, in particular reducing or ceasing foreign aid to the country. The Commonwealth has suspended members on four occasions and threatened sanctions against Fiji in 2000. In contrast, the OIC has only shown comparatively soft responses, mainly concern statements and rhetorical condemnations.

Figure 3.13: Choice of different instruments by RO

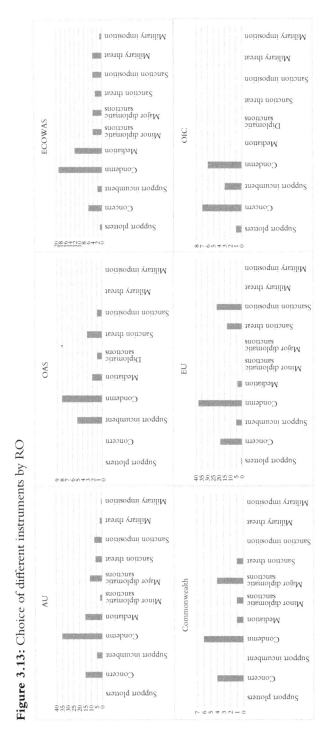

Source: Author's depiction, based on the collected data

Apart from the fact that ROs seem to have preferred strategies, the most striking observation is that ROs do not consistently apply the same instruments to every case. Instead, their responses differ considerably in strength and severity. ECOWAS serves as a prime example: the RO mostly ignores unsuccessful coups in West Africa (6 responses after 26 failed coups). In contrast, the organization shows a plethora of different responses to the successful takeovers in the region. It has not shown any response to seven cases and, in the case of Gambia in 1994, even expressed its implicit approval of the coup plotters' actions by allowing them to participate in the next ECOWAS Summit. The coups in Côte d'Ivoire (1999), Guinea-Bissau (1999) and Niger (1999) were rhetorically condemned, yet no further action was taken. ECOWAS tried to mediate between coup plotters and the ousted government in Sierra Leone (1992), Niger (2010), Guinea-Bissau (2003, 2010) and Burkina Faso (2014, 2015).Although the West African organization took a rather conciliatory attempt in all these cases, a handful of coups were severely punished: ECOWAS imposed diplomatic and economic sanctions against Togo (2005) and Guinea (2008). In the cases of Mali (2012), Guinea-Bissau (1998) and Sierra Leone (1997), these measures were combined with the threat to use military force against the coup plotters and in Guinea-Bissau (2012) ECOWAS actually intervened militarily to restore constitutional rule.

Other organizations, such as the AU and the OAS have striven for more continuity in their responses by outlining official procedures and potential measures in their statutes. For instance, the AU has an official policy of suspending any member state in which a coup has taken place (Leininger, 2014). Nevertheless, the organization refrained from suspending the Central African Republic (2003), Guinea-Bissau (2003) or Zimbabwe (2017) after coup plotters had taken successfully taken control of the states. Besides, while in some cases, such as after the coups in Egypt (2013), Guinea-Bissau (2012), Mauritania (2005) and Niger (2010) the formal suspension of the state was the only major action taken by the AU, in other instances the organization also threatened or imposed economic sanctions (Burkina Faso in 2014 and 2015; Burundi in 1996; Comoros in 1999; Guinea in 2008; Madagascar in 2009; Mali in 2012; Mauritania in 2008; in Togo 2005) or even military force (Burundi in 1993; São Tomé and Príncipe in 2003). Also the EU has a selective approach towards coups: The EU has condemned 11 failed coups, yet in turn 17 successful coups did not receive a response. After 19 successful coups, the EU only voiced its concern or condemned the coup rhetorically, but in another 22 cases, the EU additionally imposed economic sanctions, mainly via reducing or suspending foreign aid.

To summarize, ROs use rhetorical, diplomatic, economic and military measures to respond to coups. The frequency with which the measures are used is antiproportional to their strength. The weakest instrument, rhetorical response, is by far used most frequently, followed by a significantly lower number of diplomatic and economic measures. Military responses to coups by ROs are rare. While the usage of medium-strength instruments like mediation or suspension of states from regional bodies have become more frequent, there is no general trend towards significantly stronger responses to coups. Most noticeably, the responses of ROs to coups are characterized by a tremendously high degree of heterogeneity: patterns of responses to coups differ between regions and ROs, but also within ROs a high degree of inconsistency is visible. ROs increasingly follow the request to reject and oppose coups, yet they do so through a plethora of different instruments.

Discussion

Having presented the empirical evidence, the implications of the findings for the role of ROs after coups are discussed in this section. Besides, the potentials and limitations of the data and the question which conclusions can be drawn from it are briefly laid out. The insights from the descriptive analysis indicate that the role of ROs after coups has clearly been strengthened over time. The empirical evidence shows that gradually more regional actors have started to reject and oppose coups. The general level of activity of ROs has significantly increased and the probability that a coup happening now will evoke responses from surrounding ROs is noticeably higher than it was 10 or 20 years ago. Notwithstanding, the data also show that many ROs are still hesitant to address coups and even very active ROs do not respond to all unconstitutional takeovers alike. Hence, despite the increasingly influential role of ROs after coups, responding to such events does not seem to be an automatism.

There are two plausible explanatory factors for this: on the one hand, almost all ROs suffer from a constant shortage of financial, personal and military resources, making decisive and strong responses to each and every coup in their member states difficult. On the other hand, ROs are also often confronted with the challenge to reach consensus among their member states to agree on measures after coups. When member states evaluate the circumstances and impact of a coup differently, this can be an especially challenging endeavour.

In addition, the data show that ROs differ tremendously regarding how they respond to coups. As the mapping of the data shows, ROs use four groups of instruments to respond to coups: rhetorical, diplomatic, economic and military means. The frequency with which ROs use these policy instruments of varying strength differs across regions, organizations and cases. In sum, rhetorical measures are used most frequently by ROs after coups – diplomatic and economic measures occasionally and military measures very rarely. There is no apparent trend towards the use of more robust and intrusive measures over time. This does not necessarily imply that ROs refrain from following and exerting the normative guidelines of the anti-coup norm in itself. Instead, the finding may reflect the fact that despite a normative commitment to the anti-coup norm, the limited resources of most ROs can lead to a hesitancy of ROs to enforce the anti-coup norm with stronger, yet also very cost-intensive and risky means like economic sanctions and military operations.

The diverse strategies of different ROs also suggest that there is not one tried and tested way of responding to coups. ROs have a variety of instruments to choose from to respond to coups and, as the data illustrate, they actively make use of it. The availability of diverse instruments and the possibility to combine them, for example by first rhetorically condemning a coup and later imposing economic sanctions against the coup plotters, provides ROs with a high degree of flexibility over how they respond to a coup. Yet the data presented in this chapter do not tell us how ROs make use of this flexibility. For a better understanding of the role of ROs after coups further reflection on why ROs choose weaker or stronger responses after coups is needed.

To sum up, the point is that one needs to be careful about jumping from the observed empirical patterns of RO responses to coups to causal claims. The fact that ROs apparently play a more active role does not tell us why they do so, and which aims they pursue when criticizing or sanctioning coup plotters. Therefore, for further exploring the role of ROs in the context of coups, one has to exceed the descriptive analysis. This step is taken in the two subsequent chapters. In Chapter 4, the factors determining how strongly a RO responds to a particular coup are analysed in detail with quantitative methods. After that, the qualitative analysis in Chapter 5 goes beyond the question which instruments ROs apply after coups and focuses on the post-coup solutions they seek to achieve through applying these instruments.

Summary

In this chapter, the first research question of what measures ROs use to respond to coups was empirically assessed. The data show that since the anti-coup norm has been adopted by many important ROs, potential insurgents have become more hesitant to stage coups and the incidence of coups has declined. In addition, ROs increasingly comply with the request to oppose coups and they have become more active after coups. Yet the role of ROs after coups is characterized by a strong degree of heterogeneity and variation. Not only do ROs choose different instruments to respond to coups, but they also do not consistently apply them to all coups alike. Whereas some coups are followed by severe measures such as suspension from regional bodies, economic sanctions or even military interventions, other takeovers only face comparatively mild criticism, are ignored or, in extreme cases, are even welcomed and supported by certain ROs.

This finding resonates strongly with the few existing comparative studies on the issue, which point towards a high degree of variation in the way ROs respond to coups. For example, Shannon et al (2015), Tansey (2017) and Thyne and Hitch (2020) emphasize the generally inconsistent approach of international actors towards coups. Focusing specifically on the role of African ROs, Souaré (2014), Nathan (2016c) and Wet (2019) likewise argue that despite a rising consensus against the acceptance of coups, ROs are still far from consistently addressing every coup in their region. In presenting the first comprehensive global overview of the responses of ROs to coups, this chapter advances the academic knowledge on the issue. The detailed mapping shows not only that ROs vary in their responses to coups but provides deep insights on the varying level of activity of different actors, region-specific particularities and the tremendous differences in the use of a continuum of instruments, ranging from non-reactions to rhetorical, diplomatic and economic to military means.

This high extent of variation implies that although the anti-coup norm seems to play an important role for many ROs, this role is not tightly defined. ROs have quite some leeway in how they interpret and apply the anti-coup norm when faced with coups. This observation constitutes a perfect transition towards the second research question. The presence of responses in some cases, yet not in others and the choice of instruments of diverging strength after coups does not necessarily mean that ROs randomly or arbitrarily apply the anti-coup norm. To thoroughly assess the role of ROs after coups, it is important to understand which factors drive the decisions of ROs over whether to get active after a coup and which instruments to use to do so. Accordingly, in the following chapter, the second research question, which factors influence the choice of stronger or weaker RO responses to coups, is examined.

4

Explaining the Strength of RO Responses to Coups

The data collected and presented in Chapter 3 show that the responses of ROs to coups are tremendously diverse. Some ROs are generally more active and tend to impose stronger measures than others. Yet also one and the same RO often shows stronger responses to one coup than to another. Which factors drive such differential responses? In Chapter 2, a series of potential explanations were developed which account for this inter- yet also intra-RO variation. In the present chapter, an explanatory statistical analysis is conducted to put these theoretical expectations regarding the strength of RO responses to coups to an empirical test. In other words, the chapter seeks to explain why RO responses to coups differ so much in their strength and which factors are responsible for this diversity.

Examining this question is a crucial step for understanding the role of ROs after coups. Only if we understand which capacities, motives and considerations influence RO responses to coups can we thoroughly assess which roles ROs play in combatting coups and exerting the anti-coup norm. The decision over how to respond to a coup is a complex one. In Chapter 2, it was argued that the decision-making process of ROs leading to stronger or weaker responses includes two steps: first, the decision to get active or not, and second the choice of an instrument of particular strength. Methodologically, this duality is taken care of by using zero-inflated probit models, which explicitly model this two-step decision-making process. Based upon these models, the plausibility of the expectations from Chapter 2 is tested. The analysis shows that democracy as well as stability-related factors play an important role in shaping the strength of RO responses. The respective empirical results are presented and their implications for the role of ROs after coups are critically discussed.

The chapter is structured as in the following way: first, the potential explanations for diverging RO responses are briefly revised. Next, the data structure and model selection as well as the operationalization of the dependent and independent variables into empirical indicators are described. Subsequently, the results from the statistical analysis are reported, described and visualized. As zero-inflated probit models are not straightforward to interpret, particular emphasis is put on illustrating the effects found in the models. The most important findings and their implications for the role of ROs after coups are critically discussed. The chapter ends with a short summary, in which the empirical findings are wrapped up.

Theoretical expectations on RO responses

As Chapter 3 shows, RO responses to coups vary across regions, organizations and cases. I argue that three major groups of factors influence the choice of weaker or stronger responses by ROs: RO-specific characteristics, democracy-related aspects of a coup as well as security factors. Confronted with a coup, ROs have to take a dual decision: whether to respond at all to a coup and which instruments to choose to do so. The first part of this decision is influenced by three factors. ROs are more likely to respond to coups if they happen in their own member states, if the coup plotters are successful in taking power and if the RO has an official mandate to address such unconstitutional leader changes.

With regard to the strength of responses, the characteristics of the RO in question play an important role. ROs with a more democratic membership are assumed to take stronger action after coups. Likewise, ROs are expected to show stronger responses to coups if they hold more economic and military power in relation to the country. Democracy-related aspects of the coup also matter. If a government ousted by a coup is democratic, RO responses to the incident are expected to be stronger. Likewise, ROs are assumed to take more severe measures after exclusively military coups. If a coup is preceded by popular protests, RO responses are expected to be weaker as the legitimacy of the incumbent is already undermined. Security-related aspects are another important issue. Successful coups are a higher security risk than failed ones and should therefore evoke stronger responses by ROs. Besides, ROs are assumed to respond more decisively if a coup is accompanied by major violence. ROs are also expected to show stronger responses after coups in countries which are close trading partners. Finally, it is expected that the democracy-related explanations (prior level of democracy, civilian vs. exclusively military coup and prior protests) play a more important role for democratic ROs than for autocratic ones.

Data and methods

In this section, the structure of the data, the respective model specifications used for the analysis and the operationalization of the dependent and independent variables into empirically measurable indicators are briefly described.

Data structure and model selection

The data on RO responses to coups as collected for Chapter 3 forms the basis for the following analysis. As the research interest lies on the strength of the responses by ROs to coups, the unit of observation is the RO–coup dyad. Hence, the data were transformed into a dyadic structure. For example, the combination *AU – coup in Zimbabwe 2017* constitutes one observation in the dataset. To each of the 135 coups recorded in the data, each of the 78 ROs can potentially show a response. This resulted in a dataset with 8,080 observations.[1]

Yet the number of cases in which ROs actually show a response to a coup is much smaller. In none of the coups recorded in the data have more than six out of the 78 ROs have simultaneously taken action. On average, a coup leads to responses by only 1.726 ROs (see Chapter 3). Thus, in the overwhelming majority of the dyads, no response is recorded. From a theoretical angle, this is not surprising. Obviously not all ROs can reasonably be expected to respond to each and every coup. For instance, it is not plausible to assume that a coup in Fiji will evoke responses from all ROs around the globe, including small ROs in Africa or Latin America. Put differently, not all ROs are likely candidates to respond to a particular coup.

Recent studies have emphasized the need to distinguish between relevant and non-relevant dyads in conflict studies and IR (Xiang, 2010). The challenge is to do so methodologically. A promising approach are zero-inflation models. Put simply, zero-inflation models handle the challenge of an excessive number of zeros by assuming that observed non-responses in the data can be distinguished into two latent groups. An observation with a value of zero can either belong to a first group in which the observations have a probability of zero of showing a response or it can belong to a second group in which the observations have a non-zero probability of showing a response, but still do not respond (Long & Freese, 2006). In the present case, this can be illustrated as follows: after a coup in a state, there is a comparatively large group of ROs not affected and concerned by the coup, which have consequently no motive at all to intervene. Besides, there is a smaller group of ROs which are affected by the takeover and might potentially show a response, yet within this group still some ROs might decide not to respond. As the two groups are latent, they cannot a priori be distinguished. However, zero-inflation techniques are capable of modelling (Escribà-Folch, 2013) the likelihood of observations to belong to either group, as well as of calculating the probability of showing an actual response if the observation belongs to the 'relevant' group (Bagozzi et al, 2015). In doing so, zero-inflation models proceed in two steps, using two sets of variables. The first set determines the chance of a RO belonging to either of the two latent group, while the second set models the effects on the actual dependent variable. The two set of variables can be distinct, yet may also include the same variables (Long & Freese, 2006). Applying this approach to the present data, a first set of variables is used to model which ROs are likely to take action in the first place, while a second set determines the strength of the responses. This corresponds with the theoretical expectations from Chapter 2 that different factors drive the decision of ROs whether to become active and how strongly to respond.

Apart from the overrepresentation of non-responses in the data, the nature of the dependent variables is also challenging for the analysis. The first question, whether a RO takes action after a particular coup, is captured by a binary dependent variable. The second dependent variable, measuring the strength of the responses is more problematic in this regard. As the strength of responses is an ordered categorical variable, the use of standard OLS regression is not appropriate. Instead, an ordered-probit model must be applied (Long & Freese, 2006). Zero-inflation techniques can be used for the analysis of different sorts of dependent variables. Due to the categorical nature of the dependent variable a Zero-inflated Ordered Probit (ZiOP) model is the appropriate choice in the present case (Bagozzi et al, 2015). While ZiOP models constitute an elegant statistical solution to the challenges of the present data structure, their interpretation deserves special care. The size of the coefficients of an ordered probit model cannot be directly interpreted as unit changes in the dependent variable. Therefore, a section is dedicated to an extensive visualization and discussion to the size and significance of the effects tested in the analysis.

An additional challenge for the present analysis is the issue of a violation of the assumption of independence of the observations. The response of a RO to a particular coup might be influenced by the responses of the RO to other takeovers, as path dependencies, previous experiences and unobserved idiosyncratic characteristics of the ROs come into play. Likewise, the responses of different ROs to one specific coup might also be dependent on each other, as ROs can cooperate and coordinate their responses to a coup or compete for influence. In order to address this challenge, the standard errors are clustered on the coup level in all models.[2]

Operationalization

For thoroughly examining which factors account for the variation in RO responses to coups, two aspects are important. First, the question whether a RO responds to a particular coup at all, and second, how strong this response is. Both measures are based on the new dataset on RO responses

Table 4.1: Operationalization of strength of response

Score	Highest form of response shown
0	No response
1	Concern
2	Support for incumbent
3	Condemnation
4	Mediation
5	Minor diplomatic sanctions
6	Major diplomatic sanctions
7	Economic sanction threats
8	Economic sanction imposition
9	Military intervention threat
10	Military intervention imposition

to coups (for details on the data collection process see Chapter 3). The first dependent variable consists of a simple binary indicator capturing whether a RO responds to a given coup or not. For the second dependent variable, an ordered response score is constructed. As illustrated in Figure 2.2, the responses of ROs to coups can be ordered along a continuum of increasing intensity.[3] Using this order, the second dependent variable captures the strength of the strongest response shown by a RO after a coup, with higher numbers implying more severe responses.[4] While the scale for measuring the second dependent variable thus has a transitive order, the distances between the different measures cannot be interpreted meaningfully.[5] Therefore, the second dependent variable is ordinal in nature and is treated accordingly in the subsequent statistical models. Table 4.1 summarizes the scale of the second dependent variable.[6]

The theory chapter introduced a number of factors which potentially explain the variation in the responses of ROs to coups. In the following, the operationalization of these factors is outlined. The first set of expectations concerns the question which factors impact the probability that a RO takes action at all.

Expectation 1a states that a binding democratic commitment provides ROs with a mandate to deal with severe democratic flaws such as coups. The presence of such binding democratic commitments is established by analysing the statutes of the ROs, including documents like (founding) treaties, amendments to the former and formal protocols. Only ROs which call democratic standards a central prerequisite for membership in their statutes are coded with 1, while ROs whose statutes contain only vague declarations to promote democracy or no democratic references at all are assigned a 0.[7]

According to Expectation 1b, ROs are focused on coups within their own boundaries and rarely respond to external coups. Therefore, a binary indicator captures whether a country in which a coup takes place is a member in a RO. Information on the membership of ROs is retrieved from the respective RO websites and, in case they do not provide such data, is supplemented by additional research. Only states with full membership are taken into account, whereas countries with a status as observer or associated member are not counted.

Expectation 1c claims that successful coups have a higher chance of being followed by RO responses than failed coups. A binary indicator captures the success of a coup. All coup incidents, in which the coup plotters succeed in at least temporarily taking over power are coded as successful, whereas coups which were immediately defeated by the government are coded as failures.[8]

The second set of potential explanations captures RO-related factors, which are expected to impact the strength of responses. According to Expectation 2a, ROs with a dominantly democratic membership should show stronger responses to coups than ROs which include many autocratic states. There are many ways of measuring democratic standards in political science. For the present analysis, it was decided to use the PolityIV index (Marshall et al, 2018), as the fine-grained scale ranging from −10 (highly autocratic) to 10 (highly democratic) is well suited to capture differences between less and more democratic member states of ROs. Besides, it is a widely used measure and data are available for almost all countries over a long time period. As the raw data are only available on the country level, the RO level of democracy is determined by taking the average of the values of the full member states of the RO.

Expectation 2b states that the strength of response of a RO is also shaped by the capacity of a RO to successfully exert pressure on a state in which a coup has happened. This capacity depends on the relative power of the respective state vis-à-vis the RO. Two alternative indicators are used to capture the relative power of a state towards a RO. The first indicator measures the economic power of a state vis-à-vis a RO by dividing the gross domestic product (GDP) in USD billions of the state by the combined GDP in USD of all RO member states. The second indicator grasps the relative military power by dividing the size of the army of the state by the combined number of military forces of all RO members. Data for both measures are taken from the World Development Indicators of the World Bank (2019). As the data distribution is extremely skewed, both measures were logarithmized.

The third set of expectations captures normative considerations about the effects of coups on democratic standards. Expectation 3a suggests that the level of democracy of a country prior to the coup plays a role and that ROs should respond more strongly to coups in democracies. As for the measure of the RO level of democracy, the PolityIV index is used as data source (Marshall et al, 2018) to assess the level of democracy in the respective country.

Expectation 3b formulates that the responses of ROs depend on the domestic attitude towards the coup plotters and the ousted incumbent. If the former government has already been challenged by prior violent protests, ROs should show more muted responses towards the coup. Data from the Mass Mobilization Data Project (Clark & Regan, 2019) are used to construct a binary indicator on whether a coup was proceeded by mass protests against the incumbent government or its policies.

According to Expectation 3c, ROs should show stronger responses to exclusively military coups compared to coups in which civilian actors take a leading role. Data for this binary indicator are taken from the coup dataset by Marshall and Marshall (2019), which lists the identity of coup plotters. For the cases not included in this dataset, the data were extended by own research on the identities of the coup plotters. All exclusively military coups are assigned a 1, whereas coups which include leading civilian actors are coded with 0.

The fourth set of expectations stems from pragmatic considerations of ROs about coups. Expectation 4a states that ROs are not only more likely to respond to successful coups than to failed ones but should also show stronger responses towards them. The rationale behind this is that the unsuccessful coups constitute a less immediate threat or pressing problem for a RO. The same binary indicator capturing the success of a coup as for Expectation 1c is used.

Expectation 4b states that coups which are accompanied by high levels of violence should lead to stronger responses by ROs, as they bear a higher risk of spillover to neighbouring countries. Data on the level of violence associated with a coup, in the form of the absolute number of casualties, is taken from the dataset of Marshall and Marshall (2019). For the cases not included in the Marshall and Marshall data and for the missing values in their dataset, additional research in the EIU reports and newspaper articles was conducted. Coups which led to more than 100 casualties are coded as coups with major violence (1), whereas coups with lower numbers are assigned a 0.

Finally, Expectation 4c argues that ROs do not only take threats for security, but also for the economy into account. Accordingly, ROs are expected to show stronger responses towards coups in countries which are important trading partners for them. Consequently, a variable captures the share of trade of the country in which the coup happened with the RO in relation to the total trade flows of the RO in the respective year. Data on trade flows in USD billions are retrieved from the direction of trade statistics of the International Monetary Fund (IMF, 2019). As the distribution of the data is extremely skewed, the measure is logarithmized.

In addition to the theorized explanatory variables, three control variables are included in the analysis. The first accounts for the fact whether the country in which a coup takes place has faced prior coups in the recent past. A sequence of coups in a country is an indicator for lasting political instability. Accordingly, ROs might evaluate the chances of successfully intervening in the country as less favourable and be therefore more hesitant to show strong responses. The count variable used in the analysis captures the number of previous coups in a ten-year time span prior to the coup.[9] Data on previous coups are taken from the coup data of Marshall and Marshall (2019) and Powell and Thyne (2019). The second control variable accounts for temporal dynamics. The observation period covers 30 years from 1990 to 2019, a time span in which major changes in world politics took place, in particular regarding the role and significance of regional actors. Therefore, a time variable capturing the year of the coup controls for temporal dynamics in the data. Finally, not only temporal, but also geographical differences can play a crucial role. To account for the particularities and differences between world regions, a categorical variable captures the continent where a coup happens.[10]

Statistical analysis

In the subsequent section, the plausibility of the potential explanations is tested and the results of the statistical analysis are reported. Before starting the actual analysis, potential problems of multi-collinearity between the different independent variables were checked for. In general, the correlations between the explanatory factors are low and where exceeding a value of 0.25 the variables where not included in the same models.[11]

Combined model

As theorized in Chapter 2, three sets of factors are expected to shape the strength of RO responses: characteristics of the RO concerned, as well as democracy- and stability-related factors. Respective expectations were formulated and in Table 4.2 a series of models containing different combinations of variables from the three explanatory approaches are shown. In a first step, the factors in the inflation stage of the model, which determine whether a RO takes action or not, are examined. The results provide strong empirical support for the theoretical expectations. First, ROs with a democratic mandate are more likely to take action after coups than organizations lacking such a mandate. Second, ROs are also significantly more likely to intervene in their member states than in third-country states. Third, ROs seem to respond more frequently to successful coups than to failed coup attempts.[12]

Table 4.2: Combined model with effects of explanatory factors on strength of responses

Response	Model 1	Model 2	Model 3	Model 4	Model 5	Model 6	Model 7	Model 8
Democracy level RO			0.066** (0.023)	0.075*** (0.021)			0.058** (0.020)	0.063** (0.020)
Economic position					-0.152*** (0.031)	-0.171*** (0.030)		
Military position							-0.088* (0.036)	-0.110** (0.033)
Democracy level state	0.040* (0.018)	0.035 (0.021)	0.037* (0.018)	0.030 (0.021)	0.031 (0.017)	0.022 (0.019)	0.032 (0.017)	0.022 (0.020)
Prior protests	0.127 (0.198)	-0.016 (0.246)	-0.043 (0.188)	-0.199 (0.179)	0.116 (0.155)	0.029 (0.170)	0.023 (0.167)	-0.081 (0.178)
Military coup		0.625** (0.227)		0.541** (0.207)		0.564** (0.190)		0.573** (0.192)
Success	1.560*** (0.219)		1.368*** (0.224)		1.338*** (0.173)		1.317*** (0.182)	
Major violence	0.624*** (0.186)	0.627* (0.258)	0.649*** (0.167)	0.676*** (0.204)	0.740*** (0.171)	0.756*** (0.200)	0.695*** (0.163)	0.728*** (0.195)
Trade relations	0.022 (0.040)	0.017 (0.045)	0.047 (0.037)	0.060 (0.039)				

(continued)

Table 4.2: Combined model with effects of explanatory factors on strength of responses (continued)

	Model 1	Model 2	Model 3	Model 4	Model 5	Model 6	Model 7	Model 8
Prior coups	0.039	0.034	0.035	0.025	-0.024	-0.039	0.008	-0.008
	(0.049)	(0.064)	(0.050)	(0.060)	(0.044)	(0.056)	(0.045)	(0.056)
Year	0.016	0.016	0.012	0.011	0.016	0.017	0.011	0.012
	(0.011)	(0.013)	(0.011)	(0.012)	(0.010)	(0.011)	(0.011)	(0.011)
Region								
Asia	.	.	.	.	.	.	.	
	(.)	(.)	(.)	(.)	(.)	(.)	(.)	(.)
Africa	0.433	0.642*	0.685	0.797**	0.354	0.429	0.514	0.535
	(0.340)	(0.286)	(0.352)	(0.290)	(0.293)	(0.249)	(0.317)	(0.288)
America	0.690	0.915*	0.641	0.728*	0.858*	1.024***	0.690*	0.787**
	(0.424)	(0.368)	(0.364)	(0.308)	(0.350)	(0.296)	(0.338)	(0.304)
Europe	1.594***	2.418***	1.098**	1.521***	1.783***	2.424***	1.310***	1.895***
	(0.403)	(0.449)	(0.385)	(0.424)	(0.347)	(0.366)	(0.365)	(0.414)
Oceania	0.257	0.738	0.204	0.517	-0.075	0.267	-0.062	0.229
	(0.782)	(0.897)	(0.644)	(0.565)	(0.616)	(0.577)	(0.627)	(0.593)
Inflate								
RO member	2.063***	1.961***	2.232***	2.167***	2.287***	2.134***	2.330***	2.201***
	(0.157)	(0.175)	(0.174)	(0.148)	(0.154)	(0.135)	(0.165)	(0.143)

Table 4.2: Combined model with effects of explanatory factors on strength of responses (continued)

	Model 1	Model 2	Model 3	Model 4	Model 5	Model 6	Model 7	Model 8
Democratic mandate	1.329***	1.269***	1.331***	1.290***	1.395***	1.316***	1.363***	1.296***
	(0.105)	(0.128)	(0.111)	(0.114)	(0.120)	(0.109)	(0.118)	(0.110)
Success	-0.052	0.584***	-0.034	0.599***	-0.018	0.617***	-0.004	0.612***
	(0.142)	(0.130)	(0.148)	(0.135)	(0.146)	(0.138)	(0.143)	(0.136)
Constant	-2.759***	-3.194***	-2.727***	-3.130***	-2.762***	-3.173***	-2.766***	-3.162***
	(0.155)	(0.163)	(0.165)	(0.166)	(0.164)	(0.164)	(0.167)	(0.163)
N	6004	6004	6004	6004	6004	6004	6004	6004
AIC	1877.872	1918.554	1869.603	1907.138	1860.375	1896.870	1866.499	1902.816
BIC	2038.676	2079.358	2037.107	2074.643	2021.180	2057.674	2034.003	2070.320

Clustered standard errors in parentheses, * $p<0.05$, ** $p<0.01$, *** $p<0.001$

Having discussed the first decision – whether a RO reacts at all – the following paragraphs address the second and more complex decision, the choice of instruments of diverging strength to do so. Here, three sets of factors (RO characteristics, democracy- and stability-related factors) are examined. The statistical models show that there is compelling evidence for the first set of these factors. ROs with a more democratic membership were assumed to show stronger responses to coups. As Models 3, 4, 7 and 8 illustrate, the more democratic the membership of a RO is, the stronger are its responses to coups. Not only the level of democracy, but also the capacities of ROs play a decisive role. The strength of RO responses to coups declines, the more powerful the position of the affected state is vis-à-vis the RO in economic (Models 5 and 6) and military (Models 7 and 8) terms. Put differently, if a RO has a strong leverage towards a state hit by a coup, it will show stronger responses compared to situations in which the affected state has a strong economic or military position in relation to the RO.

Regarding the second set of factors, democracy-related aspects of the coup, the evidence is less conclusive. There is some tentative support for the claim that coups in democracies lead to stronger responses, yet the respective coefficient is only statistically significant at a 5 per cent level in two of the eight models (Models 1 and 3). An additional assumption was that prior popular protests decrease the strength of RO responses. But prior protests do not seem to exert a noticeable effect in any of the models. In contrast, the findings for the last democracy-related aspect robustly support the respective theoretical expectation. Coups with an exclusively military leadership evoke stronger responses than coups in which civilian political leaders are involved (see Models 2, 4, 6 and 8).

The third and final block of explanatory variables refers to the stability-related considerations. For the first factor, the success of a coup, the empirical findings are in line with the theoretical expectations. As assumed, RO responses to successful coups are noticeably and robustly stronger than those to failed coups (see Models 1, 3, 5 and 7). Likewise, the extent of violence associated with a coup and the resulting risk of spillover seems to be an important factor. If a coup is accompanied by a major amount of violence, ROs are more likely to impose stronger policy instruments against a state (see Models 1–8). In contrast to the security aspects of regional stability, economic considerations do not turn out to be decisive factors in the analysis. The density of the trade network between a state hit by a coup and the RO concerned does not seem to influence the choice of stronger or weaker policy instruments (see Models 1–4). The control variables do not deliver particularly noteworthy results. Neither the number of prior coups nor a temporal trend per se seem to drive the findings. The strength of RO responses varies between continents, with significantly stronger RO responses to coups in Europe and America and partly also Africa compared to Asia. Yet given the unequal global distribution of coups, with very few incidents in Europe and Oceania, these findings should be treated with care. Respective region-specific analyses are reported at a later point.

To conclude, RO characteristics, including the level of democracy as well as the economic and military leverage of the organization vis-à-vis the respective state are important predictors for the strength of responses. Besides, stability-related considerations about the success and level of violence of a coup play an important role. In contrast, the expectations formulating democracy-based considerations about the level of democracy of the ousted regime or public support for the coup do not receive conclusive support by the analysis. Only the civilian or military identity of coup plotters is a stable predictor in this set of factors.

The statistical analysis shows that zero-inflated ordered probit models are a good tool to model the two interconnected decisions of whether and how to respond to a coup. Yet a central challenge of models with ordered categorical data is to quantify and illustrate the effect sizes. Put simply, what difference do the various explanatory factors actually make? The interpretation of the coefficients in a zero-inflated ordered probit model is not as straightforward as for linear models. Therefore, the statistical tool of predicted probabilities is used to visualize some central findings of the analysis in tables and graphs.

Determinants of RO action

The first step of the analysis was concerned with the question of which factors have an impact on the likelihood that ROs respond to coups. The empirical analysis revealed that a combination of the three variables – RO membership, democratic mandate of a RO and success of coup – are well-suited to explain if a RO takes action after a particular coup. Figure 4.1 depicts the predicted probabilities that a RO responds to a coup for the eight possible combinations of these three variables based on the regression results of the inflation equation.[13]

The graph effectively shows that RO membership is the most important criterion for ROs to take action after coups. All four upper combinations show considerably higher values than the lower four. Besides, the presence of a binding democratic commitments within a RO also considerably increases the chances that a RO takes action: for instance, the chance of a failed a coup within a RO to evoke a RO response is more than three times higher in ROs with a democratic mandate (63.10 per cent) than in ROs lacking such a mandate (16.81 per cent). Furthermore, also the outcome of a coup is a crucial criterion, as success constantly increases the likelihood of RO responses (for example from 3.10 per cent for failed coups outside ROs to 10.48 per cent for similar cases ending successfully). Finally, Figure 4.1 illustrates the large differences in the resulting predicted probabilities. Whereas the likelihood

Figure 4.1: Predicted probabilities of RO response

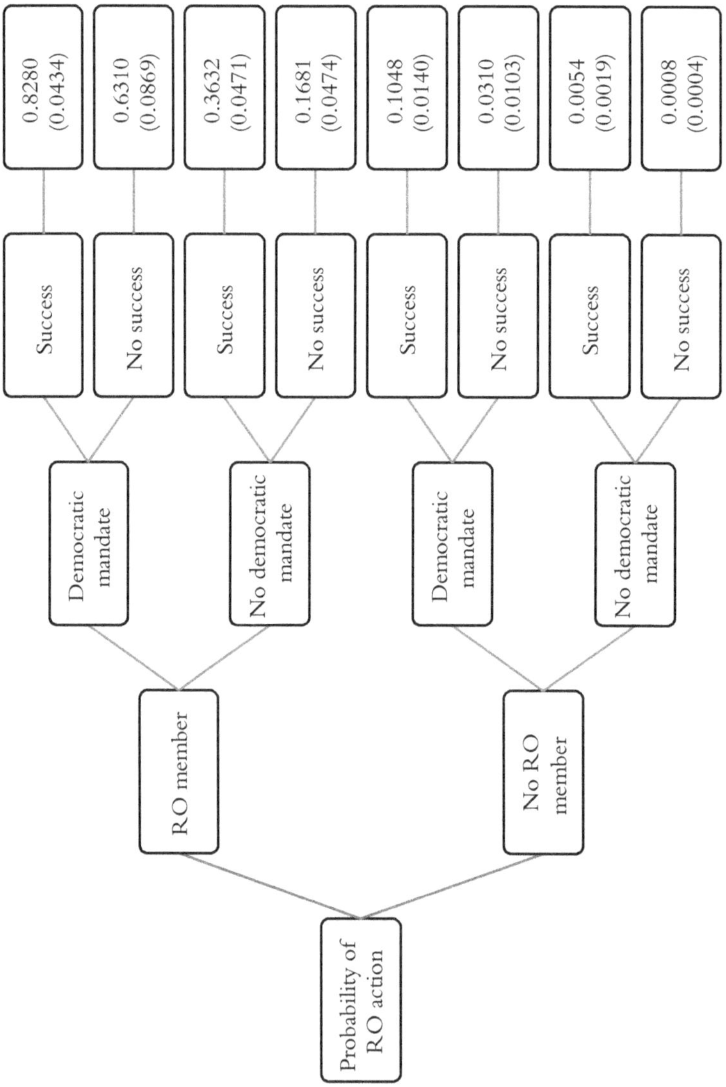

Source: Author's depiction, based on regression results

of a RO without democratic mandate to respond to a failed coup outside its boundaries is only 0.08 per cent, a successful coup within a member state of a RO with a democratic mandate holds a 82.80 per cent chance of being addressed. This large range underlines how important it is to explicitly model the relevance of different RO–coup dyads in the analysis. To meaningfully analyse why ROs choose instruments of different strength after coups, it is essential to focus on those cases in which a response is likely at all.

Strength of responses

Although the question of when ROs respond to coups is an interesting and important one, it does not completely capture the variety of RO responses to coups. Therefore, the second step of the analysis focuses on the question regarding which factors influence the choice of instruments of different strength. The effects of the most important of these factors and their implications are visualized and discussed in the following. Table 4.3 reports the average predicted probabilities that the response of a RO reaches a particular level of strength, conditional on the fact that the RO is a potentially active or relevant RO.[14]

Table 4.3: Average predicted probability of the different responses for relevant ROs

Reaction score	Highest form of reaction	Mean	Standard deviation	Minimum	Maximum
0	No reaction	0.5086	0.2123	0.0542	0.9851
1	Concern statement	0.0509	0.0104	0.0048	0.0600
2	Support for incumbent	0.0285	0.0064	0.0021	0.0341
3	Condemnation	0.1903	0.0602	0.0068	0.2493
4	Mediation	0.0418	0.0196	0.0005	0.0690
5	Minor diplomatic sanctions	0.0390	0.0210	0.0003	0.0739
6	Major diplomatic sanctions	0.0318	0.0195	0.0002	0.0712
7	Economic sanctions threatened	0.0185	0.0125	0.0001	0.0484
8	Economic sanctions imposed	0.0772	0.0679	0.0001	0.3524
9	Military intervention threatened	0.0085	0.0110	0.0000	0.0877
10	Military intervention imposed	0.0049	0.0082	0.0000	0.0900

Source: Author's own depiction, based on regression results

The results reveal that even among the ROs which might potentially enforce the anti-coup norm, the likelihood of staying silent after a coup (50.86 per cent) is slightly higher than the chance of responding. Among the RO responses, the majority only reaches a rhetorical level, with the chance of a coup being condemned as the strongest response scoring by far the highest (19.03 per cent). The probability of different diplomatic and economic measures as the toughest form of response ranges between 1.85 per cent (sanction threats) and 7.72 per cent (actually imposed sanctions). The comparatively high difference between sanction threats and actually imposed sanctions can be explained by the fact that economic sanctions are often used as an immediate punitive signal after coups. In this case, sanction threats are omitted, which on other occasions are often used as a preliminary step to warn and coerce states to change their behaviour (Nooruddin, 2002; Bapat et al, 2013; Bapat & Kwon, 2015). Finally, the data show that the probability of relevant ROs to respond to a coup by military means is extremely low (0.85 per cent and 0.49 per cent respectively). The values reported in Table 4.3 are average values. As the statistical analysis has shown, the actual probability of a specific RO to respond to a particular coup in a certain way strongly depends on a number of characteristics of the RO as well as on democracy- and stability-related aspects of the coup itself and the country in which it took place. The impact of some of these factors is illustrated in the following.

Leverage against member states

The analysis revealed that when deciding on instruments to respond to coups, ROs are guided by questions concerning feasibility and the chance of successfully exerting pressure on a state affected by a coup. The empirical findings indicate that ROs are less likely to show stronger responses against powerful states. This effect is illustrated in Figure 4.2. As strength of responses is an ordered categorical variable, no linear effects of the explanatory factor on the strength of responses can be plotted. Therefore, Figure 4.2 depicts the effect of the economic position on the likelihood that the responses of the group of potentially active ROs reach selected levels of strength. For the sake of better readability, only six instead of all ten stages are exemplarily plotted, which still cover the effect for the whole continuum of RO responses ranging from a non-reaction over rhetorical (condemnation), diplomatic means (mediation and suspension), economic (sanctions) to military means. The graphs show that the economic position of a state is a highly influential factor. The likelihood that relevant ROs do not respond to a coup constantly rises from only 23.36 per cent for the least influential states to 91.89 per cent for the most influential ones (upper left graph). Hence, coup plotters in economically powerful countries have a significantly higher chance of evading penalties from the relevant ROs. This dynamic is confirmed in the

Figure 4.2: Effect of economic leverage on selected forms of response

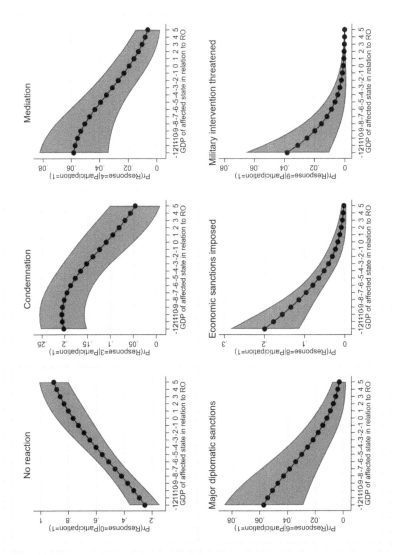

Source: Author's depiction, based on regression results

illustrations for responses using the different punitive instruments: coups in the least powerful states have a probability of 19.93 per cent of being condemned (upper middle graph), a more than four times higher likelihood than for the most powerful ones (4.08 per cent). Also the likelihood of mediation (upper right graph) and major diplomatic sanctions such as a suspension from the RO (lower left graph), decreases from 5.85 per cent to 0.53 per cent and from 6.29 per cent to 0.25 per cent with increasing economic influence. Most noticeably, the probability of facing economic sanctions (lower middle graph) drops from 21.07 per cent to 0.26 per cent with increasing economic power of the respective state. Besides, the effect on the probability of the threat of military means (lower right graph) is remarkable. While the average probability for such measures is only 0.49 per cent (compare with Table 4.3), the least influential countries have a chance of 4.22 per cent of being threatened with military interventions by ROs. In contrast, the risk for economically powerful states is almost non-existent (0.01 per cent).

Level of democracy in country

RO responses to coups are not only contingent on the power of the RO vis-à-vis the state. The present analysis also suggests that ROs are at least partly guided by normative concerns about the expected effects of coups on the state of democracy in the affected country. For instance, some of the models show that ROs take the regime type of the ousted government into account when deciding on their responses to coups. Yet this effect is less accentuated than the effect of economic power, which also becomes visible in the visual illustration in Figure 4.3.

With an increasing level of democracy, the chance that a relevant RO completely ignores a coup constantly declines from 60.43 per cent to 38.60 per cent (upper left graph). In turn, the probability of punitive responses rises. While the effect is comparatively small for condemnations (upper middle graph, 17.60 per cent for highly autocratic vs. 22.12 per cent for highly democratic states), the probability of major diplomatic sanctions (lower left graph, 2.29 per cent vs. 4.53 per cent) almost doubles, and for economic sanctions (lower middle graph, 4.06 per cent vs. 12.22 per cent) almost triples between the two ends of the democracy continuum. Yet the confidence intervals for all plotted effects are large, implying that the statistical predictions of the effect are less certain.

Major violence

Apart from the intuitive finding that successful coups attract stronger responses than failed ones, one major result from the pragmatic considerations is that highly violent coups increase the severity of RO responses. The size

Figure 4.3: Effect of level of democracy of country on selected forms of response

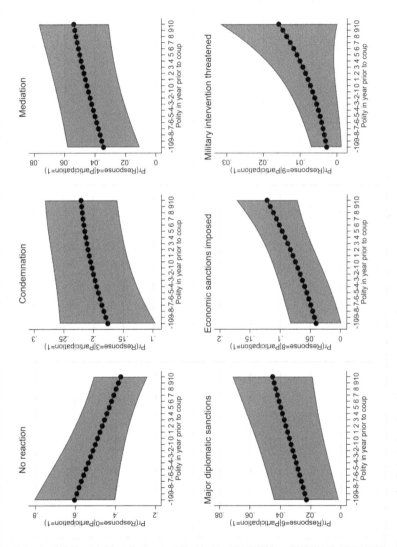

Source: Author's depiction, based on regression results

of this effect is illustrated in Table 4.4, which shows the likelihood that the responses of the relevant ROs reach certain levels of strength.

First, less than a third of the coups accompanied by major violence were completely ignored by the relevant ROs (28.43 per cent), compared to more than half of the coups with fewer than 100 casualties (52.14 per cent). When comparing rhetorical instruments of RO responses, it becomes apparent

Table 4.4: Effect of major violence on probability of different responses

		Margin	Stand. error	z	P>z	95 % Conf. Interval	
No reaction	No major violence	0.5214	0.0598	8.72	0.000	0.4042	0.6385
	Major violence	0.2843	0.0554	5.13	0.000	0.1757	0.3929
Concern	No major violence	0.0513	0.0105	4.91	0.000	0.0309	0.0718
	Major violence	0.0451	0.0091	4.93	0.000	0.0272	0.0630
Support for incumbent	No major violence	0.0287	0.0110	2.60	0.009	0.0071	0.0503
	Major violence	0.0268	0.0103	2.61	0.009	0.0067	0.0470
Condemnation	No major violence	0.1891	0.0305	6.20	0.000	0.1293	0.2488
	Major violence	0.2140	0.0278	7.69	0.000	0.1595	0.2685
Mediation	No major violence	0.0408	0.0097	4.19	0.000	0.0217	0.0598
	Major violence	0.0577	0.0131	4.39	0.000	0.0319	0.0834
Minor diplomatic sanctions	No major violence	0.0377	0.0101	3.74	0.000	0.0179	0.0575
	Major violence	0.0589	0.0157	3.74	0.000	0.0281	0.0897
Major diplomatic sanctions	No major violence	0.0305	0.0095	3.21	0.001	0.0119	0.0491
	Major violence	0.0527	0.0141	3.74	0.000	0.0251	0.0803
Economic sanctions threatened	No major violence	0.0176	0.0071	2.49	0.013	0.0037	0.0314
	Major violence	0.0331	0.0131	2.53	0.012	0.0074	0.0588
Economic sanctions imposed	No major violence	0.0715	0.0170	4.20	0.000	0.0382	0.1048
	Major violence	0.1753	0.0374	4.68	0.000	0.1019	0.2487
Military intervention threatened	No major violence	0.0074	0.0039	1.90	0.057	-0.0002	0.0151
	Major violence	0.0291	0.0121	2.40	0.016	0.0054	0.0527
Military intervention imposed	No major violence	0.0040	0.0026	1.56	0.118	-0.0010	0.0091
	Major violence	0.0230	0.0133	1.73	0.083	-0.0030	0.0490

Source: Author's own depiction, based on regression results

Figure 4.4: Effect of prior protests for autocratic and democratic ROs

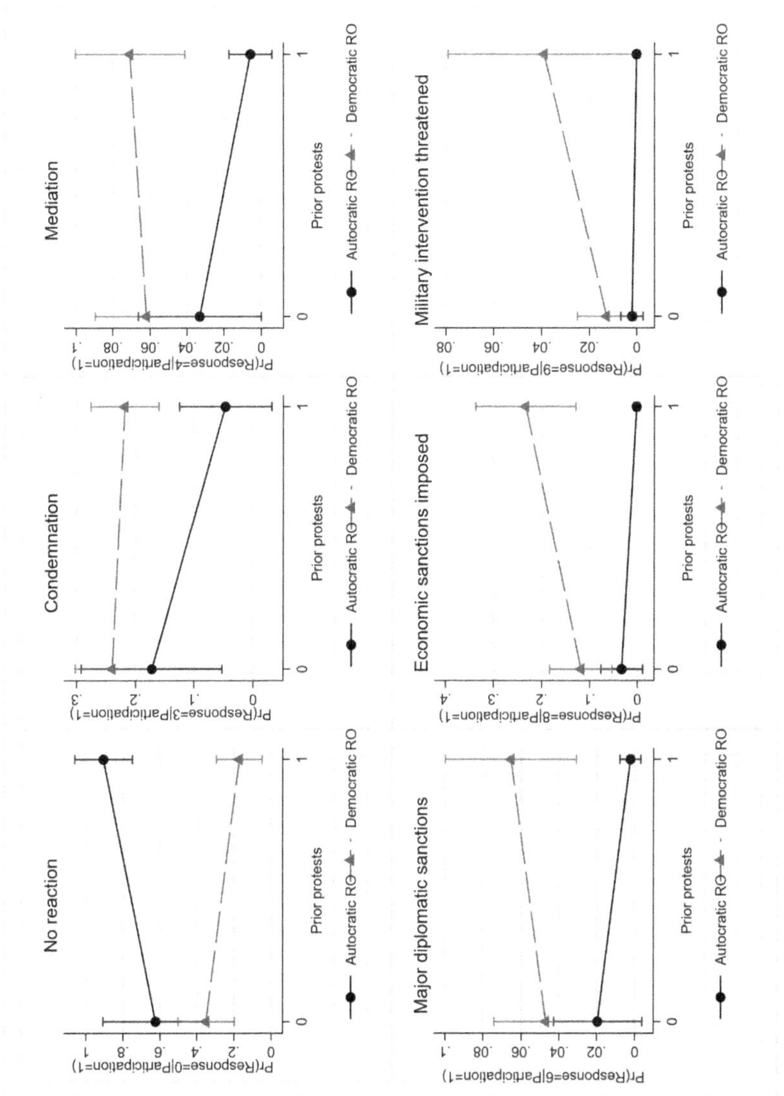

Source: Author's depiction, based on regression results

that the difference between violent and non-violent coups is comparatively small (for example 2.87 per cent vs. 2.68 per cent for support statements of the incumbent). However, for stronger responses, the difference is more nuanced. For instance, while the predicted probability of a violent coup to be followed by major diplomatic sanctions is 5.27 per cent, the value for non-violent coups is considerably lower (3.05 per cent). The chances of coups leading to economic sanctions by RO more than double for violent takeovers (17.53 per cent vs. 7.15 per cent). For military interventions as the most severe form of response the likelihood is generally low, yet more than five times higher after violent coups compared to non-violent ones (2.30 per cent vs. 0.40 per cent).

Prior protests

A final topic of interest is the importance of the domestic population in a coup. According to Expectation 3b ROs are less likely to take strong measures against a coup if the ousted incumbent had already faced domestic protests as an indicator or popular discontent. The analysis featured inconclusive results in this regard. The reason is that popular protests have a divergent effect on autocratic and democratic ROs. Figure 4.4 plots the diverging effect of prior protests for highly autocratic (blue line) and democratic ROs (red line). The findings indicate that if coups are preceded by popular protests, democratic ROs are less likely to ignore the event (17.17 per cent) than in the case of coups without protests (34.97 per cent). In addition, they are more likely to impose stronger measures such as diplomatic, economic or military sanctions when protests are a feature of the coup. Interestingly, the effect is reverse for autocratic ROs. While they generally have a lower likelihood of addressing coups, proceeding popular protests even further decline their willingness to take action. 90.60 per cent of the coups without protests evoked no responses of highly autocratic ROs, whereas for coups with prior protests the likelihood is only 62.50 per cent.

Differentiated effects

The previous analysis has provided convincing evidence that many of the tested variables exert a relatively robust effect, independent of sample size, combination of variables or model specification. In order to gain further confidence in the results, a number of additional robustness checks were conducted.[15] While the effect sizes and significance levels of some variables slightly change in the robustness checks, none of the additional tests contradicts the findings from the main analysis reported so far. Instead, the additional tests strongly foster the confidence that the reported effects are actually important explanatory factors and not just statistical artefacts.

However, not all explanatory factors might be of equal importance for all ROs, regions and measures. The ROs included in the sample are highly diverse in terms of their capacities, but even more so with regard to their ideational values and commitments. Likewise, the examined regions are extremely diverse. In the following, further analyses are conducted to illustrate region-as well as RO-specific patterns and phenomena.

Separate analyses for different measures

As conceptualized in Chapter 2, RO responses to coups follow a continuum of increasing strength, ranging from rhetorical statements over diplomatic and economic sanctions to military measures. However, in some cases the order of these instruments might be disputed, for instance when we compare severe diplomatic measures such as suspensions from ROs to weaker economic instruments like mainly symbolic sanctions. Besides, it could be the case that some explanatory factors do not generally lead to an increase in the severity of RO responses but have a measure-specific effect: for instance, ROs with a close trading network with a state hit by a coup could be more inclined to choose import/export restrictions as an instrument instead of diplomatic or military means because they know that this measure will create considerable economic pressure on that state.

To account for such differences, a further separate analysis for each of the four response types of rhetorical, diplomatic, economic and military action was conducted. Generally, the results of this analysis correspond closely to the main analysis and confirm many of the theoretical expectations.[16] Some interesting specific effects are described in the following. For instance, the main analysis showed that if coups are accompanied by major violence ROs tend to show stronger responses than after bloodless or 'soft' coups. The separate analysis specifies that the extent of violence primarily increases the likelihood that ROs take two sorts of responses, namely rhetorical and military ones. An explanation could be that highly violent coups create more attention in the news. Accordingly, more ROs feel inclined to at least comment on the event, voice their concern or condemn it. At the same time, a high level of violence constitutes a 'red flag' for a major emerging security issue, which increases the chances that ROs address the problem with military means to stabilize the affected country.

A second interesting finding concerns the average level of democracy of ROs. The main analysis illustrated that ROs with dominantly democratic member states are more likely to take stronger action against coup plotters. When focusing on the different sorts of measures, we see that more democratic ROs actually tend to use rhetorical and economic measures significantly more frequently than ROs with more autocratic member states. Hence, they are for instance more likely to condemn coups or to impose economic sanctions. Interestingly, this tendency is also visible for diplomatic measures, yet the effect is not so clear (see Figure 4.5). One potential reason could be that democratic and autocratic ROs alike frequently engage themselves as mediators after coups and mediation forms an important part of diplomatic measures.

Interaction effects

Apart from specific effects of some explanatory factors on particular forms of responses, there are also influential differences between ROs. The ROs examined in the analysis are not a homogeneous group. Some ROs have a highly democratic membership, while others are profoundly autocratic. One can reasonably assume that democracy-related aspects play a more important role for more democratic ROs. But the empirical findings reported in Table 4.5 do not support this notion.

Regarding the level of democracy in the countries, it is not the case that more democratic ROs pay more attention to the regime type of a country prior to the coup. There is an interaction effect between prior protests and the democracy level of ROs (Model 6). Yet, like the initial effect, it runs counter to the theoretical expectation. An average democratic RO shows a (although not significantly) weaker response to coups which are proceeded by prior protests. But the more democratic a RO becomes, the smaller this effect gets. Highly democratic ROs even show stronger responses to coups with prior protests. In the last model, there is no significant interaction effect. The identity of the coup plotters and the democracy-level ROs turn out to be solid criteria, but it does not seem to be the case that democratic ROs pay more attention to this aspect than others.

Based on the models presented, there is little empirical evidence that the evaluation of coups systematically differs between democratic and autocratic ROs. Hence, one cannot say that ROs with a more democratic membership generally pay more attention to democracy-based criteria. Yet the fact that the expected interaction effects are not statistically significant in the analysis do not mean that absolutely no differences between organizations exist. To illustrate this, the interaction effect between the level of democracy among the member states of a RO and the significance of democratic standards in a country hit by a coup is plotted in Figure 4.6. The blue line represents a RO with a highly autocratic membership, whereas the red line shows the effect for a highly democratic RO.

The graphs for the different forms of strongest responses do not only show that more autocratic ROs are generally less likely to take significant action against coup plotters and more likely to do nothing. In addition, the comparably flat blue lines indicate that autocratic ROs do not make their decision on how strongly to respond to a coup contingent on the

Figure 4.5: Effect of average democracy level of RO for different sorts of measures

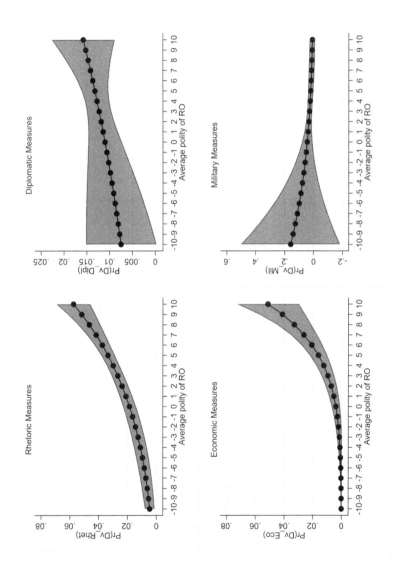

Source: Author's depiction, based on regression results

Table 4.5: Interaction effect between value-based variables and democracy level of RO

	Model 1	Model 2	Model 3	Model 4	Model 5	Model 6	Model 7	Model 8	Model 9
Response									
Democracy level state	0.055★ (0.022)	0.046★ (0.020)	0.038 (0.024)						
Prior protests				0.442★ (0.201)	0.110 (0.211)	−0.220 (0.240)			
Military coup							0.538★ (0.258)	0.443★ (0.187)	0.406 (0.238)
Democracy level RO		0.065★★★ (0.019)	0.061★★ (0.020)		0.068★★★ (0.020)	0.037 (0.020)		0.067★★★ (0.019)	0.062★ (0.028)
Democracy level state# Democracy level RO			0.003 (0.004)						
Prior protests # Democracy level RO						0.083★★ (0.032)			
Military coup # Democracy level RO									0.009 (0.035)
Prior coups	0.060 (0.059)	0.039 (0.057)	0.041 (0.058)	0.090★ (0.045)	0.056 (0.061)	0.067 (0.059)	0.062 (0.052)	0.036 (0.056)	0.035 (0.056)
Year	0.008 (0.019)	0.006 (0.011)	0.007 (0.011)	−0.010 (0.012)	0.012 (0.012)	0.014 (0.012)	0.011 (0.034)	0.016 (0.013)	0.016 (0.013)
Region									
Asia									

Table 4.5: Interaction effect between value-based variables and democracy level of RO (continued)

	Model 1	Model 2	Model 3	Model 4	Model 5	Model 6	Model 7	Model 8	Model 9
	(.)	(.)	(.)	(.)	(.)	(.)	(.)	(.)	(.)
Africa	0.844**	0.918***	0.960***	0.387	0.810**	0.814***	0.693	0.747**	0.750**
	(0.307)	(0.271)	(0.255)	(0.674)	(0.263)	(0.243)	(0.379)	(0.275)	(0.270)
America	0.794*	0.710*	0.700*	0.363	0.871**	0.897**	0.896	0.878**	0.884**
	(0.348)	(0.286)	(0.283)	(0.687)	(0.289)	(0.283)	(0.588)	(0.296)	(0.290)
Europe	2.114***	1.472***	1.553***	1.524*	1.452**	1.708***	2.274**	1.684***	1.717***
	(0.381)	(0.384)	(0.407)	(0.742)	(0.493)	(0.435)	(0.719)	(0.446)	(0.450)
Oceania	1.076	0.492	0.488	1.497*	0.693	0.766	1.449	0.648	0.645
	(2.712)	(0.791)	(0.754)	(0.673)	(0.956)	(0.882)	(1.012)	(0.689)	(0.675)
Inflate									
RO member	1.909***	2.132***	2.132***	1.731***	2.092***	2.140***	1.806***	2.107***	2.117***
	(0.300)	(0.152)	(0.150)	(0.086)	(0.186)	(0.152)	(0.184)	(0.166)	(0.167)
Democratic mandate	1.186***	1.209***	1.213***	1.100***	1.192***	1.202***	1.136***	1.197***	1.199***
	(0.179)	(0.123)	(0.123)	(0.086)	(0.124)	(0.121)	(0.113)	(0.123)	(0.123)
Success	0.647***	0.673***	0.678***	0.609***	0.672***	0.687***	0.606***	0.621***	0.622***
	(0.128)	(0.126)	(0.126)	(0.111)	(0.125)	(0.128)	(0.118)	(0.130)	(0.130)
Constant	-3.260***	-3.219***	-3.214***	-3.311***	-3.222***	-3.223***	-3.262***	-3.187***	-3.186***
	(0.167)	(0.174)	(0.176)	(0.138)	(0.173)	(0.176)	(0.171)	(0.172)	(0.174)
N	7607	7607	7607	7607	7607	7607	7607	7607	7607
AIC	2095.451	2086.261	2087.422	2093.767	2094.323	2089.948	2093.898	2085.970	2087.895
BIC	2234.187	2231.934	2240.032	2232.503	2239.996	2242.558	2232.635	2231.643	2240.505

Note: Clustered standard errors in parantheses, * p<0.05, ** p<0.01, *** p<0.001

Figure 4.6: Effect of level of democracy of country for autocratic and democratic ROs

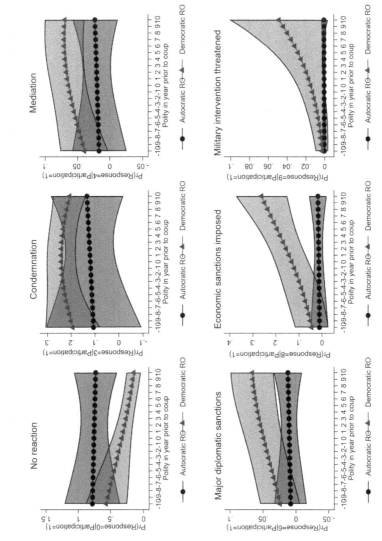

Source: Author's depiction, based on regression results

democracy level of the affected country. In contrast, as shown by the red lines, highly democratic ROs are more likely to address coups in democratic countries with stronger means and less likely to ignore them. For instance, the probability that an autocratic RO imposes diplomatic measures does not differ much after coups in highly autocratic (0.81 per cent) and highly democratic states (1.17 per cent). In turn, democratic ROs have a higher likelihood to impose sanctions in the latter (6.61 per cent) than in the former case (2.42 per cent). Interestingly, the shape for the relatively weak form of response of condemnation has a flat reversed u-shape. One explanation might be that democratic ROs tend to ignore the fall of highly autocratic rulers altogether, condemn the fall of semi-democratic rulers and take stronger action after the fall of more democratic rulers

Region-specific differences

As Chapter 3 has shown, the global distribution of ROs is far from even. Likewise, the norms, competencies and thereby also the general level of RO activity varies between regions. In an analysis of a global sample, region-specific patterns and trends might be masked, even if including region as a control variable in the analysis. Therefore, I conducted region-specific analyses for coups in Africa, Latin America and Asia and Oceania.[17] In general, these tests support the notion that a combination of RO-specific characteristics, and democracy- as well security-related factors account for the strength of RO responses.[18] Yet interestingly, the importance of these factors seems to be weighted differently across regions. The results from the global analysis indicated that the level of democracy in a state prior to a coup plays a role, although a relatively weak one. When differentiating between the regions, we see that the question whether an ousted government was democratic or not seems to be no key factor in Africa and Asia and Oceania. In contrast, in Latin America the democratic legitimacy of the ousted incumbent is an important aspect for ROs. Figure 4.7 illustrates exemplarily that whereas higher levels of prior democracy significantly increase the prospects of condemnations and economic sanctions in Latin America this is not the case in Africa, Asia and Oceania.

In these regions other factors play a more dominant role. If a coup in Africa, Asia or Oceania is accompanied by major violence, this increases the prospects that ROs take action noticeably. In contrast, in Latin America the amount of violence associated with a coup does not have such a strong impact on the responses of ROs. Likewise, the effect of exclusively military coups vs. coups with civilian involvement are more accentuated in Africa, Asia and Oceania.

Figure 4.7: Effect of level of democracy of country in different regions

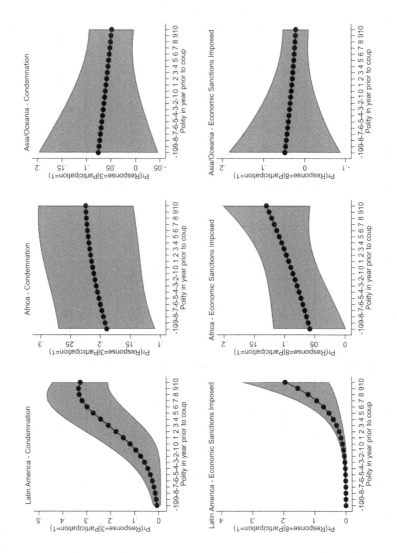

Source: Author's depiction, based on regression results

124

The particular role of the EU

One organization plays a very particular role after coups. The extent of integration within the EU as well as the capacities and resources available to the EU by far exceed those of other ROs, which has prompted debates about the comparability of the EU with other ROs in general (Lombaerde et al, 2010). Chapter 3 has also shown that the EU reveals a highly atypical pattern of behaviour towards coups. It is the only RO which responds to coups in non-member states on a regular basis. This 'external' engagement has important implications. The coups addressed by the EU do not happen in EU member states bound to the democracy norms and rules of the EU. Instead, the EU responds to coups in other countries, which are usually organized in their own set of local ROs with sometimes very different norms and values from the EU. The external role also influences the choice of available instruments: the EU lacks the possibility to initiate local mediation mechanisms or to suspend countries. Instead, the EU imposes economic sanctions more often than other ROs, as the dependency of many states on EU development cooperation, European investment and trade offers an opportunity to exert considerable pressure on coup plotters.

The EU has been the most active and also one of the most influential ROs after coups. Its cooperation with ROs facing coups in their member states like the AU or ECOWAS has been significantly expanded and strengthened in recent years. Therefore, it is important to include the EU in the analysis to give a complete picture of the role of ROs. The EU has been a key actor after numerous coups, and omitting it would do not good. Yet one also must make sure that the results found in the statistical analysis with the complete sample accurately depict the dynamics for all ROs and are not driven in a significant way by the EU as a powerful outlier. Therefore, in a next step, an outlier analysis excluding the EU from the models is conducted. Table 4.6 reports the results for the analysis without the EU. For the sake of brevity, only the differences from the analysis of the full sample are discussed.

The first remarkable difference concerns the democracy levels of RO member states. In the prior models, ROs with a higher average level of democracy tended to respond more decisively to coups. Yet a test without the EU reveals that this effect is mainly driven by the extremely high level of activity and strong responses of the EU with its democratic membership. For the remaining ROs, the form of governance of the member states does not seem to exert a noticeable effect on the severity of responses (Models 3, 4, 7 and 8). Likewise, the relative power of a RO becomes less influential once the EU is excluded. The effect of economic leverage of a RO vis-à-vis a state is weaker, yet still holds (Models 5 and 6), while the effect of military strength disappears (Models 7 and 8).

Furthermore, the comparatively weak evidence for the effect of regime type of the affected state on the strength of RO responses from the prior

Table 4.6: Combined model without EU

	Model 1	Model 2	Model 3	Model 4	Model 5	Model 6	Model 7	Model 8
Response								
democracy level RO			0.017 (0.040)	0.018 (0.039)			0.017 (0.038)	0.017 (0.037)
Economic position					-0.100* (0.043)	-0.122** (0.043)		
Military position							-0.038 (0.050)	-0.070 (0.046)
Democracy level state	0.024 (0.020)	0.019 (0.023)	0.022 (0.020)	0.018 (0.023)	0.020 (0.019)	0.017 (0.022)	0.022 (0.019)	0.018 (0.023)
Prior protests	0.083 (0.234)	-0.109 (0.258)	0.056 (0.238)	-0.126 (0.259)	0.075 (0.201)	-0.090 (0.221)	0.052 (0.226)	-0.132 (0.241)
Military coup		0.914*** (0.252)		0.905*** (0.250)		0.826*** (0.242)		0.884*** (0.246)
Success	1.463*** (0.271)		1.457*** (0.266)		1.348*** (0.238)		1.402*** (0.260)	
Major violence	0.663*** (0.201)	0.778** (0.272)	0.665*** (0.199)	0.774** (0.271)	0.741*** (0.198)	0.837*** (0.249)	0.690*** (0.195)	0.815** (0.263)
Trade relations	0.016 (0.050)	-0.012 (0.048)	0.017 (0.048)	-0.013 (0.048)	-0.024 (0.054)	-0.027 (0.066)	0.003 (0.054)	-0.002 (0.067)
Prior coups	0.016 (0.060)	0.002 (0.070)	0.016 (0.061)	0.003 (0.070)				

Table 4.6: Combined model without EU (continued)

	Model 1	Model 2	Model 3	Model 4	Model 5	Model 6	Model 7	Model 8
Year	0.041**	0.049***	0.039**	0.048***	0.040**	0.046***	0.038**	0.045**
	(0.013)	(0.015)	(0.013)	(0.014)	(0.012)	(0.014)	(0.013)	(0.014)
Region								
Asia	(.)	(.)	(.)	(.)	(.)	(.)	(.)	(.)
Africa	0.847	0.900	0.861	0.903	0.789+	0.799	0.812	0.780
	(0.617)	(0.606)	(0.616)	(0.607)	(0.479)	(0.496)	(0.534)	(0.558)
America	1.306	1.587*	1.233	1.523*	1.410**	1.582**	1.279*	1.468*
	(0.740)	(0.703)	(0.670)	(0.659)	(0.538)	(0.553)	(0.556)	(0.601)
Europe	1.551*	2.574***	1.345*	2.416**	1.575**	2.476***	1.390*	2.405***
	(0.655)	(0.782)	(0.606)	(0.767)	(0.544)	(0.658)	(0.576)	(0.712)
Oceania	0.690	1.150	0.646	1.105	0.479	0.833	0.517	0.877
	(0.954)	(0.965)	(0.926)	(0.950)	(0.837)	(0.859)	(0.873)	(0.873)
Inflate								
RO member	2.559***	2.483***	2.573***	2.489***	2.655***	2.542***	2.622***	2.520***
	(0.197)	(0.178)	(0.204)	(0.181)	(0.184)	(0.171)	(0.188)	(0.174)

(continued)

Table 4.6: Combined model without EU (continued)

	Model 1	Model 2	Model 3	Model 4	Model 5	Model 6	Model 7	Model 8
Democratic mandate	0.929***	0.871***	0.911***	0.861***	0.920***	0.865***	0.918***	0.873***
	(0.136)	(0.122)	(0.138)	(0.123)	(0.145)	(0.126)	(0.143)	(0.128)
Success	0.002	0.631***	0.003	0.634***	0.017	0.662***	0.001	0.643***
	(0.222)	(0.179)	(0.223)	(0.180)	(0.236)	(0.186)	(0.225)	(0.183)
Constant	-3.098***	-3.566***	-3.094***	-3.567***	-3.078***	-3.555***	-3.083***	-3.554***
	(0.246)	(0.250)	(0.244)	(0.250)	(0.247)	(0.256)	(0.246)	(0.252)
N	5892	5892	5892	5892	5892	5892	5892	5892
AIC	1267.245	1286.305	1268.975	1288.195	1262.352	1279.930	1268.367	1286.286
BIC	1427.598	1446.658	1436.008	1455.229	1422.705	1440.282	1435.401	1453.320

Note: Clustered standard errors in parentheses, * $p<0.05$, ** $p<0.01$, *** $p<0.001$

models disappears completely in the current analysis (see Models 1–8). An additional analysis with only the EU indicates that the EU actually shows stronger responses after coups in democracies compared to coups in autocratic settings.[19] However, as Table 4.6 reveals this does not apply to ROs in general. In other words, the question whether an ousted government was democratically elected or not does not seem to be essential for many ROs.

Discussion

Table 4.7 summarizes the findings for all potential explanations. The results indicate that there is not one superior approach to explain the responses of ROs to coups. Instead, a mixture of RO-related factors, democracy-based as well as stability-oriented considerations is well suited to do so. What do these results imply for the role of ROs in the context of coups? In the following, the implications of some of the key findings are discussed.

Preconditions for RO action

Put simply, ROs become active after coups if they have a respective mandate, the coups are successful and happen in their member states. To begin with, the positive effect of democratic mandates on the chance that ROs take action strengthens the dominant notion of the anti-coup norm as a democratic norm. It is in line with existing studies that ROs with a formal commitment to democratic norms should have a higher likelihood of enforcing these norms in the case of blatant norm violations (Dandashly, 2015; Odinius & Kuntz, 2015). Hence, the desire to protect democratic standards is a key motive of ROs when responding to coups.

Second, the fact that ROs are more likely to take action against successful coups than failed ones indicates that ROs play a more important role after the former than after the latter. ROs tend to rather enforce the anti-coup norm in successful cases, where coups pose a more daunting threat, while failed coups are less urgent sources of concern. This confirms the idea that also stability is a major issue for ROs.

Finally, the strong effect of membership suggests a division of labour between different regional actors: ROs tend to respond to the coups in their own member states, while usually staying silent on those in external countries. The idea that domestic conflicts and democratic crises can be most effectively solved by the respective regional actors is very common in the literature (Ackermann, 2003; Hammerstad, 2005; Kirchner & Dominguez, 2011; Donno, 2013). Hence, it is intuitive that coups might also be most effectively dealt with by those ROs in which the affected state is a member. Due to the simultaneous membership of most states in several ROs (Panke & Stapel, 2018), usually not one but multiple ROs are directly

Table 4.7: Overview findings research question 2

Aspects	Expectations	Empirical evidence
RO activity	E1a: If a RO has official democratic provisions codified in its statutes, it is more likely to respond to a coup.	supported
	E1b: If a coup happens in a member state of a RO, the RO is more likely to respond to the coup.	supported
	E1c: Successful coups are more likely to lead to RO responses than failed ones.	supported
Strength of responses: RO factors	E2a: The more democratic the member states of a RO are, the stronger are the responses to a coup.	partly supported (effect strongly driven by EU)
	E2b: The more leverage a RO has vis-à-vis a state affected by a coup, the stronger are the responses by ROs.	supported
Strength of responses: democracy-based considerations	E3a: The more democratic an ousted government has been, the stronger are the responses of ROs to the coup.	partly supported (not in all models and effect is driven by EU)
	E3b: If the ousted regime has been challenged by popular protests prior to the coup, ROs show weaker responses.	not supported
	E3c: If a coup is exclusively conducted by military actors, ROs should show stronger responses.	supported
Strength of responses: stability-based considerations	E4a: If a coup is successful, ROs should show stronger responses than to a failed coup.	supported
	E4b: The higher the number of casualties in a coup, the stronger the responses shown by ROs.	supported
	E4c: The more important a state is for a regional trade network, the stronger the responses shown by ROs.	not supported
Strength of responses: interaction effects	E5a: The positive effect of the democracy level of the ousted government on the strength of RO responses should be more accentuated for ROs with a democratic membership.	not supported
	E5b: The negative effect of prior popular protests on the strength of RO responses should be more accentuated for ROs with a democratic membership.	not supported
	E5c: The positive effect of exclusively military coups on the strength of RO responses should be more accentuated for ROs with a democratic membership.	not supported

affected by a coup. The question of what impact this has on the likelihood of RO responses is of key interest. On the one hand, it is plausible that a RO might decide not to address the issue if another RO is already taking action against a coup. The rationale behind this would be that the problem is already taken care of by another actor and therefore does not require the additional attention and resources of the RO. On the other hand, it is also conceivable that strong action by one actor could lead to a 'cascade effect' of additional responses by other ROs. For instance, a suspension of a state from the AU after a coup is a strong statement, which can inspire economic sanctions of the EU and additional measures by sub-regional African ROs. Studying the dynamics of such processes over time and focusing on potential coordination mechanisms such as contact groups or joint mediation missions constitutes a promising avenue for future research.

Leverage of ROs against states hit by coups

Without denying that the anti-coup norm is an important guiding motive for the responses of ROs to coups, one can clearly state that the enforcement of the norm is contingent on the economic and military potential of ROs vis-à-vis the respective country. Thus, ROs tend to impose stronger sanctions against weaker states, while they act more cautiously against powerful states. The implications of this finding for the role of ROs in the context of coups is worrying. On the one hand, this result is intuitive and in line with previous findings (von Soest & Wahman, 2015; Hartmann, 2017). Most ROs suffer from a constant shortage of resources, which makes careful consideration about their own capacities to successfully engage in particular conflicts absolutely essential. On the other hand, the unequal treatment of countries undermines the aspiration of a universal rejection of coups and abets criticisms of a selective application of the norm by ROs.

Democratic legitimacy of ousted governments

There is some evidence that ROs evaluate coups in democracies differently than the ousting of autocrats. The fact that ROs seem to take the regime type of ousted governments into account indicates that democracy protection is actually an issue for ROs when responding to coups. Strictly speaking, the different treatment of coups in autocracies and democracies could be considered an inconsistent application of the anti-coup norm. But it can also be interpreted as a sensitivity of ROs towards the circumstances and expected consequences of a coup. Apparently, ROs consider the ousting of autocrats as more justifiable than coups against democratically legitimized leaders. If one perceives coups primarily as violations of democratic Principles, this makes absolute sense, as coups in democracies usually impair the level of democracy, while coups in autocracies simply replace one autocratic leader with another (Marinov & Goemans, 2014).

Yet it is also important to take a differentiated view on this issue. The EU is a very active RO after coups, which puts a great deal of emphasis on the democracy aspect. Likewise, the extent of democratic legitimacy of an ousted government is a key factor for ROs in Latin America when responding to coups. In contrast, in Africa, Asia and Oceania, the question of whether coups hit autocratic or democratic governments does not play such a key role. This indicates that not only the general extent of internalization of the anti-coup norm varies across regions. Also the weighing process of the two competing aims of the anti-coup norm – democracy and security – seems to be structurally different across world regions.

Popular protests and coups

Recent literature has emphasized the domestic relevance of protests for coups, as they can signal popular discontent with a state leader (Casper & Tyson, 2014; Johnson & Thyne, 2016; Gerling, 2017). Regarding the international effects of protests prior to coups, the findings of the analysis are less straightforward to interpret. On the one hand, the findings indicate that ROs with a more democratic membership are responsive to popular protests in member states in the sense that they perceive them as alarming signs of political instability which require their involvement. Hence, the stability argument seems to play a strong role here. On the other hand, democratic ROs in particular seem to struggle to align the inflexible condemnation of coups enshrined in the anti-coup norm with popular demands of removal of disliked leaders. Put differently, the anti-coup norm sometimes obliges democratic ROs to protect incumbents who have obviously lost the trust and support of their population against attempts to topple them.

Coups and violence

ROs show stronger responses to coups which claim more casualties. This finding indicates that ROs perceive coups not only as a violation of democratic and constitutional principles. Instead, ROs also treat coups as a potential source of instability and turmoil. When coups are conducted in a swift way, claim few casualties and quickly restore a certain level of stability in a country, it is less urgent for ROs to respond to them. In contrast, domestic conflicts which are accompanied by a high level of violence bear the potential of a spillover of instability to the region, threatening also other member states of the RO (Miller et al, 2018). Consequently, ROs have an incentive to become more heavily engaged.

This does not mean that the anti-coup norm does not matter for these ROs. However, within the framework of the anti-coup norm the choice of responses of diverging strength by ROs depends on stability issues. In sum, only 20.85 per cent of the non-violent coups with a low risk of domestic and regional destabilization are sanctioned by ROs with measures stronger than rhetoric criticism of the events. In contrast, 42.98 per cent of the violent coups, associated with a higher risk of spillover into the wider region, are followed by diplomatic, economic or military sanctions. Hence, independent of democracy-based considerations ROs are much more likely to show strong and decisive responses if a coup constitutes a serious threat to regional stability. This supports the notion that stability is actually a key value pursued by ROs after coups. Interestingly, this aspect seems to be particularly important for ROs in Africa, Asia and Oceania, while the effect after coups in Latin America is less accentuated.

Summary

To conclude, in the present chapter, the theoretical expectations about the factors influencing the likelihood and strength of RO responses to coups were tested. Despite a recent trend towards examining not only coups themselves, but also the international reactions to them, few studies have systematically examined the factors determining the strength of RO responses to coups. Most studies contend themselves to comparing the responses of ROs to several coups, seeking to draw conclusions on the 'consistency' of the application of the anti-coup norm by the respective organization (Boniface, 2002; Ikome, 2007; Omorogbe, 2011; Wet, 2019). A noticeable example is a quantitative study by Shannon et al (2015), which suggests that coups against democracies and wealthy states are more likely to receive international attention.

By systematically examining the strength of RO responses, this chapter adds to the sparse literature on the issue. The analysis revealed that three main factors determine whether a RO takes action after a coup: membership of the affected state in the respective organization, the presence of binding democratic provisions, which provide ROs with a mandate to address democratic flaws and success of the coup plotters in taking over power. These findings are well suited to explain why some ROs are so much more active after coups than others: the unequal global distribution of coups confronts some ROs with (successful) coups in their member states much more frequently than others. Besides, the results emphasize that the formally adopted and codified democratic norms in RO statutes are influential guiding themes for the responses of ROs to violations of these norms. ROs with binding democratic provisions take action against coups more frequently than ROs lacking such provisions. On the one hand, these are promising news for the consistent application of the anti-coup norm, suggesting that with further democratization of ROs, negative responses and punitive measures against coup plotters could become the rule for more ROs.

On the other hand, the statistical analysis also revealed that ROs vary tremendously in the strength of their responses. Several factors can help us to understand this choice of instruments of diverging strength. While ROs take democracy-related aspects, such as the distinction between civilian and military coups and the regime type of the ousted government, into account, stability-based considerations, including the feasibility to successfully exert pressure on a state, the success of a coup and the risk of spillover of major violence also play a major role. Hence, one can clearly state that ROs do not treat all coups alike. In general, ROs follow the anti-coup norm in the sense that they express their disapproval of and opposition to coups. However, when deciding on the strength of their responses, ROs take a very close look at the situation at hand and make the strength of their response contingent on a number of democracy-based, but even more so on stability-based considerations.

This approach bears risks, but also potentials. On the one side, the obvious different treatment of more and less powerful states, violent and non-violent coups, civilian and military coups, takeovers in democracies and autocracies, gives ammunition to critics claiming that the anti-coup norm is actually selectively imposed by ROs. Arceneaux and Pion-Berli (2007) argue that 'OAS behavior has remained remarkably consistent since the early 1990s: it defends democracies selectively.' In a similar manner, Ikome (2007) criticizes the AU because 'responses to coups have not been uniform, and [...], generally speaking, the response has been too soft to serve as a deterrent to aspiring coup-plotters'. If coup plotters can gamble that under certain conditions they may only face mild criticism, not only the deterrent power of the anti-coup norm to potential rebels is at risk. Likewise, the reputation of ROs as consequent, impartial and credible enforcers of a jointly agreed-upon regional norm may suffer.

On the other side, a flexible approach with responses of different strengths allows us to account for the high diversity of coups. Coups can have a variety of different reasons for taking place, are conducted in different ways and, as the debate about the democratization potential of coups shows, they can under certain circumstances, also have positive effects (Marinov & Goemans, 2014; Powell, 2014a; Thyne & Powell, 2016). In order to account for this diversity, some authors have called for a more differentiated approach from ROs in their fight against coups. For instance, Omorogbe (2011: 154) demands that 'it would be preferable if the AU adopted a more nuanced policy [towards coups]'.

In the end, the question is maybe not whether it would be desirable that ROs treat all coups alike, but whether they can reasonably be expected to do so. Coups touch upon vital questions of democracy, stability and state sovereignty. Thus, it is only natural that ROs face a constant tension between unconditionally and uniformly enforcing the anti-coup norm and accounting for the particularities of a given takeover. To sum up, the anti-coup norm is an essential motive guiding the responses of ROs to coups. Yet for understanding the role of ROs in specific cases, one cannot look at the anti-coup norm in isolation; we must also take the circumstances of coups, as well as the capacities and interests of ROs, into account.

5

Examining Differential
Post-coup Solutions

Having examined what measures ROs use to respond to coups (research question 1) and which factors drive the choice of stronger or weaker responses (research question 2), this chapter moves one step further. The policy instruments applied by ROs after coups, as studied in the two prior chapters, are not ends in themselves, but usually means to achieve particular post-coup solutions. The third research question asks what sort of post-coup solutions do ROs pursue through their responses and why.

The period starting from the moment when coup plotters have successfully taken power until the point when a stable political order is restored is defined as post-coup trajectory or aftermath of a coup. The implementation of the anti-coup norm in such situations poses a challenge for ROs. Whereas the anti-coup norm requests ROs reject coups as a political means, it does not prescribe that ROs are automatically obliged to 'reverse' coups and to reinstate an ousted government. Oftentimes, coups do not topple democratic, stable and economically successful governments, but rather repressive and autocratic regimes with a poor governance record (Lindberg & Clark, 2008). As most ROs are not particularly eager to unconditionally support such leaders, a frequent solution after coups is to push for the formation of a new constitutionally and democratically elected government. Alternatively, ROs sometimes also try to negotiate power-sharing agreements between the ousted government and the coup plotters or acknowledge the coup plotters as the new rulers of the country.

This chapter examines which of these solutions the AU, EU and ECOWAS/SADC pursued after four coups in Madagascar (2009), Niger (2010), Burkina Faso (2015) and Zimbabwe (2017). The case studies show that the stance of regional partners towards coup-born regimes varies tremendously and is highly context dependent. The subsequent sections seek to shed light on the question which circumstances and conditions shaped the choice of ROs for either of the potential post-coup solutions. The chapter is structured as follows: first, the case study approach and case selection as well as the data collection and coding process are briefly described. Next, the empirical evidence on the positions of ROs in the aftermath of the coups in the cases of Madagascar (2009), Niger (2010), Burkina Faso (2015) and Zimbabwe (2017) is presented. Subsequently, a comparative view on the cases is taken in order to evaluate the plausibility of the expectations from Chapter 2 and to draw generalizable insights from the analysis. In the final part, the results are summarized and their implications for the role of ROs after coups are discussed.

Case selection and data

In this final part of the analysis, a comparative case study is conducted to examine the third research question. The rationale of this decision and the case selection strategy are briefly outlined in the following. Subsequently, the data used for the analysis are described.

Case study design and case selection

To examine why ROs decide to pursue different post-coup solutions, four cases were selected and analysed. Four coups after which ROs pursued four different post-coup solutions were chosen: a power-sharing between ousted government and coup plotters (Madagascar in 2009), a formation of new government of actors not involved in coup (Niger in 2010), a reinstatement of the ousted government (Burkina Faso in 2015) and the consolidation of the rule of the coup plotters (Zimbabwe in 2017). This selection offers several advantages.

First, the case selection follows a diverse case design, capturing the complete spectrum of variation on the dependent variable (Seawright & Gerring, 2008). Hence, the four chosen cases include one example for each potential post-coup solution ROs may pursue after coups. By covering the complete range of potential outcomes, a diverse case design holds the distinct advantage: the chosen sample of cases is highly representative of the full population of all post-coup solutions (Seawright & Gerring, 2008). Figure 5.1 shows that the four chosen cases cover the whole spectrum of post-coup trajectories as conceptualized in Chapter 2.

After the coup in Burkina Faso in 2015, the AU, EU and ECOWAS successfully pressed for the reinstatement of the government. After the coup in Niger in 2010, the same ROs advocated for free and fair elections, which brought a new government in charge. In Zimbabwe in 2017, the AU, EU and SADC accepted the rule of the coup plotters, which was belatedly confirmed in highly controversial elections. Following a coup in Madagascar in 2009, these ROs pushed for a power-sharing agreement, resulting in a political deadlock of almost four years. Thus, the four selected cases allow

Figure 5.1: Post-coup solutions favoured by ROs and selected cases

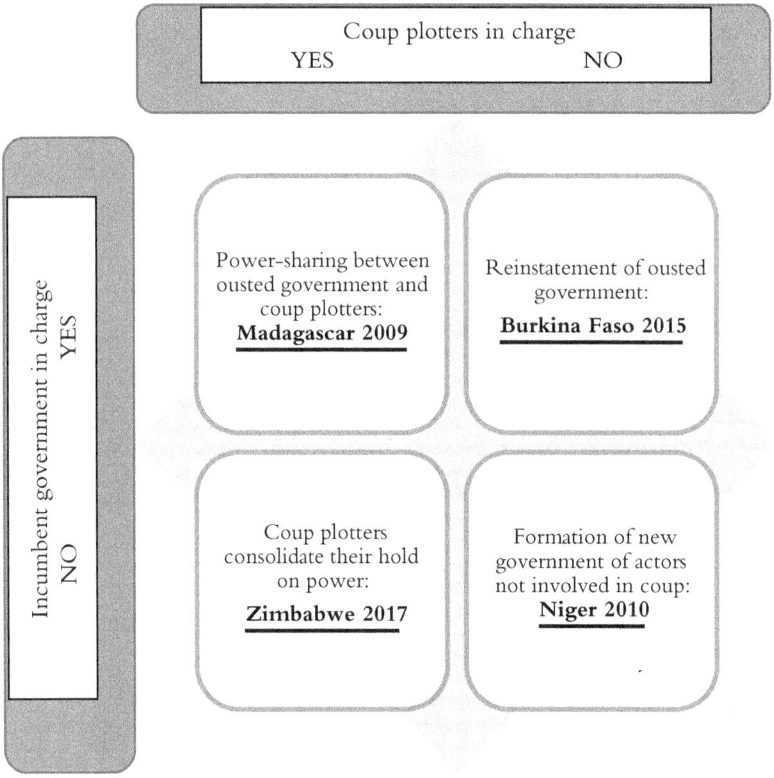

us to examine the complete variation of potential post-coup trajectories. Besides, the combination of two relatively recent cases in 2015 and 2017, with two slightly older cases from 2009 and 2010, accounts for a potential temporal dynamic in the data.

Second, it was ensured that the selected cases are comparable with regard to key parameters (Gerring & Thomas, 2005). All four coups were successful in the sense that the coup plotters achieved to take power at least temporarily. Hence, the coup attempts were not immediately defeated. Besides, all four coups happened on the same continent. Furthermore, the ROs responding to the coups were very similar: in all four cases, the AU, EU and the most powerful subregional RO (ECOWAS/SADC) were the main actors addressing the coup. Additionally, the four countries are roughly comparable with regard to key macroeconomic and military indicators such as GDP and military spending. Thus, the four states are neither among the smallest and most vulnerable targets for strong RO action, nor are they among the most powerful nations of the continent, which often tend to evade strong external criticism.

Some thoughts about the generalizability of the results are needed (Onwuegbuzie & Leech, 2010). Two issues are of particular concern in the present analysis. First, all four coups represent cases in which the respective ROs (AU, EU, ECOWAS/SADC) had a strong rationale for addressing the coups. All four ROs have a democratic mandate, the incidents happened in RO member states (apart from the EU) and the coups were successful. Hence, they can be considered as 'most-likely cases'.

Given the present research question, this choice is reasonable. There is no point in examining the pursued post-coup solutions of ROs in cases which they did not even address. The downside is that the insights from the four cases tell us relatively little about coups with weaker RO engagement. Second, the focus on coups in Africa limits the generalizability to a global scale. The choice of four African coups enhanced the comparability of the cases tremendously, increasing the validity of the results. Yet future studies should examine whether the results also hold for the post-coup solutions pursued by other ROs on different continents and with varying levels of democratic commitment.

Notwithstanding that, the comparative case study has a value reaching beyond the four cases. Each of the selected cases stands as a representative of one of the four groups of potential post-coup solutions all cases can be categorized into. The systematic comparison of cases over time and across two different African sub-regions strengthens the confidence in the findings. The case selection was done with great care, with the aim being to choose the cases in an unbiased and transparent manner. Furthermore, the strategy of selecting diverse cases holds the advantage of a comparably high level of representativeness (Seawright & Gerring, 2008).

Data collection

For the qualitative analysis of the four cases, data from a multitude of sources was compiled. In a first step, all available official RO materials concerning the four respective coups and post-coup trajectories were collected. These materials comprise decisions, resolutions, official communiqués and declarations. The documents were mainly retrieved directly from the websites of the respective ROs. In case their databases were incomplete (in particular for ECOWAS and SADC), further research was conducted to find relevant documents. In the cases of Madagascar and Burkina Faso, multilateral mediation and consultation groups were founded. Also the statements, declarations and decisions of the International Contact Group on Madagascar (ICG-M) and the International Follow-Up and Support Group for the Transition in Burkina Faso (GISAT-BF) were collected. Additionally, speeches and statements by RO officials and state leaders, press declarations and interviews with media outlets were searched for and collated. Some of this information could also be directly found on the websites of the respective ROs, yet many of these materials required further research on the cases.

In order to assess the quality of the electoral campaigns and processes following the coups, the reports and communiqués of different internal election observation missions to the countries were collected and analysed. These include reports from the electoral observation missions of the AU, the Carter Center, COMESA, the Commonwealth, the Electoral Institute for Sustainable Democracy in Africa (EISA), the EU, the Joint Mission of the International Republican Institute and the National Democratic Institute (IRI/NDI), the OIF and SADC.

The information obtained from these sources was cross-checked and supplemented by a systematic media analysis covering regional as well as international newspapers. For the media analysis the data bank of Lexis-Nexis was used, which compiles a large amount of news coverage from national, regional as well as international outlets and allows for systematic keyword searches. Besides, reports from a variety of independent think-tanks, institutes and NGOs were used for background information on the cases and to track developments concerning the economic, political and human rights situation. Finally, existing scientific articles and book chapters on the four cases were also reviewed to gain further insights into how the respective coups were evaluated by the academic community. The resulting qualitative evidence provides a remarkably rich, detailed and nuanced picture of the four cases.

Operationalization

The object of interest of the last research question are post-coup solutions. The term 'post-coup solution' comprises a political solution which leads to the end of the instable political situation following immediately after a coup. As illustrated in Figure 2.3, the diverse post-coup solutions which ROs can pursue comprise the reinstatement of the ousted government, a power-sharing agreement between the rival parties, the formation of a completely new government or the acceptance of the coup plotters as new rulers (see Chapter 2).

Which post-coup solution ROs pursue in a particular case can be derived from their statements, demands and actions. Regularly, verbal RO reactions to coups include parts in which the ROs formulate explicit demands regarding the post-coup solution. For instance, African ROs regularly request new elections without the participation of the coup plotters after coups (Nathan, 2016c). Oftentimes, ROs seek to emphasize the urgency of their demands by combining them with threats of punitive measures in case the coup plotters do not give in. Particularly economic and diplomatic sanctions are often tied to explicit requests (Charron, 2013). Sometimes the demands of ROs regarding a post-coup solution also are obvious from their actions, for example when they seek to mediate a power-sharing agreement between the coup plotters and the ousted government.

Empirically, each of the four chosen cases represents one of the conceivable post-coup solutions. In Burkina Faso (2015), ROs pushed for the reinstatement of the ousted government. In Niger (2010), the respective ROs promoted timely new elections, which led to the formation of a new civilian government. In Madagascar (2010), the ROs sought to mediate a power-sharing agreement between the rival domestic actors. In Zimbabwe (2017), the ROs accepted the consolidation of the rule of the coup plotters. As explained before, the focus lies on the role of the AU, EU and ECOWAS (in the cases of Niger and Burkina Faso) and the AU, EU and SADC (in the cases of Madagascar and Zimbabwe). This decision was made to enhance the comparability between the cases and to limit the analysis to a reasonable scope. While the focus of the analysis clearly lies on which stance these ROs took towards the events and which requests they voiced, it is important to embed their positions in the general international attitude after coups. Therefore, also the positions of other key state and IO actors involved in the four cases are briefly sketched where necessary.

In order to explain the variation regarding the different post-coup solutions in the cases, four expectations were formulated in Chapter 2. These expectations concern four conditions which are expected to drive the choice of differential post-coup solutions by ROs: the unequivocal applicability of the anti-coup norm, the democratic legitimacy of the incumbent, the chances of a democratic transition under the new leaders and the domestic power constellation. To evaluate the plausibility of these expectations, several factors were considered.

According to the sixth expectation, the extent up to which the anti-coup norm unequivocally applies to a leader change matters. If a leader change clearly qualifies as a coup and thereby unequivocally triggers the anti-coup norm, ROs enjoy less leeway to pursue post-coup solutions favourable for the coup plotters and are more likely to push for the reinstatement of the ousted government or new elections. Recent literature indicates that coup plotters use two strategies to frame their action in a more positive light and evade the application of anti-coup provisions. They either try to cast doubts that a takeover qualifies as coup or provide a narrative why their forceful interference in the politics of a country was necessary and beneficial (Yukawa et al, 2020). Accordingly, the unequivocal applicability of the anti-coup norm to a situation is captured in the following way.

First, the circumstances of a coup are examined and it is assessed whether the event clearly fulfils all criteria of a coup. According to the working definition of this book, coups are coercive and illegal attempts by parts of a country's elites to grab executive power from the ruling government. Coup plotters as well as international actors can challenge the definition of an event as coup on for several reasons. They may claim that the leader change was not violent and therefore not coercive, they may question the illegality of the action or argue that their action is not targeted against the government itself (Marsteintredet & Malamud, 2019). Hence, it is evaluated whether any of the aspects of the definition of a coup is in doubt. Information on this issue was mainly drawn from reports and news coverage of the exact proceedings of the coup and the narratives presented by the coup plotters, the ousted governments and respective ROs.

As an alternative to directly denying that a coup has taken place, coup plotters may admit that they staged a coup, but provide justifications why they did so. In many cases, coup plotters provide a storyline portraying their forceful intervention as an unfortunate, yet indispensable step to save the country (Miller, 2011). Usually, such narratives are grounded upon perceived or actual failures of the incumbent to effectively rule the country (Gassebner et al, 2016). If coup plotters succeed in framing their actions in this way, such 'mitigating circumstances' can cast doubts that the anti-coup norm is unequivocally applicable to the case. Therefore, the presence of a narrative seeking to excuse a coup is captured. Information on this issue was mainly derived from the (press) statements, speeches and interviews given by coup plotters after a coup, as well as from the reactions of the ROs to them.

The seventh expectation refers to the democratic legitimacy of the incumbent. As mentioned, coups hardly ever happen in established liberal democracies (Powell & Thyne, 2011). Notwithstanding, states hit by coups vary a lot regarding their state of democracy. Three aspects are used to measure the extent of democratic legitimacy of the incumbent: first, electoral legitimacy, referring to the question of whether the ousted ruler had come into office through an electoral contest which had dominantly been acknowledged as free and fair by domestic and international observers. For assessing this aspect, information on and reports of the last elections from political scientists, NGOs and electoral observation teams were examined.

Second, respect of the incumbent for the constitutional provisions was taken into account. This concerns the question whether the incumbent has sought to strengthen his or her power at the expense of the legislative or judicative or violated term limits in order to stay in power longer than provided for in the constitution. Coups have repeatedly been triggered by state leaders who themselves sought to violate constitutional provisions in order to enhance their power (Trithart, 2013). For evaluating this aspect, the study mainly relied on reports of NGOs and independent think-tanks and research institutes such as the EIU and the ICG, but also used RO statements on these issues as well as secondary literature.

The third aspect of democratic legitimacy is that the incumbent does not engage in major forms of democratic misconduct, including political violence, the suppression of opposition forces, the violation of civil rights and corruption. Again, information on this issue was drawn from the reports of NGOs, independent think-tanks and research institutes, as well as secondary literature.

The eighth expectation concerns the prospects of a democratic transition under a new leadership. Assessing such prospects is particularly challenging, as all coup plotters have incentives to make promises about a democratization process to the international community (Grewal & Kureshi, 2019). For evaluating how seriously coup plotters are about their democratization plans, is the analysis captured whether they present a precise and binding schedule for timely elections as a first aspect. Information on this issue is mainly derived from press statements of the coup plotters and news coverage on the plans themselves, as well as international reactions to them. An additional valuable source in the cases of Madagascar and Burkina Faso constituted the progress reports of the international contact groups.

As a second aspect, it was assessed whether the coup plotters initiate further democratic reforms in addition to setting an electoral schedule. These include the formation of a civilian interim government, an interim parliament, as well as the foundation of an independent electoral commission to grant the fairness of the upcoming elections. Information on this indicator was collected from reports of the ROs themselves as well as of the contact groups, the EIU and the ICG.

The ninth and final expectation relates to the domestic power constellation in a country. Three aspects are captured here: the support of the population, the political parties and the armed forces (including military, paramilitary and police forces) for the ousted incumbent and the new rulers. The position of the armed forces and political parties vis-à-vis the coup plotters and the ousted state leader can be relatively easily derived from statements of their respective leadership. Popular opinion after a coup is harder to assess, as reliable and independent opinion polls are difficult to conduct in the respective countries. Yet still it is important to take the popular opinion into account. To do so, mainly reports of protests, demonstrations and strikes in favour of or against the leader change in the country were used. When available, data on the popular opinion from the Afrobarometer were also included.

The aspects used to evaluate the conditions are summarized in Table 5.1. As the table illustrates, each of the four conditions expected to affect the choice of different post-coup solutions is measured by several aspects. The evaluation of the aspects is based on the qualitative analysis of the collected materials for the case studies. In reaching a final evaluation for each condition, all respective aspects are taken into account. The aspects for each condition are weighed equally, as none of them is assumed to be more important than another. The final evaluation of the respective conditions is gradual rather than absolute. For instance, it is not the case that an ousted leader

Table 5.1: Overview operationalization of post-coup conditions

Conditions	Aspects	Descriptions
E6: Unequivocal applicability of the anti–coup norm	Event clearly meets all criteria of the coup definition	Consensus on the fact that the takeover was violent, illegal and directed against the government.
	Mitigating circumstances	No denial that a coup took place, but arguments justifying the coup: (Economic) misrule, state failure, autocratic tendencies of incumbent.
E7: Democratic legitimacy of the incumbent	Electoral legitimacy	The ousted incumbent has been elected in an at least dominantly fair electoral contest.
	Respect of constitutional provisions	The incumbent respects constitutional provisions, especially regarding the independence of other state organs (courts, parliaments, etc.) and term limits.
	Absence of major misconduct	The incumbent does not engage in major forms of democratic misconduct, including political violence, the violation of civil rights, the suppression of opposition forces and corruption.
E8: Prospects of post-coup democratic transition	Precise electoral schedule	The coup plotters provide a precise and binding schedule for timely elections.
	Democratic reforms	Democratic reforms are initiated following the coup (for example formation of a civilian interim government and parliament, independent electoral commission).
E9: Domestic power constellation	Support of the population	Popular protests, demonstrations, strikes in favour of either the ousted government or the new rulers.
	Support of political parties	Support of major political parties for either the ousted government or the new rulers.
	Support of the armed forces	Support of police forces, the army and para-military forces for either the ousted government or the new rulers.

either enjoys absolute democratic legitimacy or lacks it completely. Instead, democratic legitimacy is perceived as a continuous concept, which may range from high (all three aspects of electoral legitimacy, respect of constitutional provisions and absence of major misconduct are fulfilled) to medium (one or two indicators are fulfilled) to low (none of the indicators is fulfilled). The same logic applies to the other conditions.

Case studies

In the following, the post-coup solutions which the AU, EU, ECOWAS and SADC pursued in Madagascar, Niger, Burkina Faso and Zimbabwe are analysed. The section proceeds in chronological order starting with the case of Madagascar (2009), to be followed by the analyses of Niger (2010), Burkina Faso (2015) and Zimbabwe (2017). For each of the cases, the coup itself and the responses of the respective ROs are first described, before analysing the case in terms of the potential explanatory factors formulated in the expectations: the unequivocal applicability of the anti-coup norm, the democratic legitimacy of the incumbent, the prospects of democratization under the new regime and the domestic power constellation.

Madagascar, 2009

In March 2009, the Malagasy President Marc Ravalomanana was ousted by his rival Andry Rajoelina, the mayor of the capital Antananarivo. Rajoelina took over after a prolonged power struggle between the two politicians, in which Rajoelina had accused the elected president of engaging in a broad array of undemocratic and illegal practices. Following the leader change in Madagascar, the AU, EU and SADC condemned the coup, in line with COMESA, the OIF and the UN. But they also sought negotiations and attempted to broker a power-sharing solution between the ousted government of President Ravalomanana and the coup plotters backing Rajoelina. Owing to a series of drawbacks and failures, it took almost five years until a newly elected president was sworn in in January 2014.[1]

The case of Madagascar is a prominent and well-researched example of how coups can result in protracted deadlock and how international mediation attempts can fail (Lanz & Gasser, 2013; Nathan, 2013; Witt, 2013, 2017). The focus of the present study is not on why the mediation attempts failed to produce a timely solution. Instead, the research interest lies in why ROs sought to establish a power-sharing agreement in the first place. After the unconstitutional ousting of the elected president, this solution was clearly not compatible with the initial provisions of the anti-coup norm. Hence, why did the respective ROs push for a power-sharing agreement? After briefly describing the regional responses to the coup in Madagascar, this question is addressed by analysing the case against the four criteria, the unequivocal applicability of the anti-coup norm, the democratic legitimacy of the ousted government, the prospects of post-coup democratization and the domestic power constellation.

RO responses and positions: a cacophony of voices

On 17 March 2009, the Malagasy President Marc Ravalomanana was forced to hand over power to the military, which subsequently transferred it to his political rival Andry Rajoelina. International responses to the coup followed promptly afterwards. A series of ROs, including the AU, SADC, the EU, but also COMESA and the OIF addressed the coup, as did the UN and several single countries, most importantly the United States and France, the former colonial power of the island state. The lowest common denominator of the responses was the understanding that constitutional and democratic order had to be restored in Madagascar (Witt, 2017, 2020). Yet how this goal was to be achieved and under whose leadership a government should be formed turned out to be challenging.

Interestingly, SADC initially took the fiercest stance vis-à-vis the coup. At an extraordinary summit on 30 March 2009, the organization 'condemned in the strongest terms the unconstitutional actions that have led to the illegal ousting of the democratically elected Government of Madagascar' (SADC, 2009). Notably, the summit further directly suspended Madagascar, explicitly refused to recognize Rajoelina as new head of state, demanded Ravalomanana's reinstatement and threatened that 'in the event of non-compliance with the above decisions, SADC shall, in collaboration with the African Union and United Nations, consider other options to restore constitutional normalcy' (SADC, 2009).

The open formulation of 'other options', potentially also allowing for the use of military force, was exceptionally fierce for SADC. COMESA supported the stance of SADC and encouraged it in 'examining all options, including the possibility of military intervention' to resolve the crisis (Reuters, 2009). However, many other actors took a more moderate position. The EU only voiced its deep concern and 'urge[d] all parties to engage in dialogue and to show restrain' (EU, 2009b). Most notably, the AU also refrained from directly condemning the coup. Instead, the organization only '[n]ote[d] the resignation by decree, today, of President Marc Ravalomanana, under pressure from the civilian opposition and the army' and '[u]rge[d] the Malagasy parties to uphold the spirit of dialogue and compromise in order to find, as soon as possible, a peaceful and consensual solution to the crisis' (AU, 2009a).

The idea of finding a consensual and inclusive solution to the constitutional crisis soon gained momentum among regional and international partners. Swiftly, several ROs and other international actors decided to initiate mediation attempts to bring the hostile camps of Ravalomanana and Rajoelina together with the aim of holding consultations about a power-sharing deal and the formation of a joint interim government. Only days after the coup, special envoys from the UN (Tiébilé Dramé), the AU (Ablassé

Ouédraogo) and the OIF (Edem Kodjo) arrived in the country. Despite its initially unconciliatory stance, also SADC sent an envoy (Themba Absalom Dlamini). In addition, on 20 June, SADC appointed Joaquim Chissano as the lead mediator of the organization, tasked with bringing about an agreement between the opposing political forces in Madagascar (Witt, 2017). In order to coordinate and align the activities of the comparatively large number of international and regional actors involved in the mediation process, the International Contact Group on Madagascar (ICG-M) was founded, in which inter alia representatives of the AU, EU, COMESA, the Indian Ocean Commission (IOC), the OIF and SADC regularly met (ICG-M, 2009).

In sum, the evidence clearly indicates that a form of power-sharing was the preferred solution of the AU, EU and SADC. At first glance, the rationale of these ROs to strongly prefer a negotiated solution between the political opponents in Madagascar is not immediately evident. After all, the democratically elected President Ravalomanana had been violently toppled and forced to flee the country by the coup plotters backing Rajoelina. So first, there was little reason to reward Rajoelina with participation in a joint interim government. Second, given the severe antipathy between the two rival politicians and their supporters, it was also not clear why ROs expected that such a deal would materialize and work out.

Unequivocal applicability of the anti-coup norm: a popular revolution?

An analysis of documents of the ICG-M indicates that the question whether the events in Madagascar in March 2009 actually constituted a coup, hence invoking the anti-coup norm, was not at the centre of debate at that time. International and regional actors unanimously agreed in the contact group that 'the process of devolution of power that occurred in Madagascar took place in flagrant violation of the relevant provisions of the Malagasy Constitution and that the subsequent decision to confer the office of President of the Republic to Mr. Andry Rajoelina constitutes an unconstitutional change of Government' (ICG-M, 2009).

The fact that the event fulfilled the criteria of a coup was not contested. Notwithstanding, the circumstances of Ravalomanana's fall are essential for understanding how and why regional actors responded to the event. A central argument of Rajoelina for justifying his claim to power was the framing of the sequence of events as a popular revolution (Chauprade, 2009). In fact, the forced resignation of Ravalomanana had been preceded by popular demonstrations against the president (Lanz & Gasser, 2013). However, coups are often accompanied or even triggered by popular protests, as they signal domestic dissatisfaction with the incumbent and a certain weakness of his or her position (Gerling, 2017). As such, protests can change the standpoint of elites over whether to stage a coup or not, but they do not modify the nature of coups themselves. In the case of Madagascar, the protests had certainly weakened Ravalomanana's position. Yet the ultimate trigger leading to Ravalomanana's fall was the move of the Malagasy army to withdraw their confidence and backing for the president (EIU, 2009a).

The second argument against the allegation that Rajoelina had ousted Ravalomanana in a coup was that Rajoelina had not directly taken power from Ravalomanana. Rajoelina argued that Ravalomanana himself had transferred power to the military and that he had only been subsequently mandated with transitionally governing the country by the armed forces. Yet this line of argumentation contains some obvious flaws. To begin with, on 31 January, Rajoelina had announced the creation of the High Authority of the Transition (HAT) and declared himself head of state (Lanz & Gasser, 2013). Thus, he had very actively sought power. In a phone interview with the news agency Reuters, Rajoelina himself had announced: 'Of course it is me who is giving the army orders. I am in permanent contact with them' (Rajoelina, 2009).

Besides, the Malagasy constitution does not foresee any transfer of executive power from the elected government to the armed forces. Likewise, the military does not hold any constitutional competencies to designate an interim president (Connolly, 2013). Furthermore, there are credible doubts whether Ravalomanana's decision to hand over power to the armed forces was of his own volition, given that the army had openly threatened the president and announced that the military would no longer take orders from him (EIU, 2009a). In the aforementioned phone interview his rival Rajoelina had also threatened: 'For now we are waiting for him to resign. If he doesn't, then we have other options ... I can't say if that means a military intervention' (Rajoelina, 2009).

In a nutshell, one can hardly contest that the ousting of Ravalomanana in Madagascar in 2009 fulfilled the criteria of a coup, defined as coercive and illegal attempts by parts of a country's elites to grab executive power from the ruling government. The analysis shows that there was a strong international consensus that the regime change had been unconstitutional and that the argument about mitigating circumstances of the coup was weak. As such, the event should have clearly triggered the anti-coup norm. However, the fact that Ravalomanana's resignation was preceded by large-scale public protests and the subsequent transfer of power from Ravalomanana to the army and then to Rajoelina at least partially impaired the unequivocalness of the takeover and allowed for an alternative, if feeble, framing of the chain of events.

Democratic legitimacy: press freedom as a stumbling block

Yet the framing from the Rajoelina camp of the events as popular revolution was not the only factor explaining why ROs decided to favour a solution according to which a democratically elected president was supposed to share power with the man who had ousted him. For understanding the only conditional support for Ravalomanana, it is essential to take a closer look on his record of governance as Malagasy president. The analysis of the state of democracy in Madagascar prior to the coup points to some essential deficits.

Madagascar's political history is characterized by instability, autocratic tendencies and turmoil. Since the country's independence from France in 1960, several governments have been toppled by political violence and uprisings (Maunganidze, 2009). In 2001, Ravalomanana, then popular mayor of the capital Antananarivo was elected as President of Madagascar following a violent and disputed presidential run-off against the incumbent, Didier Ratsiraka. In the next parliamentary elections in 2002, Ravalomanana and his party, the Tiako-I-Madagasikara (TIM), reached a comfortable electoral victory. In the 2006 presidential elections, Ravalomanana was re-elected, though opposition parties vocally criticized the uneven conditions of electoral campaign and the unfair treatment of opposition candidates (Ratsimbaharison, 2016). For instance, Ravalomanana gave orders to deny Pierrot Rajaonarivelo, an opposition candidate with good prospects, access to the country to apply for candidacy, thereby securing his own certain victory (Cheeseman & Klaas, 2018). A constitutional referendum in 2007 strengthened the president's powers, in particular his right to legislate by decree during a state of emergency.

Apart from the described limitations of electoral fairness and an increasing concentration of power in the hands of the president, corruption and restrictions of civil rights and freedoms became an issue. Despite favourable natural conditions and comparatively high amounts of development cooperation, Madagascar is among the poorest countries in the world (Horning, 2008). The island state regularly ranks at the bottom of development indices (Hinthorne, 2011). In 2001, the election of the self-made millionaire Ravalomanana raised hopes for an improved economic policy of the country. However, Ravalomanana ruthlessly intermingled his private economic interests with those of the state, favouring his own firms and misusing state resources for private purchases (Maunganidze, 2009). For instance, the president was sharply criticized for leasing large parts of the island's cultivated land to a South Korean company and purchasing a second expensive superfluous presidential aeroplane (ICG, 2010a). Furthermore, allegations of a high level of corruption were repeatedly voiced against the government (ICG, 2014).

In addition to the allegations of economic mismanagement, the analysis points towards restrictions of freedoms of opinion, of speech and of the press, which emerged as central sources of discontent. In the course of his presidency, Ravalomanana closed a series of newspapers, television and radio stations, in an attempt to silence critical reporting on his rule

(Ratsimbaharison, 2016). On 13 December 2008 the situation escalated when Ravalomanana decided to shut down the media outlet VIVA. The television station, owned by his political rival Rajoelina, had broadcast an interview with the former president Ratsiraka, in which he voiced critique about Ravalomanana's style of governance (ICG, 2010b). In response to the closure, Rajoelina called for demonstrations and a general strike against Ravalomanana. The government's response to the protests was harsh. Security forces repeatedly violently surpressed demonstrations causing at least 135 fatalities and many more injured people over the course of three months (Maunganidze, 2009). The growing tension reached its tragic climax on 6 February 2009. On this day, 28 unarmed protesters against Ravalomanana were shot in front of the presidential residence (EIU, 2009b). News about the event quickly spread over the country.

Also on the international stage, the increasingly autocratic tendencies of the Ravalomanana regime and its use of violence against protesters did not go unnoticed and evoked rising concern. Prior to the coup, the AU had already sent an envoy to facilitate talks between the government and the protesters with the goal of finding a political solution and bringing an end to the violence (ICG, 2010b). After the events of 6 February, the AU 'urged all stakeholders to exercise restraint, refrain from any action likely to aggravate the current situation' (AU, 2009b). Likewise, the EU demanded to 'continue the reforms that are needed to respond to the urgent calls for greater social justice and democracy and the sound management of public affairs' (EU, 2009a).

To summarize, the analysis indicates that the limited electoral legitimacy and the flawed state of democracy under the Ravalomanana regime was an important reason why regional actors refrained from unconditionally siding with Ravalomanana's government and supported a negotiated power-sharing deal instead. Like many of his successors, the Malagasy president had sought to concentrate power in his hands and to marginalize his opponents. To reach this goal, he had not only manipulated the electoral process, but had also misused state resources and assets, had constrained political rights and freedoms and had violently repressed popular protests against his government. As a result, Ravalomanana's reputation as a democratic state leader was seriously impaired, despite his official electoral legitimization.

Post-coup democratization: restricting presidential power?

According to the expectations formulated in Chapter 2, ROs do not only take the democratic record of the incumbent into account, but also the chances of democratization under the new regime. Consequently, the present section examines this aspect in the case of Madagascar. In the view of many ROs, the fact that the Malagasy military immediately and voluntarily transferred power to a civilian government under the leadership of Andry Rajoelina was a promising starting point for a successful democratic transition. The prospect of enduring military rule would have been hard to swallow for ROs, particularly for the AU (Ratsimbaharison, 2017). In contrast, the civilian political movement under the leadership of Rajoelina faced less open criticism. In the days and weeks to follow the coup, Rajoelina and his supporters made efforts to gain internal and external legitimacy.

An essential prerequisite for reaching these goals was the presentation of a credible democratization agenda. Thus, after his rival Ravalomanana had fled the country, Rajoelina promised not only new elections, but also fundamental political and economic reforms (Witt, 2017). Rajoelina publicly announced that the mission of the HAT was 'to lead to the return to constitutional order' and that the regime would strengthen the rights of the legislative assembly vis-à-vis the president, further the separation of powers and reform the electoral process with the goal of creating equal opportunities for all candidates (Chauprade, 2009).

Regional and international actors did not believe these pledges wholesale. After all, promising democratic reforms is a common strategy of coup plotters to gain international acceptance (Thyne et al, 2018). And apart from promises and announcements, the HAT and Rajoelina undertook few tangible steps towards democratizing the country (ICG, 2014). Yet still, Rajoelina's suggestions to restrict the presidential powers hit a nerve. Madagascar had for years suffered from the uncontrolled and absolute power of a series of presidents who had put their personal interests above the development of the poor island state (ICG, 2010b). Consequently, one main argument in favour of a power-sharing agreement was that it would force the opposed political factions of Ravalomanana and Rajoelina to cooperate and to find compromises on central issues (ICG-M, 2009).

To conclude, concerns about the chances of democratization in Madagascar were a central reason for regional actors to push for a consensual and inclusive solution. Rajoelina had emphasized his commitment to initiate democratic reforms, conduct elections and restrict presidential powers. Yet the AU, EU and SADC had reasonable doubts whether Rajoelina could be trusted to implement them on his own. Instead, they believed that an inclusive interim government would facilitate dialogue and compromise, ultimately strengthening the state of democracy in Madagascar.

Domestic power constellation: a Malagasy stalemate

The idea of a power-sharing agreement as a feasible solution to the crisis in Madagascar did not arise solely from hopes about timely democratization. Instead, an examination of the case indicates that also a pragmatic assessment of the domestic power constellation played a decisive role therein. During his years as president, Ravalomanana had built up a considerable support base and his party, the TIM, constituted the most influential political force in the country. The opposition in Madagascar was splintered between a large number of small parties (Freedom House, 2008). Yet in the months before the coup, Rajoelina had emerged as the unifying leader of the opposition. Like Ravalomanana in earlier years, also Rajoelina was mayor of the capital, Antananarivo. Given the strongly centralized nature of the Malagasy state and the marginalization of rural areas, the mayor's office in the capital was an influential political post (Maunganidze, 2009). When Rajoelina mobilized against Ravalomanana and founded the HAT, his support base rapidly increased.

In the aftermath of the coup, the political polarization of Malagasy society became even more apparent. While Rajoelina supporters publicly celebrated the coup and cheered the removal of the former regime, also large pro-Ravalomanana demonstrations emerged, calling for the return of the ousted president from exile (EIU, 2009a; Ratsimbaharison, 2017). Faced with a deeply divided society, international actors attempted to overcome the cleavages by initiating talks between four political movements, representing the supporters of the ousted president Ravalomanana, his challenger Rajoelina, but also the former presidents Didier Ratsiraka and Albert Zafy.[2]

An additional factor leading towards a power-sharing agreement was the position of the military. The Malagasy army has not played a particularly dominant role in the country's troubled history, yet the analysis shows that the military turned out to be a decisive factor in the political crisis starting in 2009. During his term, Ravalomanana had not built up strong linkages with the army (ICG, 2010b; Ratsimbaharison, 2016); hence, when Rajoelina's revolt took place, the army sided with the challenger (Hauge, 2010). This move further consolidated Rajoelina's position and made it difficult for ROs to enforce a solution, which would have excluded the Rajoelina faction from power.

In sum, the preference of ROs for a power-sharing agreement including the ousted president's faction as well as that of his challenger Rajoelina, also emerged from pragmatic considerations. The analysis shows that while Ravalomanana still had a considerable support base in Madagascar, also Rajoelina had gathered support from the population, as well as from military and political elites. In order to resolve this stalemate, ROs sought to establish a joint interim government as the most feasible and promising solution.

Niger, 2010

The coup in Niger in 2010 is well suited to illustrate why ROs frequently prefer new elections to the reinstatement of ousted governments. The Nigerien President Mamadou Tandja had initially been democratically elected and enjoyed international support. Yet when he approached the end of his second and according to the Nigerien constitution final term as President, Tandja displayed increasingly authoritarian tendencies. When he announced his intention to extend his rule for another presidential term, against the constitutional provisions, senior army leaders staged a coup. The stance of internal and particularly regional actors against the coup was clearly critical, yet Tandja had lost most of his international support as well. As a result, strong international pressure quickly led to the formation of a civilian interim government and free and fair elections took place under a year after the coup.[3]

At first glance, the positions of regional actors vis-à-vis the coup in Niger seem to be perfectly in line with the provisions of the anti-coup norm. Yet why did the AU, EU and ECOWAS take such a clear stance in this case, while being more lenient in other cases, such as that of Madagascar, described in the previous section? In order to examine the motives and considerations of the respective ROs after the coup in Niger, the case is analysed along the four criteria of the unequivocal applicability of the anti-coup norm, the pre-coup democratic record, the prospects of post-coup democratization and the domestic power constellation.

RO responses and positions: muted indignation

On 18 February 2010, soldiers under the leadership of Major Salou Djibo ousted the Nigerien president Mamadou Tandja. In a classical coup, they arrested the government, dissolved the existing institutions and established the Supreme Council for the Restoration of Democracy (CSRD), a transitional council to temporarily rule the country (EIU, 2009c). Stunningly, the international response to the coup was muted. Admittedly, most international actors did not openly greet the coup and dutifully condemned the unconstitutional move. However, although the responses of ROs and other actors expressed international concern about the situation, the majority of statements only formally denounced the coup. The EU High Representative Catherine Ashton 'condemn[ed] the seizure of the power by a military coup in Niger and call[ed] upon all actors to engage immediately in a democratic process allowing for rapid establishment of the constitutional order in the country' (EU, 2010b).

ECOWAS also condemned the coup and called on both sides to resolve the constitutional crisis through dialogue and negotiations (RTT News, 2010). Following the coup, ECOWAS President Mohammed Ibn Chambas not only criticized the coup plotters, but Tandja as well: '[T]his is a throwback to the past in the region, a situation which obviously is unacceptable. We have a policy now of zero tolerance for violent change of government just as we find totally unacceptable attempts by governments to hang on to power through manipulation of constitutions' (Clottey, 2010).

The AU took the strictest stance on the issue. At a meeting of the Peace and Security Council, the organization decided to suspend Niger according to the provisions of the AU's anti-coup regime. Besides, the AU 'demand[ed] the speedy return to constitutional order based on democratic institutions and affirm[ed] the readiness of the AU, in close collaboration with ECOWAS, to facilitate such a process' (AU, 2010a).

Interestingly, while all three regional actors condemned the coup as a procedural means of leader change, they refrained from calling for the reinstatement of the ousted government. Instead, all organizations stressed that they would prefer the formation of a new government via free and fair elections. Only days after the coup, the Chairman of ECOWAS, the president of neighbouring Nigeria Goodluck Jonathan, received a delegation of the coup plotters to be briefed on their roadmap towards democratization (*Daily Independent*, 2010). As Ibn Chambas stated in the name of ECOWAS, '[w]e will work hand in hand with the African Union to ensure that there is restoration of consensus around the constitution in Niger' (Clottey, 2010). The fact that the ROs did not even take the reinstatement of the former government or a power-sharing agreement into account and immediately pushed for new elections raises questions about the Nigerien coup and its evaluation by ROs. In the following, the impact of the four criteria of the unequivocal applicability of the anti-coup norm, the pre-coup democratic record, the prospects of post-coup democratization and the domestic power constellation are examined.

Unequivocal applicability of the anti-coup norm: the dilemma of guardian coups

With regard to the unequivocal applicability of the anti-coup norm, the situation was remarkably clear. When soldiers led by Major Djibo took over power and arrested President Tandja and his cabinet, the move could hardly be perceived as anything other than a coup. As a result, all three ROs referred to the events as a coup and basically no discussion about whether the incident invoked the anti-coup norm or not emerged. As illustrated in the next section, the AU, ECOWAS and the EU followed the norm to the letter by condemning the coup and calling for a return to democratic and constitutional order (Zounmenou & Loua, 2011). According to the provisions of the Lomé Declaration, the AU was also obliged to suspend Niger and did so swiftly. However, while the respective ROs took a formally negative position, they also sent silent signals that the coup plotters would not face the full force of possible RO responses (EIU, 2010b). In particular, the emphasis of the AU, EU and ECOWAS that they would stand ready to assist the transition underlined that the ROs were not completely hostile towards the coup plotters.

The apparent contradiction of this approach can be explained by the fact that although all three ROs agreed that the events in Niger in February 2010 constituted a coup and therefore required formal rejection, it was also clear that it was a very peculiar coup characterized by certain mitigating circumstances. Coups can come about as a result of a broad range of different motivations (Gassebner et al, 2016). One particular case is the so-called 'guardian coup' or 'corrective coup' (Baudais & Chauzal, 2011). The underlying idea of this concept is that in young and unstable democracies, the military serves as a guardian of the political process. When political actors violate key democratic rules or severe political turmoil emerges, the military intervenes to get the country back on track. From this perspective, coups are perceived as unfortunate, regrettable, yet sometimes necessary measures. The narrative presented by the Nigerien coup plotters perfectly fitted into this concept. In an interview in the aftermath of the coup, Djibo framed his actions as follows:

> You know very well that it was a very difficult moment for Niger. The political situation was critical. We decided to take responsibility to put an end to the drifting of the institutions that could have brought about disasters. That's the reason why we, the defence and security forces, sacrificed ourselves. (RFI, 2010)

Apparently, the concept of guardian coups is hard to reconcile with the unconditional rejection of any coup embedded in the anti-coup norm (Zounmenou & Loua, 2011). Yet, interestingly, the case of Niger illustratively shows that despite the far-reaching commitment of the anti-coup norms within ROs, the notion of justified guardian coups seems to continue to exist within ROs. At least, the positive framing of the coup by the army was not vocally questioned. As the respective ROs accepted the justifications of the coup plotters for their action, the coup plotters neither faced judicial consequences nor international sanctions. This indicates that although the ROs could not formally endorse the coup, they were willing to turn a blind eye to the issue.

To sum up, in the case of Niger, neither the coup plotters nor the respective ROs questioned the applicability of the anti-coup norm and the latter formally met the requirements enshrined in the norm. However, the relevant ROs did not take action which exceeded the minimally requested steps, as they perceived the takeover in the West African country as a guardian coup intended to protect the country from authoritarian backsliding. The rationale of adopting this perspective becomes clearer when taking a closer look at the background of the Nigerien case and the events leading to the fall of President Tandja.

Democratic legitimacy: term limits and constitutionality

The anti-coup norm rejects coups as a substantial threat to democratic and constitutional standards, yet obviously coups are not the only potential threat to democracies. Electoral fraud and violence, democratic backsliding and the restriction of civil rights and liberties, as well as incumbents' refusal to give up power after electoral defeat or due to the end of term limits constitute considerable risks to democratic governance (Arceneaux & Pion-Berli, 2007). When coups hit legitimate democratic state leaders, the issue of how to assess the events is usually straightforward. Yet when coups target leaders who have themselves engaged in undemocratic practices, the question of which position to take after a coup and which post-coup solutions to pursue is more difficult for ROs.

The case of Niger serves as a prime example to illustrate how coups against uncontestably undemocratic state leaders pose a challenge for ROs. Niger has a troubled political history. Since the country's independence in 1960, Niger has seen no fewer than four successful coups.[4] As a result of the inherent political instability and sluggish economic growth, Niger was among the world's least developed countries at the time of the coup (Bertelsmann Stiftung, 2010). When Mamadou Tandja was elected as president in 1999, in elections which were declared free and fair by international election observers, this raised hope for the country (Mueller, 2013). Tandja's re-election in 2004 also followed democratic rules and standards and was generally interpreted as a sign of emerging political stability in Niger (Elischer & Mueller, 2019).

Notwithstanding the fact that Tandja had come to power via democratic means, he was not a democratic poster child, as a closer analysis of his record as president reveals. While his first term was characterized by stable cooperation of his own party, the National Movement for a Society of Development (MNSD) with its coalition partner, the Democratic and Social Convention (CDS), during his second term, Tandja increasingly sought to marginalize and prosecute potential political rivals.[5] In addition, freedom of press and opinion, the impartiality of the judicial system and corruption were a source of concern (Pawlitzky, 2009). When a major food crisis hit the country in 2005, Tandja not only failed to effectively tackle the crisis, but also attempted to cover up the desperate humanitarian situation in large parts of the country and to restrict media coverage of the issue (Mueller, 2013).

In 2009, Tandja's rule came close to an end, as the Nigerien constitution held a term limit, unequivocally stating that the president can only be re-elected once. However, in December 2008, Tandja suddenly announced his plans to hold a referendum to change the constitution in a way which would allow him to run in the elections again. He explained this sudden change of mind nonchalantly by the fact that he would need more time 'to finish some projects' (Baudais & Chauzal, 2011).

Tandja's plan to change the constitution did not only violate the Nigerien constitutional provisions, which clearly rule out a change of the respective articles, but also the Protocol on Democracy and Good Governance of ECOWAS, which stipulates that '[n]o substantial modification shall be made to the electoral laws in the last six (6) months before the elections, except with the consent of a majority of Political actors' (ECOWAS, 2001). Such a consent was clearly not given. The remaining political parties strongly opposed Tandja's endeavour and the Nigerien constitutional court ruled twice against changing the constitution and holding a respective referendum (Elischer, 2013). Large-scale popular protests against the Tandja regime emerged, triggered by the ongoing economic crisis and outrage about the undemocratic manipulation of the constitutional provisions (Mueller, 2018).

A glance at the international response reveals that the external reactions to Tandja's plans were dominantly critical. While Gaddafi, the ruler of Niger's northern neighbour, expressed some sympathy for Tandja, the AU, ECOWAS and the EU, as well as a large number of single states warned Tandja not to manipulate the constitution (EIU, 2009d). For instance, in June 2009 the ECOWAS Authority of Heads of State and Government 'expressed their concerns about the possible consequences of recent developments on the constitution of the country' and 'appealed to the authorities in Niger to respect the constitution and rule of law which have been the basis for the consolidation of peace and security during the last ten years of consensual democracy in the country' (ECOWAS, 2009b).

Ignoring domestic opposition and international warnings, Tandja went ahead with his plans. He dissolved the parliament as well as the constitutional court (EIU, 2010a). After holding the referendum, which was boycotted by the opposition parties and their supporters, Tandja stayed in power. As a result of the move, the EU partly suspended its development cooperation with the Nigerien government (EU, 2010a). ECOWAS attempted to mediate between Tandja's government and the opposition, yet simultaneously suspended the country for breaking the democratic provisions of the organization (ECOWAS, 2009a). In this situation, the military finally intervened and ousted Tandja's and his regime.

To conclude, the analysis of the extent of democratic legitimacy of the ousted incumbent shows that although Mamadou Tandja was the democratically elected President of Niger, his attempt to change the constitution allowing him to stay in power constituted a clear breach of democratic and constitutional principles. By ignoring not only domestic opposition, but also stern international warnings, Tandja had seriously damaged his reputation as democratic leader and had lost a great deal of credit with his international supporters. Accordingly, the analysis indicates that while the AU, EU and ECOWAS criticized the procedural manner in which the president was replaced, they turned out to be unwilling to come to his rescue due to his lack of democratic legitimacy.

Post-coup democratization: leading Niger back on track

Against the background of autocratic backsliding under the auspices of Tandja, the prospect of timely elections and the formation of a new government constituted a far more promising alternative for restoring democratic order. Analysis of the post-coup strategy of the coup plotters shows that the junta under the leadership of Major Djibo put a lot of effort in emphasizing that their goal was not to keep power for themselves and to govern Niger permanently via a military regime. Instead, in a first statement, the military council stated that their goals were to 'make Niger an example of democracy and good governance' and to 'save Niger and its population from poverty, deception and corruption' (Perry, 2010). Tellingly, the coup plotters also named their new military council 'Supreme Council for the Restoration of Democracy (CSRD)', which did not only underline their intention to initiate democratic reforms, but also resonated well with the narrative of a guardian coup outlined in the previous section.

Admittedly, such justifications and reassurances are frequently voiced after coups and oftentimes not fulfilled. Yet the Nigerien CSRD sent credible signals that the military council was serious about its democratization plans. Within two days, most members of Tandja's former government were released and the CSRD announced that it would appoint a civilian transitional government (EIU, 2010b). Mahamadou Danda, an experienced and internationally acknowledged administrator and diplomat, was appointed as interim civilian prime minister to chair a government mainly consisting of civil servants and technocrats. The junta promised to prepare an electoral schedule and to conduct constitutional reforms, after holding consultations with all political parties (Trithart, 2013). After a draft for a new constitution had been agreed on and electoral laws were reformed, the CSRD scheduled elections for January 2011 – within a year of the coup.

All these steps reassured regional and international actors. The progress made on the way towards restoring stable democratic conditions was repeatedly acknowledged and praised by regional actors. For instance, the AU Peace and Security Council 'welcomed the elaboration of a clear programme for the Transition by the de facto authorities in Niger for the restoration of constitutional order' (AU, 2010b) and the EU promised that '[A]dvances made by the Niger authorities on the way towards restoring constitutional order will be reflected in gradual resumption of EU development assistance' (EU, 2010a). The personal commitment and leadership impressed the AU, ECOWAS and the EU and gained trust from regional actors in the process of post-coup democratization. A central prerequisite for this constructive relationship between the coup plotters and the respective ROs was the early and unequivocal statement that the coup plotters had actually no ambition to cling to power and that therefore no member of the CSRD or the transitional government would run in the 2011 elections (Zounmenou & Loua, 2011).

Once the elections took place in early 2011, election monitoring teams from the AU, ECOWAS and the EU were invited to observe the process in order to enhance trust in the democratic nature of the procedures (AU, 2011; EU, 2011b). In the presidential contest, opposition candidate Mahamadou Issoufou was elected as president, and the parties supporting him reached a majority in the legislative assembly. The international assessment of the electoral contest was generally positive, despite critique of minor organizational deficiencies. The Head of the ECOWAS mission called the elections 'free, fair, transparent and credible' (Ahmad, 2011). The report of the European observer mission drew a similar positive judgement (EU, 2011a). The High Representative, Catherine Ashton referred to the elections as 'a milestone in the process of transition to democracy and a major step towards the restoration of full cooperation between Niger and the European Union' (EU, 2011c).

In a nutshell, the analysis indicates that the credible and specific roadmap towards a democratization process outlined by the coup plotters significantly contributed to the preference of regional actors for a new government over a reinstatement of the Tandja regime or its participation in a power-sharing agreement. Once it became evident that the CSRD actually planned to conduct democratic reforms, to hold new elections and to hand over power to elected civilian authorities, the AU, ECOWAS and the EU strongly supported this process and signalled their preference for a new government. Inter alia, the EU contributed more than €20 million to financing the Nigerien parliamentary and presidential elections (EU, 2011d).

Domestic power constellation: the Nigerien army and civil society

While the increasing authoritarian tendencies of Mamadou Tandja and his attempt to violate the constitutional and democratic provisions, as well as the credible promise of post-coup democratization, played an important role in shaping RO positions after the coup, a close examination of the case indicates that more practical factors were also at play. In his efforts to cling to power, including the dissolution of parliament and the constitutional court, Tandja had lost the support and confidence of the vast majority of domestic actors. At first, not all participants in the popular protests in 2009 and 2010 had been generally opposed to the idea of 'tazartché', the Hausa term for continuity, which President Tandja had used to frame his endeavour to stay in power for additional three years (Mueller, 2018). However, once he started to prosecute political rivals, to dissolve democratic institutions and to rule through presidential decrees, his base of support quickly vanished.

When the army intervened and ousted the Tandja regime, this act did not evoke popular resistance, but led to mass demonstrations in favour of the coup in the capital and several other cities (EIU, 2010b). For instance, according to media reports several thousands of people rallied outside the parliament in Niamey after the coup to express their approval of and support for the actions of the military junta (AFP, 2010; DPA, 2010). In addition, the Nigerien army was united behind the junta of Major Djibo. Apart from the strong domestic support of the population and the military, opposition parties and civil society groups also cautiously sided with the coup plotters and welcomed the overthrow of Tandja (EIU, 2010b; Trithart, 2013). While the opposition parties did not exactly welcome the coup, they mostly blamed Tandja for the situation, as the statement of an opposition official illustrates: 'We've been in a crisis situation. This is exactly what we were afraid of, a military resolution. Tandja could have avoided this' (Nossiter, 2010).

Yet although it was evident that the coup plotters could count on a large support base, the most important political actors and also the rest of the Nigerien military, this support was not unconditional. Although the fall of Tandja was predominantly greeted, protesters, opposition parties and civil society groups immediately called for elections (Reuters, 2010). Against the background of Niger's troubled history of repeated military coups, the idea of continued military rule was unacceptable for large parts of the Nigerien society. As a result, the relevant ROs strongly favoured the formation of a new government legitimized by free and fair elections. Thereby, the ROs did not support the Tandja regime, which had lost domestic backing, but also refrained from sustaining military rule, an idea rejected by large parts of the Nigerien society.

Burkina Faso, 2015

The coup in Burkina Faso in 2015 constitutes one of the comparatively rare cases in which the pressure of international and especially regional actors has actually succeeded in reversing a coup. Following an earlier coup in 2014, an interim government under the leadership of Michael Kafando had been put in place and charged with organizing elections. When the army staged a coup against the transitional authorities in September 2015, the move was fiercely condemned by the international community, which pushed for its reversal. Strong and coherent pressure from the AU, EU and ECOWAS and other international actors finally enforced the reinstatement of the ousted Burkinabe government and elections were held as scheduled in November.[6]

Why is it that regional actors uncompromisingly applied the anti-coup norm in this case and insisted on the reinstatement of the Burkinabe interim government? As mentioned before, the reinstatement of an ousted government after coups is the exception rather than the rule. It is even more puzzling that the government of Kafando, which did not even hold electoral legitimacy in the narrow sense of the term, was so fervently supported and defended by regional actors and the international community. Hence, why did the AU, EU and ECOWAS insist on the reinstatement of the Burkinabe transitional authorities?

RO responses and positions: outrage and fury

On 16 November 2015, soldiers of a Burkinabe military elite unit, the Régiment de sécurité présidentielle (RSP), under the leadership of General Gilbert Diendéré staged a coup against the transitional government, arresting interim president Michael Kafando, his prime minister Yacouba Isaac Zida, as well as their cabinet. As a brief examination of the responses of the respective ROs shows, the move evoked a hitherto unknown extent of outrage both outside and within the African continent. The EU immediately criticized the coup, denouncing the event as 'an unacceptable attack on the ongoing process of transition' (EU, 2015b). More remarkably, the organization instantaneously threatened the coup plotters with sanctions, in case the EU's request for an immediate release of the transitional government should not be met.

African ROs took a similarly determined stance. Following the coup, ECOWAS condemned the event in clear terms and sent the ECOWAS Chairman, the Senegalese President Macky Sall and President of Benin Thomas Boni Yayi to mediate in the crisis. While the ECOWAS mediators talked to both sides, the organization made it very clear that it would not accept any form of rule by the coup plotters and 'enshrine[d] the decision to immediately reinstate the transition institutions and H.E Michel Kafando as Transition President' (ECOWAS, 2015). The AU even went one step further. In addition to condemning the event as coup and recalling the organization's general rejection of coups, the AU also denounced the move of the RSP as 'a terrorist act which should be dealt with as such by the entire international community' (AU, 2015a). The use of the term 'terrorism' in the context of coups constituted a remarkable precedent in the AU's general anti-coup strategy. Yet the organization did not only voice rhetorical condemnation. Without setting a deadline for the coup plotters to relent, the AU instantaneously suspended Burkina Faso and decided on economic sanctions, including inter alia travel bans and asset freezes against the coup plotters. The goal of these measures of the AU was clearly stated in the respective communiqué of the Peace and Security Council as 'a return to the *status quo ante*', hence a reinstatement of the ousted government (AU, 2015a).

The international consensus that the coup plotters' move was absolutely unacceptable and that the former government had to be reinstated was not only expressed by the statements, speeches and decisions of the single ROs, but also in a joint press release of the UN, the AU and ECOWAS, in which the organizations 'strongly condemn[ed] this gross violation of the Constitution and the Charter of the Transition and demand[ed] that the defence and security forces submit to the political authorities and in this case, the transition government' (AU et al, 2015). A similar statement was also issued by GISAT-BF, a contact group which had been founded to coordinate international action after the fall of Compaoré in 2014 (GISAT-BF, 2015c).

From a theoretical angle, the decisive and irreconcilable response of ROs to the coup and their clearly expressed position that they would only accept a reinstatement of the ousted government is not surprising. After all, the far-reaching anti-coup provisions of the respective ROs imply that coup plotters should not be accepted as new rulers and that ROs should exert pressure on them. Yet empirically, the 2015 coup in Burkina Faso clearly contrasts with a large number of cases in which the AU, ECOWAS and the EU have taken a much more moderate tone. Hence, why is it that the ousting of the Kafando government evoked such a decisive outcry for the reinstatement of the ousted regime by regional actors? In the following, I attempt to shed light on this question.

Unequivocal applicability of the anti-coup norm: a coup waiting to happen

To understand the context of the 2015 coup, it is important to briefly outline the events that took place one year earlier, which led to the formation of the government of interim president Kafando. In October 2014, mass protests against then-president Blaise Compaoré led the military to stage a coup against the long-time ruler (Engels, 2015). Following strong domestic and international pressure, the military agreed to hand over power to a dominantly civilian interim government tasked with organizing a democratic transition and organizing elections within a year. While progress in this regard was generally assessed as satisfying, the army remained a constant threat to the transitional process (ICG, 2015a, 2015b).

A particularly worrying role in this regard was played by the RSP. In general, the Burkinabe army is badly organized, poorly equipped and not well qualified. Yet the RSP, initially founded as 'special unit' to guard then-president Compaoré, had always been favoured by being given higher salaries, better training and equipment (Andrews & Honig, 2019). Interim president Kafando had made Yacouba Isaac Zida, a former colonel within the RSP, his prime minister and members of the army held other official and unofficial posts in the cabinet (EIU, 2015a). The question of how to proceed with the RSP loomed over the transitional process. Civil society organizations called for the dissolution of the unit and its integration into the regular army. Kafando manoeuvred, torn between the wish to fulfil popular demand and fear of confronting the powerful army unit (ICG, 2015b). During the transition period, the RSP repeatedly interrupted and jeopardized the transition process in Burkina Faso by disturbing cabinet meetings or threatening politicians, such as Zida, who had distanced himself from his former peers (EIU, 2015b; ICG, 2015a).

These acts gravely concerned the AU, which on several occasions warned the military 'to scrupulously respect the transitional institutions and Charter' (AU, 2015c), and to 'exercise utmost restraint and to refrain from any action likely to undermine the smooth conduct of the Transition' (AU, 2015d). The warnings of the AU fell on deaf ears. Once the coup happened in September 2015, it conformed to all stereotypes: a disgruntled and power-hungry army took power by violent means. The sequence of events leading to the arrest of Kafando's government could hardly be described as anything other than a coup and the coup plotters did not even bother to conceal or whitewash their actions. Consequently, the international response to the events in Burkina Faso was uniformly highly critical and external actors agreed that the ousting of Kafando and his cabinet clearly constituted a case invoking the anti-coup norm (Bjarnesen & Lanzano, 2015; Omede et al, 2018). As illustrated by the statements cited in the prior section, the AU, EU and ECOWAS all referred to the event as a coup and then acted perfectly in line with the anti-coup norm and exerted strong pressure on the coup plotters, with the explicit goal of reversing the coup and reinstating the ousted government.

To summarize, the obvious nature of the coup and the undisguisedly selfish motives of the coup plotters made it easy for regional actors to denounce the events as a coup and to apply the anti-coup norm in its full strength. Notwithstanding the logic of this argument, it is puzzling why the AU, EU and ECOWAS made such strong efforts to reinstate a transitional government which had never been legitimized through elections, given that in many other cases these very same ROs have refrained from pushing for the reinstatement of elected governments. Therefore, the next section analyses the democratic legitimacy of the ousted interim government.

Democratic legitimacy: the stony path towards elections

The issue of democratization played a decisive role in shaping the post-coup positions. Burkina Faso has a troubled political history. Since the country's independence in 1960, it has been hit by seven successful coups (Dwyer, 2017).[7] When Blaise Compaoré toppled the still popular revolution leader Thomas Sankara in 1987, he established a semi-democratic regime. Although Compaoré was repeatedly re-elected in elections in 1991, 1998, 2005 and 2010, his regime was never considered to be completely democratic, as electoral fairness in all contests suffered from biased media coverage and the misuse of state resources for campaigning, marginalizing any opposition's chances of winning (Bertelsmann Stiftung, 2014). Also political rights and freedoms were only partially realized, despite the fact that the country was internationally regarded as an anchor of stability and reliability in conflictual and fragile region.[8] Changing and manipulating the constitution, Compaoré managed to run for the presidency several times, accumulating to 27 years of uninterrupted rule. Yet when he attempted to revise the constitution once again in 2014, a wave of popular protests and a resulting military coup swept him from office (Andrews & Honig, 2019).

Following the fall of Compaoré, a transitional government under the leadership of Michael Kafando was formed, accompanied by high external and domestic expectations. Immediately after the coup, the military junta had declared its intention to lead the transition itself and the formation of a largely civilian interim government was considered a major concession to international pressure for democratization (EIU, 2015a). As an interim government, the new authorities were not directly legitimized through popular elections. Yet predominantly civilian interim authorities were strongly requested and welcomed by the Burkinabe population. The head of the new interim government, Michael Kafando, was an experienced diplomat with a good international as well as domestic reputation (Bjarnesen & Lanzano, 2015). Many posts within the cabinet were filled with skilled civil servants and technocrats, however, some important ministries, such as the Ministry of Mines and Energy and the Ministry of Territorial Administration, Decentralization and Security were held by the military (ICG, 2015b).

The most important task for the interim government was to initiate a democratic transition and to prepare elections within a year, in which no member of Kafando's cabinet would be allowed to run. Therefore, the interim authorities were mainly considered as impartial and without own aspirations to retain power. The steps towards democratization and new elections had been codified in an encompassing transition agreement signed by all affected parties and enthusiastically greeted by regional actors (AU, 2014; ECOWAS, 2014; EU, 2014). Together with other international actors, the AU, EU and ECOWAS had 'noted with satisfaction the adoption of the Transitional Charter, the consensual appointment of the President of the Transition, the formation of the Government and the establishment of the CNT' (GISAT-BF, 2015a).

The analysis indicates that the steps of the interim government to implement the provisions of this agreement were largely evaluated as promising. As stated in the agreement, additional institutions, including a National Transition Council (CNT) as interim parliament and a Commission of National Reconciliation and Reform were founded (Transitional Charter of Burkina Faso, 2014). The National Independent Election Commission (CENI) was well on the way to preparing free and fair elections within the electoral schedule, despite major administrative challenges. A debate arose about one aspect of the newly adopted electoral law, which forbade all persons who had supported Compaoré's attempt to stay in power for an additional term to run as candidates in the upcoming elections (ICG, 2015a). Arguing that the law discriminated against supporters of Compaoré's former party, Congress for Democracy and Progress (CDP), opponents of the law appealed to the Community Court of ECOWAS. Following a verdict of the court that the law in its current form was actually discriminatory and violated the electoral rights of citizens, the transitional authorities argued that the court had no jurisdiction to hear the case and ignored its ruling (Ariotti, 2016).

Notwithstanding this incident, the steps taken by the Burkinabe interim government towards democratization were approved, commended and supported by ROs. In March 2015, the joint international contact group on Burkina Faso, the GISAT-BF 'noted with satisfaction the progress that continues to be made in the implementation of the transitional process, in conformity with the Charter of the Transition adopted on 16 November 2014' (GISAT-BF, 2015b). Likewise, in June 2015, the EU supported the transition process in Burkina Faso with an additional €120 million of budget support with the stated goal 'to consolidate the country's democratic gains following the popular uprising at the end of October 2014' (EU, 2015a).

To conclude, the analysis reveals that while the Burkinabe interim government was not legitimized through an electoral mandate, it could count on a high degree of procedural legitimacy, as it undertook credible and promising steps to restore democracy in the country. Therefore, the transitional authorities enjoyed a high degree of democratic legitimacy and support not only among the domestic population, but also with international and regional partners, which in the end increased the pressure on ROs to come to help to them after the coup.

Post-coup democratization: improbable democratizer

The previous section has shown that international and regional actors assessed the chances to complete a successful democratic transition under the leadership of the interim government of President Kafando as quite favourable. In contrast, an examination of the coup plotters' strategy suggests that they failed to present a convincing roadmap outlining how they planned to restore democracy. The pretext for justifying and framing the coup as an act geared towards protecting democracy was the contentious electoral law (Hagberg, 2015). Claiming that the current version of the law, which impeded high-level supporters of Compaoré's former attempts to change the constitution from running as candidates in the upcoming elections, had caused cleavages in the population, the coup plotters promised to organize 'appeasing and inclusive elections' (Bjarnesen & Lanzano, 2015). For this task, the coup plotters formed a new National Democratic Council (CND) tasked with overseeing the democratic transition.

Yet credibility and trust in this body were basically non-existent. The CND only included members of the coup plotters from the RSP elite unit, who were not only inexperienced in civilian political leadership but had also little reason to actually hold democratic elections, given that large parts of the population were highly critical of the RSP and its interference in Burkinabe politics (Hagberg, 2015). Besides, the infamous General Gilbert Diendéré was presented as head of the new council. Diendéré was not only considered to be the mastermind and leading figure behind the current coup, but he had also been a close ally to the former president Blaise Compaoré and his private army chief (ICG, 2013). Inter alia, Diendéré had been charged with the murder of the popular Burkinabe revolution leader Thomas Sankara, a pending unresolved crime at the time of the coup, which had paved the way to power for Compaoré in 1987 (EIU, 2016a). Hence, the ruthless reputation of Diendéré and his fellow members of the CND made them unlikely candidates to successfully conduct serious democratic reforms and to organize free and fair elections.

Finally, the blatant way in which the RSP had ignored former regional warnings not to interfere in the political process further undermined the international reputation of the coup plotters. When the coup plotters openly defied the explicit requests of the AU, the organization kept its public promise to 'hold all those who obstruct the smooth conduct of the Transition accountable for their actions' (AU, 2015d). The unilateral decision of the coup plotters to change the direction of the transition process did not sit well with international and particularly regional partners, who had made great efforts after the 2014 fall of Compaoré to initiate this very same process.

To summarize, the analysis of the coup plotters' strategy in the aftermath of the coup indicates that while the coup plotters made a shaky attempt to frame their action as a democratic coup, the composition of the CND and the defiance of the body against the explicit warnings of regional partners, gave this version of a 'democratic coup' only extremely limited credibility. Against such low prospects of a democratic transition, regional actors had few reasons to incorporate the coup plotters in any sort of post-coup solution.

Domestic power constellation: revolution reloaded

Apart from justified concerns about a failure of the democratization process, a closer examination of the post-coup situation suggests that domestic responses to the coup also played a major role. As the repeated calls for the dissolution of the RSP had shown, the elite unit was highly unpopular in the civilian population. When the RSP under the leadership of Diendéré finally staged the coup, the domestic popular response was uniform, swift and decisive. Opposition parties immediately and strongly condemned the coup. The president of the dissolved transitional parliament, Chérif Sy, went underground and urged civil society to oppose the coup (EIU, 2015b). Spontaneous large anti-coup demonstrations were quickly called in the capital of Ouagadougou and other cities throughout the country (Yarwood, 2016). Encouraged by the success of the protests less than a year earlier, which had led to the fall of Blaise Compaoré, the civilian population bravely opposed the new regime. Citizens not only participated in demonstrations, but also engaged in civil disobedience. Following the coup, trade unions called a general strike, which was enacted by large parts of the workforce, even the informal sector. In Ouagadougou, people built barricades in the streets against the soldiers, successfully challenging their control of the city (Hagberg, 2015).

Apart from directly confronting the coup plotters, the population and politicians also called for the regular military forces to oppose the move of the RSP. In a public statement, Sy addressed the armed forces and urged the 'army chief of staff and the chiefs of staff of the various military regions to immediately take measures to ensure that this act of treachery is stopped' (BBC, 2015). At first, the military hesitated. Yet on 21 September, the army followed popular calls and regiments of the regular troops moved towards Ouagadougou (EIU, 2015b). All these points illustratively show that the RSP and the CND were isolated, as they did not only face massive civilian resistance but also lacked support from large parts of the remaining armed forces.

The isolated position of Diendéré and his CND had a decisive impact on the responses of ROs to the coup. Seeing that the coup against Kafando was strongly opposed by the population, which was committed to the promised transitional process, ECOWAS and the AU, and also the EU were subjected to public and political pressure to become engaged. The strong and uniform domestic calls for the release of Kafando and his government and the dissolution of the RSP and CND made a reversal of the coup and a reinstatement of the ousted government the only viable solution. When the ECOWAS mediators presented a first draft agreement on the reinstatement of the ousted government, the agreement included a provision for an amnesty for the coup plotters. Yet a massive domestic outcry led the ECOWAS summit to reject the draft on 22 September (ECOWAS, 2015). In the end, the RSP was dissolved, Diendéré was arrested and the interim government was reinstated. The reinstatement of Kafando and his cabinet was formally attended and welcomed by the AU, ECOWAS and EU (AU, 2015b; EU, 2015c). The elections, initially scheduled for October, were delayed by several weeks, yet held in a free and fair manner in November (Ariotti, 2016).

Zimbabwe, 2017

The final case of Zimbabwe pointedly illustrates how coups can successfully be 'sold' to the international community and that regional actors are sometimes very willing to endorse coup-born regimes. For 37 years, President Robert Mugabe had ruled the formally democratic Southern African country in a manner which most opposition members and international observers described as inherently autocratic and repressive. When Mugabe was toppled after a struggle about his succession in November 2017, the majority of ROs and other international actors were hesitant to call the event a coup. Relieved about Mugabe's fall, most external actors were willing to accept Mugabe's rival Emmerson Mnangagwa as new president conditional on his promise to hold timely elections. Mnangagwa's victory in these elections was, in general, internationally accepted, despite evidence of massive electoral fraud.[9]

Obviously, this position of regional actors is not in line with the provisions of the anti-coup norm, which do not tolerate continued rule by the coup plotters. Hence, why did the AU, EU and SADC decide to acknowledge the Mnangagwa regime? In the following, the order of events of the coup and the positions taken by ROs in the aftermath are briefly described. Subsequently, potential reasons for these positions of ROs are analysed.

RO responses and positions: the king is dead, long live the king?

On 15 November 2017, armed forces under the leadership of General Constanino Chiwenga took over control in Zimbabwe, put Mugabe under house arrest and arrested several among his closest circle. Six days later, Mugabe read out a pre-formulated speech announcing his 'voluntary' resignation as President of Zimbabwe. At first glance, one would expect the coup to trigger critical responses from the relevant regional actors, in particular the AU, the EU and SADC, which have all made a strong and credible commitment to the anti-coup norm.

Astonishingly, this was not the case. Despite the fact that the coup took place in a country which is a member of the AU and SADC, hence two ROs holding strong anti-coup regimes in place, the immediate international responses to the takeover were hesitant, muted, not to say supportive. One of the most critical voices was then-President of the AU, the Guinean President Alpha Condé, stating in an interview with the French newspaper *Le Monde* that the AU assumed the leader change to be a coup and recalling the AU's general condemnation of any such events (*Le Monde*, 2017). However, the official statement of the AU carefully avoided the term 'coup d'état' and only stressed that 'it is crucial that the crisis is resolved in a manner that promotes democracy and human rights, as well as the socio-economic development of Zimbabwe' (AU, 2017a).

In a similar manner, SADC euphemistically called on the involved actors to 'resolve the political impasse amicably' (SADC, 2017b). The emerging answer to this request was the resignation of Mugabe and the inauguration of the former vice-president Emmerson Mnangagwa as new state leader. Mnangagwa, a close ally of Chiwenga, had been a driving force behind the takeover. The affected ROs quickly signalled that they were highly receptive to a solution in which the coup plotters at least temporarily remained in power. The High Representative of the EU, Federica Mogherini, stated that '[t]he decision made by President Mugabe to stand down shows that he has listened to the people's voices' (EU, 2017). The AU 'welcome[d] the decision by President Robert Mugabe to step down from his position as Head of State' (AU, 2017b) and SADC likewise 'commend[ed] His Excellency, President Robert Gabriel Mugabe, for his bold decision to step down from his position of Head of State of the Republic of Zimbabwe' (SADC, 2017c). SADC even went one step further by 'congratulat[ing] His Excellency, Emmerson Dambudzo Mnangagwa, on his swearing in as President of the Republic of Zimbabwe' and claiming that 'Zimbabweans have placed their trust in President Mnangagwa and are looking forward to his leadership in upholding the tenets of the Constitution of Zimbabwe' (SADC, 2017a).

Given that Mnangagwa had severely violated the provisions of this very same constitution and at least at the point of speaking did not enjoy any public mandate, it is striking that ROs so readily endorsed the new leadership.

Unequivocal applicability of the anti-coup norm: the loophole of 'military-assisted transition'

Recalling the definition of coups as coercive and illegal attempts by parts of a country's elites to grab executive power from the ruling government, it can hardly be contested that the leader change in Zimbabwe qualifies as a coup. The move was carried out by a small elite (army officers), it targeted executive power (the president) and coercive and illegal means (arrest of the president and threat to use force) were applied. Hence, when Zimbabwean armed forces planned the ousting of Mugabe, they were well aware that the incident would in principle evoke the anti-coup norm and that a coup would force SADC and especially the AU to follow its institutionalized anti-coup procedures.

The resulting international condemnation, political isolation and the potential imposition of sanctions would have seriously harmed Mnangagwa and his fellow coup plotters. Therefore, they took every effort to create the illusion that their steps were within the constitutional and legal boundaries, hence not qualifying as a coup. In a television statement addressing the nation, Major General 'SB' Moyo, another leading figure of the coup, emphasized that '[w]e wish to make it abundantly clear that this is not a military takeover'

(Magnani, 2018). Moyo and other members of the coup plotters substantiated that claim by arguing that the army had not actually targeted Mugabe, but criminals surrounding him, that the military had not used violence and had not suspended the constitution and that the army had only acted within its duties to protect the Zimbabwean nation (Asuelime, 2018).

From an analytical point of view these arguments are far-fetched and to a certain extent simply incorrect. Admittedly, the course of events in Zimbabwe can be classified as a 'soft coup', lacking major violence and repression.[10] Nevertheless, the unlawful interference of the military to replace one leader by another can hardly be described as anything else other than a coup. Technically, the events fulfilled all criteria of a coup, a view shared by a range of political scientists (Taylor, 2017; Asuelime, 2018; Beardsworth et al, 2019). Notwithstanding the unequivocal academic evaluation of the events, the coup plotters managed to create their own popular narrative of the course of events. Euphemistically calling the events a 'military-assisted transition' (ICG, 2017), a term which was quickly picked up by the media as well as by RO officials, they successfully evaded being doomed as breakers of the anti-coup norm.

While the clever framing strategy of the coup plotters deserves some credit, two uncomfortable questions remain. The first is why an ostensibly lawful and constitutional leader change within an at least formally democratic country would ever need to be 'assisted' by the military. The second is why ROs so willingly played along and accepted what Beardsworth et al (2019) aptly describe as 'a cleverly and carefully curated piece of political theatre'. After all, in his initial assessment, AU chairman Condé had realistically described the events as 'clearly soldiers trying to take power by force' (Saunderson-Meyer, 2017).

To conclude, the analysis of the unequivocal applicability of the anti-coup norm shows that the fall of Mugabe technically fulfilled all criteria of an incident invoking the norm. However, the coup plotters skilfully managed to present an alternative narrative, casting doubts on the illegality of their actions and euphemizing the coup as military-assisted transition. Given that these claims were not completely plausible, the question remains why the AU, EU and SADC were so readily prepared to overlook the unconstitutionality of the leader change and to support the new government. In order to answer this question, it is important to take a closer look at the events in Zimbabwe leading up to the coup, the apparent democratic deficits and the fragile overall situation of the country.

Democratic legitimacy: Mugabe, an elected autocrat

An analysis of the situation in Zimbabwe prior to the coup points towards blatant democratic flaws. Robert Mugabe was first elected as prime minister of Zimbabwe in 1980, following a violent liberation struggle against the white minority regime of Ian Smith. After a constitutional reform, he became president of the country in 1987. At the beginning of his rule, Mugabe gained international credit and was generally praised for his education, conciliatory demeanour, as well as promising reforms in the health and education sector (Marx, 2017). In the first decade of his rule, Mugabe faced only minor opposition and his party, the Zimbabwe Africa National Union – Patriotic Front (ZANU-PF),[11] constituted the only relevant political force. Yet growing popular discontent with the sluggish economy and Mugabe's authoritarian style of leadership led to the formation of the opposition party Movement for Democratic Change (MDC) guided by the charismatic former union leader Morgan Tsvangirai in 1999. In the following years, the ZANU-PF and Mugabe contested and won several presidential and parliamentary elections.[12]

However, the quality and fairness of these elections were repeatedly and sharply criticized by the opposition as well as by international election observers. In fact, ZANU-PF engaged in the whole range of methods of electoral fraud, including gerrymandering of election districts, misuse of state funds for electoral contests, denying MDC supporters access to the electoral register and manipulating election results, intimidation and massive use of violence against the opposition and their supporters (Grebe, 2010; Southall, 2013; Chimage, 2015; Cheeseman & Klaas, 2018). A sad climax was reached when the MDC gained a victory in the 2008 parliamentary and presidential elections. Announcing a run-off for the presidential office between the leading Tsvangirai and Mugabe, the regime staged a heavily violent campaign against MDC and their supporters, finally forcing Tsvangirai to withdraw from the electoral contest and granting Mugabe a comfortable victory (Barclay, 2010; Cheeseman & Klaas, 2018).[13] The extent of electoral violence and fraud only mirrored general authoritarian tendencies in the country, including harassment of opposition forces, NGOs and the press, deficits in the rule of law and the separation of powers, as well as persistent major human rights violations (ICG, 2002; Amnesty International et al, 2007; ICG, 2008, 2016).

As a result, international partners became increasingly dissatisfied with the Mugabe regime. The Commonwealth decided to suspend Zimbabwe in 2002, leading Mugabe to leave the organization for good (Magaisa, 2019). In the same year, the EU imposed first targeted sanctions, following major flaws in the parliamentary elections and illegal land invasions by the government (Giumelli, 2013). Later, development cooperation with the Zimbabwean government was also considerably reduced. The US began to exert pressure on Zimbabwe with measures subsumed under the Zimbabwe Democracy and Economic Recovery Act (ZDERA). Furthermore, the World Bank and the International Monetary Fund suspended cooperation with Zimbabwe in the wake of increasingly undemocratic conditions. The suspension of urgently needed financial means severely hit the already strained Zimbabwean economy (Grebe, 2010). With sanctions in place, including inter alia a travel ban against Mugabe himself and his participation in European–African summits became an increasingly contentious issue between European and African state leaders, evoking repeated vocal protests from several European participants (van Wyk, 2018).

While Western states denounced Mugabe for his authoritarian leadership style, regional responses were more nuanced. Mugabe's status as a hero of the liberation struggle against white minority rule granted him respect and standing among Southern African state leaders (Magnani, 2018). The SADC repeatedly protected Mugabe against accusations and requested the West to lift sanctions against Zimbabwe (SADC, 2003). Instead of directly confronting Zimbabwe, the SADC and the regional hegemon South Africa preferred an approach of 'quiet diplomacy', seeking to mediate and to facilitate dialogue and cooperation between Mugabe's regime, the opposition and international actors (Adelmann, 2004).

Assessments of the effectiveness of this strategy vary. The comparatively soft approach, particularly of the SADC mediator, the South African president Thabo Mbeki, has frequently been criticized as too lenient and ineffective (Mhango, 2012; Dzimiri, 2017; Bratton & Penar, 2018). Yet to SADC's credit, the organization brokered a power-sharing agreement between Mugabe and Tsvangirai in 2009 and criticized the political, economic and human rights situation in Zimbabwe on several occasions (SADC, 2002). Likewise did the AU, inter alia in a highly critical report of the African Commission on Human and Peoples' Rights (AU, 2002). Feeling unable to bring about political change, scared by political violence and suffering from the massive economic crisis, many Zimbabweans voted with their feet and fled to neighbouring countries, especially South Africa, Zambia, Botswana and Mozambique (Crush & Tevera, 2010; Derman & Kaarhus, 2013). The influx of estimated 3 million migrants, accounting for 20 per cent of Zimbabwe's population, put a major burden on these countries, diminishing regional support for Mugabe.

To conclude, the analysis of the situation prior to the coup shows that during the 37 years of Mugabe's rule, Zimbabwe had taken an increasingly authoritarian turn. Although formal democratic institutions and provisions continued to exist, democratic freedoms, human rights and the rule of law were regularly severely violated by Mugabe's regime. As a result of the democratic crisis, combined with the disastrous state of the Zimbabwean economy, Western partners had become openly critical towards the Mugabe regime and questioned its legitimacy. Likewise, regional support for the former liberation hero had also dwindled, yet had not completely disappeared.

Post-coup democratization: promise and perils of elections

Not only the democratic legitimacy of the incumbent, but also the prospects of democratization under a new regime are important for shaping post-coup positions. When Mnangagwa was inaugurated as president a few days after the coup, he appeared to be an unlikely candidate for genuine political change. The 75-year-old former vice-president had been part and parcel of Mugabe's regime. Nicknamed 'crocodile', Mnangagwa had not only been extensively involved in mass killings in the 1980s (known as operation Gukurahundi), but also in the brutal crackdown on the opposition after the first round of elections in 2008 (Magaisa, 2019).

Importantly, the major flaws of Mugabe's rule, described here, were not the reasons leading him to stage the coup. Instead, Mnangagwa's move can clearly be attributed to his pursuit of power. With the ageing of President Mugabe, the issue of succession had gained importance within ZANU-PF. Hence, within the ruling party two factions formed. On the one side, a group of mostly younger party officials rallied around Mugabe's wife Grace and formed a group known as G40. On the other side, an 'old guard' of party and army veterans sided with Emmerson Mnangagwa. For a long time, Mugabe himself avoided declaring his support for either faction and skilfully played them off against each other. However, on 7 November 2017, Mugabe dismissed Mnangagwa, a move widely interpreted as Mugabe's decision to support a succession by his wife. Mnangagwa struck back and with the help of his good ties to the military he successfully took power.

Notwithstanding Mnangagwa's egoistic motive to take power, the clever politician immediately understood that democratic legitimization of his rule was essential to gain national and international acceptance. In his inauguration speech on 30 November, Mnangagwa did not only promise that his new government would 'work towards ensuring that the pillars of the State assuring democracy in our land are strengthened and respected', additionally, he also publicly confirmed twice that 'the 2018 harmonised elections […] will be held as scheduled' (Mnangagwa, 2017). The binding promise to initiate democratic reforms and particularly to uphold the electoral schedule for the next year went down extremely well with regional and international actors.

Indeed, the new regime did not undertake any of the common attempts of coup plotters to delay or postpone the election date. Compared to the previous Zimbabwean experiences of fraudulent, polarized and violent electoral contests, the run-up to the 2018 election was reported to be remarkably open and peaceful. Apart from instigating electoral reforms, Mnangagwa also invited a broad range of international election observers to monitor the contest, a remarkable difference from Mugabe, who had barred entrance for observers from countries being allegedly 'hostile' to Zimbabwe.

Unfortunately, the election itself could not fulfil all the hopes invested in it. With a narrow margin of 50.8 per cent, Mnangagwa won the presidential elections and the ZANU-PF reached a two-thirds majority in the parliamentary elections. As promised, several international observer teams monitored the elections. Yet their evaluation of the fairness and transparency of the electoral process differed noticeably. Many Western observers took a rather critical stance. For instance, the EU generally praised the relatively peaceful run-up to the election, the high level of participation and competitiveness of the election and the steps of the Zimbabwe Electoral Commission (ZEC) to improve the administrative arrangements. Yet still the EU concluded that 'many aspects of the 2018 elections in Zimbabwe failed to meet international standards' (EU, 2018). International critique mainly concerned shortcomings in the registration of voters, a lack of impartiality of the ZEC and missing transparency of the final results, intimidation and coercion of voters as well as heavily biased media coverage. In contrast, the regional electoral observer missions from the AU and SADC reached predominantly positive assessments of the elections. Although reporting several administrative deficits, the AU election observation mission concluded in its final report that 'the 2018 Harmonised elections were generally peaceful and well administered' (AU, 2018). SADC similarly praised the elections, calling them 'a political watershed in Zimbabwe's history' (SADC, 2018).

In sum, the 2018 elections in Zimbabwe certainly fell short to meet gold standards of free and fair elections. Nevertheless, compared to the political charades of 'democratic' elections and the vicious outbreaks of electoral violence in the Mugabe era, the 2018 elections constituted a noticeable, though small, improvement. The analysis of the prospects of post-coup democratization shows that Mnangagwa's strategy to play the democratic card, to commit himself to democratic reforms and to uphold a timely electoral schedule worked out well in appeasing the important ROs and other international actors and paved his way to international and domestic recognition.

Domestic power constellation: power to the people, power to the army?

While the prospect of timely elections was a decisive factor for the decision of ROs to back up the coup-born regime, another important issue was the domestic power constellation. The analysis points towards a particularly strong position of the coup plotters in this regard. First, the demonstrative alliance between Mnangagwa as an established political leading figure within the ZANU-PF and key military officials including General Chiwenga and Major-General Moyo constituted an ostensibly invincible force. Over the years of Mugabe's increasingly authoritarian rule, the Zimbabwean army had become a significant political force within the country. Politicized, unprofessional and unrestricted by effective civilian supremacy, the Zimbabwean army had repeatedly overstretched its mandate and directly interfered in the political process (Maringira, 2017). A telling example is the run-up to the 2002 elections, when General Vitalis Zvinavash directly undermined the position of Mugabe's rival Tsvangirai by publicly stating that the army would 'not accept, let alone support or salute, anyone with a different agenda that threatens the very existence of our sovereignty, our country and our people' (ICG, 2002).[14]

Notwithstanding the illegality and unconstitutionality of the direct interference of the military in politics, the support of the army was a crucial factor in Zimbabwe. Once inaugurated as president, Mnangagwa immediately reinforced the alliance between himself and the army by awarding leading figures of the coup with important cabinet posts. For instance, the appointments of Air Chief Marshal Perence Shiri as lands, agriculture and rural resettlement minister and of Moyo as foreign minister can be read as clear steps towards strengthening ties between the coup plotters and the military (EIU, 2018). While the appointment of army officials as cabinet members raised some concern among international actors, the signal that Mnangagwa enjoyed strong support from the army significantly bolstered his position.

The second crucial factor emerging from the analysis, which strengthened the coup plotters' position, was the fact that they did not face much domestic opposition to their move. Supporters of Robert Mugabe or his wife's faction within the ZANU-PF were quickly, arrested, co-opted or intimidated. The opposition party MDC turned out to be supportive to the removal of Mugabe (ICG, 2017). After Mugabe's arrest, MDC leader Morgan Tsvangirai requested that '[i]n the interests of the people, Mr Robert Mugabe must resign ... immediately' and called for 'comprehensive reforms for free and fair elections to be held' (BBC, 2017).

Finally, the population took a similar positive stance towards the coup. The day after Mugabe's fall, mass demonstrations celebrating the removal of the long-lasting ruler emerged in Harare and other large cities in Zimbabwe (Müller, 2019). The generally supportive stance of the Zimbabwean population towards the leader change was not only a short-term impression. In a poll by Afrobarometer in spring 2018, 41 per cent of Zimbabweans fully endorsed the coup as 'the right thing to do', while 40 per cent stated that the coup was 'the wrong thing to do, but necessary'. In contrast, only 12 per cent clearly rejected the coup as wrong (Afrobarometer, 2018).

To conclude, the analysis of the domestic power constellation shows that the support of the Zimbabwean army, political forces and of large parts of the population significantly bolstered Mnangagwa's position vis-à-vis the AU, EU, SADC and other international actors. The lack of domestic organized opposition against the coup and the generally sympathetic stance towards the coup plotters made it difficult for the ROs to insist on their removal.

Discussion

The cases of Madagascar, Niger, Burkina Faso and Zimbabwe hint at the tremendous diversity of coups. The analysis impressively illustrates that in each of the four cases, the concurrence of a number of factors decisively shaped the position of ROs vis-à-vis the coup plotters and the post-coup solution pursued and supported by them. In all four cases, ROs with strong anti-coup provisions were affected, the AU, EU and ECOWAS/SADC.[15] Yet only in Burkina Faso did the ROs actively push for the reinstatement of the ousted government and in Niger did they insist on the formation of a new government. In contrast, in Madagascar the ROs actively sought a solution which included the coup plotters in a political power-sharing deal, and in Zimbabwe they willingly accepted the continued rule of the actors responsible for the coups (see Table 5.2). This mixed picture suggests that ROs play a diverse and complex role in finding suitable post-coup solutions. The anti-coup norm does not seem to be a non-negotiable principle in this regard. In other words, under particular conditions, ROs are willing to compromise the anti-coup norm. The following section takes a comparative view on these conditions in the four cases and seeks to examine the plausibility of the respective expectations from Chapter 2.

Unequivocal applicability of the anti-coup norm

Expectation 6 stated that if the anti-coup norm is unequivocally applicable to a particular case, ROs are more likely to push for a reinstatement of the ousted government or the formation of a new government in the aftermath of the coup. Therefore, it is expected that in cases clearly qualifying as coups, ROs have little leeway to circumvent the provisions of the anti-coup norm.

The case studies indicate that this assumption is plausible. The analysis of the four coups and their respective responses shows that the extent to which ROs stretch or circumvent the anti-coup norm depends on the unequivocalness of the respective case. Both in Burkina Faso and Niger, the sequence of events leading to the fall of Kafando and Tandja was clearly and unanimously identified as a coup. As such, there was not much room for manoeuvre to question the general applicability of the anti-coup norm and to accommodate the coup plotters. In the case of Niger, this even forced the AU to suspend the country despite the fact that the organization like most other regional actors silently welcomed the coup. But due to the general perception of the coup as a 'guardian coup' the response was less harsh than in the case of Burkina Faso.

Table 5.2: Summary of case studies

	Madagascar (2009)	Niger (2010)	Burkina Faso (2015)	Zimbabwe (2017)
Unequivocal applicability of anti-coup norm	**Medium extent of contestation** • (mainly) consent that coup took place • 'voluntary' transfer of power to the army	**Medium extent of contestation** • consent that coup took place • strong narrative of guardian coup	**Low extent of contestation** • consent that coup took place • barely any attempts of justification	**High extent of contestation** • dispute whether coup took place, 'military-assisted transition' • claims to act not against head of state
Democratic legitimacy of incumbent	**Medium extent of democratic legitimacy** • formally democratically elected, yet electoral deficits • constitutional provisions mainly respected • major deficits with democratic standards	**Low extent of democratic legitimacy** • formally democratically elected • constitutional provisions disrespected (term limits) • major deficits with democratic standards	**Relatively high extent of democratic legitimacy** • non-elected interim government • constitutional provisions fully respected • no major deficits with democratic standards	**Low extent of democratic legitimacy** • formally democratically elected, yet major electoral deficits • constitutional provisions disrespected • major deficits with democratic standards
Chances of post-coup democratization	**Low chances of democratization** • vague announcement of elections • no constitutional/ institutional reforms	**High chances of democratization** • credible announcement of timely elections • constitutional/ institutional reforms	**Low chances of democratization** • no credible announcement of timely elections • no constitutional/ institutional reforms	**Low chances of democratization** • credible announcement of timely elections • no constitutional/ institutional reforms
Domestic power constellation	**Medium position of coup plotters** • support of the military • partial support of political parties • partial popular support	**Strong position of coup plotters** • support of the military • support of political parties • popular support	**Weak position of coup plotters** • no support of the military • no support of political parties • no popular support	**Strong position of coup plotters** • support of the military • partial support of political parties • popular support
Post-coup solution	**Power-sharing**	**Formation of new government**	**Reinstatement of ousted government**	**Coup plotters consolidate their power**

In contrast, after the coups in Madagascar and Zimbabwe, the situation was more ambiguous. In the case of Madagascar, the vast majority of international actors agreed on the unconstitutionality of the leader change. Yet given the fierce power struggle between Ravalomanana and Rajoelina preceding the coup, the mass demonstrations and the use of violence by the regime against protesters, the AU, EU and SADC primarily referred to the situation as 'political crisis', thereby avoiding the term 'coup d'état'. After the coup in Zimbabwe, the ROs even went a step further. Picking up the carefully orchestrated story of the Mnangagwa regime, they euphemized the ousting of Mugabe as 'military-assisted transition' and thereby deliberately denied the applicability of the anti-coup norm after the fall of the despised dictator.

To conclude, ROs actually in some cases compromise the anti-coup norm when deciding on their preferred post-coup solutions. The degree to which compromising the norm is possible depends on the unequivocalness of the case at hand and the resulting potential for discussion about the applicability of the anti-coup norm. Hence, the analysis of the four cases of Madagascar, Niger, Burkina Faso and Zimbabwe indicates that in circumstances to which the anti-coup norm unequivocally applies, ROs are more likely to insist on the reinstatement of the government or the formation of a new government.

Democratic legitimacy of the ousted ruler

When arguing that the anti-coup norm is sometimes compromised in the context of post-coup solution, the natural question arises regarding to which factors the norm is subordinated. Given that the anti-coup norm is framed and justified as a democratic norm, democracy-related aspects are a promising starting point. Therefore, the expectation was that the preferences of ROs for particular post-coup solutions depend on the democratic legitimacy of the ousted ruler: ROs are more likely to push for the reinstatement of an ousted ruler or his/her participation in a power-sharing agreement if the ruler enjoys democratic legitimacy in the sense that he/she has been democratically elected and has respected basic democratic and constitutional principles during the period of rule.

The examined case studies provide evidence in favour of this expectation, yet the interpretation requires a degree of care. Importantly, at the time of the coup, none of the four countries qualified as an established liberal democracy, but the extent of democratic deficits varied across the cases. The interim government in Burkina Faso, the only case where the ROs actually pushed for a reinstatement of an ousted government, was not democratically elected. However, the transitional authorities under the leadership of Kafando were based on a societal consensus, could count on popular support and had taken promising steps towards democratizing the country. Therefore, in sum the government enjoyed a high degree of democratic legitimacy, which turned out to be a decisive factor in mobilizing the support of ROs after the coup.

In Madagascar, the country where the AU, EU and SADC sought a power-sharing deal between the ousted government and the coup plotters, Ravalomanana faced a variety of allegations of undemocratic conduct. While the reproaches of corruption, power centralization, limitations of the freedom of press and violence against protesters were grave, the majority of regional and international actors still considered Madagascar a democracy, albeit a deficient one. Ravalomanana was recognized as legitimate president and, therefore, there was a clear consensus that Ravalomanana could not be disregarded as part of a political solution.

In contrast, neither Tandja in Niger, nor Mugabe in Zimbabwe, enjoyed a high degree of democratic legitimacy. While Tandja had been democratically elected and had at first been greeted as a stabilizing actor, his attempts to circumvent and ignore constitutional provisions to prolong his rule, the prosecution of opposition politicians and his dissolution of legislative and parliamentary bodies, evoked not only domestic resistance, but also massive international criticism. The general interpretation was that Tandja was seeking to establish himself as an autocratic ruler, blatantly violating existing democratic provisions. Therefore, ROs showed little willingness to come to Tandja's help after the military toppled him.

Finally, in the case of Zimbabwe, severe democratic flaws under the incumbent's rule likewise led ROs to side with a new government instead of insisting on Mugabe's partial or complete reinstatement. During his 37 years of rule of the South African country, Mugabe had accumulated a remarkable number of violations against democratic principles, including massive electoral violence and fraud, brutal repression of opposition parties and civil society organizations, severe human rights violations and limitations of basic democratic rights and freedoms. Hence, while the manner of the leadership change in Zimbabwe evoked concern in many ROs, they greeted the change in itself, and even officially expressed their approval in their statements on Mugabe's resignation and the congratulation notes to Mnangagwa.

To summarize, democratic legitimacy of the ousted incumbent is a decisive factor determining which positions ROs take after a coup. The insights of the case studies show that if an ousted leader enjoys democratic legitimacy, he is more likely to be reinstated or to become at least part of a power-sharing deal. This finding resonates well with earlier results of the quantitative analysis that coups in more democratic countries in tendency are followed by stronger responses, which serve to exert stronger pressure on the coup plotters. However, the case studies also suggest that democratic legitimacy is a matter of perspective. As hardly any coups hit established liberal democracies, the evaluation of whether an ousted leader is considered democratic enough to deserve support is often challenging and subjective.

ROs may draw different conclusions in this regard depending on their general understanding of democratic standards. The cases examined in this chapter suggest that not only the question of whether the state leader came to office through (at least formally) democratic elections affect this evaluation, but also whether the incumbent respected key democratic values during his or her rule.

Credibility of post-coup democratization

The democratic record of the ousted incumbent is just one side of the equation. When agreeing on a common position in the aftermath of a coup, the affected ROs do not only take the past into account, but also focus on future chances of democratization under the leadership of the coup plotters. Following this logic, ROs are expected to push for a new government or accept the continued rule of the coup plotters if chances of democratization under such a regime are high.

The insights from the analysis with regard to this expectation tend to be supportive. In the case of Niger, the timely presented, precise and binding transitional schedule of the CSRD convinced ROs to take a supportive position and let the junta go along with their plans for political reform and holding elections for the formation of a new government. Likewise, Mnangagwa's immediate and binding promises to uphold the electoral schedule in Zimbabwe for the next year were essential factors why ROs decided to accept his continued rule, despite the fact that he had come to power by unconstitutional means. It is important to emphasize that in both cases the prospects of timely democratization were not only announced in empty promises, but substantiated by obligatory, precisely formulated commitments and concrete steps towards democratization.

Exactly such elements failed to materialize in the case of Burkina Faso. While the coup plotters brought forward vague promises to hold inclusive elections, they did not provide a credible transitional schedule, as the ousted interim government under president Kafando had done. Against this background, putting their weight behind Kafando was the obvious choice for ROs. The final case of the coup in Madagascar is a little harder to interpret. While the ideas put forward by Rajoelina to curb the presidential power and to reform the Malagasy political system were well received, the nature of these promises was vague and most ROs did not trust the junta's leader to independently conduct these reforms in a trustworthy manner. Therefore, they preferred an internationally negotiated power-sharing agreement over the continued rule of the coup plotters.

In essence, the case studies support the notion that the prospect of a democratization process is an important factor determining which position ROs take after a coup. Only when coup plotters can provide convincing proof that they are serious about initiating a democratic transition are ROs willing to accept the coup plotters themselves or a new government as the future rulers of the country. Yet the evidence from the four cases also shows that assessing the likelihood of democratic reforms under a new leadership suffers from extreme uncertainty. In particular, the coup in Zimbabwe illustrates that initially promising signals of coup plotters can later fail to lead to sustainable democratic improvements. In this case, first signs of progress towards democratization soon dwindled, leading to political deadlock and a manifestation of autocratic structures. Another challenge which needs to be discussed is the influence of other external factors on the willingness of coup plotters to initiate steps towards democratization. Depending on how much influence ROs and other international actors are able and willing to exert on coup plotters, the more or less inclined they may be to announce for instance timely elections to alleviate external pressure. Hence, the relationship between prospects of internal democratization and the choice of post-coup solutions by ROs may better be understood as a reciprocal than a unidirectional one.

Domestic power constellation

The last expectation was that apart from the anti-coup norm and concerns about democratic standards, also pragmatic considerations about the domestic power constellation are taken into account by ROs. More specifically, ROs should be more likely to accept coup plotters as new rulers or seek their participation in a joint government when the coup plotters hold a powerful and stable domestic position. The insights from the four cases tend to back this expectation.

In Burkina Faso, the position of the coup plotters was fragile from the start. The RSP faced not only massive popular resistance, visible in well-attended anti-coup demonstrations, protests and strikes, but ultimately also the opposition of the regular Burkinabe military forces. In combination with the promising democratic record of the ousted interim government and the lack of a credible democratization agenda of the coup plotters, the fragile position of the coup plotters made it easy for the respective ROs to agree on reinstating the Kafando regime.

In contrast, in all three other cases, the coup plotters had a comparatively strong position. In Zimbabwe, Mnangagwa and his allies enjoyed the support of the army as well as popular assent. Hence, despite the unconstitutionality of their actions, the coup plotters quickly consolidated their domestic position, which made it hard for ROs to take a truly hostile stance towards them. In Madagascar, the population was not so united behind Rajoelina, as Ravalomanana still had a large support base. However, as Rajoelina had also gathered large numbers of supporters behind him and furthermore enjoyed the backing of the Malagasy army, completely excluding him from a political solution for Madagascar would have turned out difficult for the AU, EU and SADC. Finally, the case of Niger seems to contradict the initial expectation. After the coup in the West African country, the coup plotters held a strong position, as they were backed by the army as well as by the population. Nevertheless, the AU, EU and ECOWAS immediately pushed for new elections, instead of taking a power-sharing agreement or an acceptance of the coup plotters into account.

As such, the Nigerien case contradicts the expectation that domestic power constellations shape post-coup solutions. Yet there are two important factors which may help to understand the dynamics in Niger: first, the popular support for the military junta was in large parts contingent on its promise to act as an impartial guardian paving the way for democratic reforms. If the junta would have shown ambitions to keep power for itself, it would have risked losing popular support quickly. Second, despite the powerful position of the military, the coup plotters immediately announced their intention to restore constitutional order via holding elections and they did not renegotiate this promise. Given that the coup plotters showed no ambition to be part of a future political solution, ROs had no reason to consider such an option. This suggests that the domestic power constellation should perhaps not be considered in isolation, but in connection with the coup plotters' ambition to rule for an extended period of time.

Notwithstanding, pragmatic considerations about domestic power constellations seem to influence the position taken by ROs after coups. As in the case of Expectation 7, the qualitative insights on Expectation 9 nicely correspond to findings of the quantitative analysis. The statistical part has shown that the power relations between ROs and the affected state are a decisive factor. The same holds true for the domestic power constellation in the qualitative part. Hence, there is strong evidence that apart from idealistic considerations about democracy, stability-based arguments also significantly shape the role of ROs in the aftermath of coups.

In sum, the findings show that the role of ROs in the aftermath of coups is actually strongly context-dependent. In some cases, ROs insist on a literal and strict interpretation of the anti-coup norm. On other occasions, they are prepared to accept or even actively strive for a solution which is not compatible with the requirements of the norm. ROs make their decisions on this question contingent on the circumstances of a coup. In Table 5.3, the findings for the four conditions which all have an impact on the role of ROs after coups are summarized. In general, the observations of all four ROs studied (AU, EU, ECOWAS, SADC) feature very similar results regarding the theoretical expectations. This gives hope that the findings of the present analysis are not RO-specific but may be transferred to further organizations. Notwithstanding, the emerging picture is not completely uniform. Whereas

Table 5.3: Overview findings research question 3

Conditions	Expectations	Empirical evidence
Unequivocal applicability of anti-coup norm	E6: If the anti-coup norm is unequivocally applicable to a particular case, ROs are more likely to push for a reinstatement of the ousted government or the formation of a new government in the aftermath of coups.	Supported by the evidence
Democratic legitimacy of incumbent	E7: Democratic legitimacy of the ousted ruler increases the chance that ROs will push for a reinstatement of the ousted ruler or his participation in a power-sharing agreement.	Supported by the evidence (with qualifications, democratic legitimacy must be understood as complex concept)
Chances of post-coup democratization	E8: If coup plotters set up a timely and credible electoral schedule, the likelihood increases that ROs will favour the formation of a new government or the consolidation of the coup plotters' rule.	Supported by the evidence (with qualifications, the assessment of chances of post-coup democratization faces uncertainties)
Domestic power constellation	E9: The stronger the domestic support of the coup plotters, the higher the likelihood that ROs will favour a power-sharing agreement or the consolidation of the coup plotters' rule.	Partly supported by the evidence (Nigerien case indicates that not only capacity but also willingness of coup plotters to keep power is important)

the ROs in all cases agreed on the general direction of post-coup solutions, the details of the pursued solutions differ. For instance, in the Zimbabwean case, the AU and SADC were more willing to accept the rule of Mnangagwa and to turn a blind eye to the irregularities of his electoral victory than the EU. Likewise, in the case of Madagascar, the SADC initially took a more hostile stance than the other two actors.

Given the diversity of the organizations examined it is not surprising that they slightly vary regarding their demands for post-coup solutions. How the preferences of ROs for different post-coup solutions affect the actual final outcomes is an interesting and largely unexplored question. The few existing studies indicate that many actors with different preferences and agendas lead to difficulties in finding stable post-coup solutions (Tansey, 2016b; Witt, 2017). The coordination mechanisms through which ROs seek to coordinate and align their positions in order to avoid mixed messages constitute very interesting study objects, which could be explored in future research.

Summary

In the present chapter, it was examined under which conditions ROs pursue particular post-coup solutions. Whereas some research exists on how ROs respond to coups and which measures they use to do so (Charron, 2013; von Soest & Wahman, 2015; Nathan, 2016c), the question of the ultimate rationales of ROs for imposing certain measures is largely unexplored. There is an interesting literature on the post-coup strategies of coup plotters, which accounts for the important role of regional and international actors (Striebinger, 2015; Thyne et al, 2018; Grewal & Kureshi, 2019; Hoyle, 2019; Yukawa et al, 2020). But all these studies take the perspectives of coup plotters, not that of ROs. In short, we know very little about what ROs actually hope to achieve in the aftermath of coups.

The final part of the analysis was intended to contribute to answer this question and examined differential post-coup solutions pursued by ROs. In doing so, it focused on the four successful coups in Madagascar (2009), Niger (2010), Burkina Faso (2015) and Zimbabwe (2017). In a comparative case study, the four coups were analysed, using inter alia official RO decisions and documents, press statements, speeches and interviews, reports of ROs, NGOs and think-tanks, news coverage and secondary literature.

The case studies provide four important insights. First, as expected, ROs actually often compromise the anti-coup norm in the aftermath of coups. Despite the categorical condemnation of coups prescribed by the norm, ROs do not always push for the reinstatement of the ousted government or new elections, but sometimes accept solutions that are more favourable for the coup plotters. The extent to which such practices are feasible is contingent on the unequivocal applicability of the anti-coup norm: the more clearly an irregular leader change is classified as a coup, the less leeway ROs have to pursue post-coup solutions which are not compatible with the anti-coup norm.

Second, the insights from the case studies indicate that the democratic record of the ousted incumbent is a central factor, determining whether ROs insist on his or her reinstatement or participation in a future government. State leaders who have themselves seriously violated democratic principles cannot automatically rely on the anti-coup norm.

Third, the prospects of future democratization also play a role. If coup plotters present a precise and credible schedule for democratization, the chances increase that ROs will not push for a return of the former authorities.

Finally, not only concerns about democracy, but also feasibility issues are important for ROs. If coup plotters enjoy domestic support from the population and the armed forces and thus hold a powerful position, ROs are more likely to pursue a post-coup solution which includes the coup plotters. However, this is dependent on the coup plotters' ambition to actually be part of such a solution.

What are the implications of these insights for the role of ROs in the context of coups? Most centrally, the analysis indicates that a certain willingness of ROs to compromise the norm in the aftermath of coups actually exists. Put differently, despite the categorical rejection of coups enshrined in the anti-coup norm, ROs occasionally pursue solutions favourable to coup plotters. The reasons why they do so require a careful interpretation. The case studies imply that democratic values and norms play a decisive role in this regard. In their decision of which post-coup solution to pursue, ROs are strongly guided by the goal of democratization. When this goal is in line with the principles of the anti-coup norm, for example if a democratic state leader is ousted by a power-hungry junta, no conflict of interest emerges, and the anti-coup norm is applied to the letter. However, sometimes the goal of democracy promotion runs counter to the inflexible principles of the anti-coup norm. When an autocratic state leader is ousted and chances of democratization are higher under a new leadership, ROs tend to subordinate the anti-coup norm to the general goal of democracy promotion. In doing so, ROs do not compromise the anti-coup norm for the sake of egoistic interests, but for another central normative principle.

Yet this is only part of the story. The results arising from the case studies suggest that while democracy is a central concern of ROs in the aftermath of coups, more tangible issues are also at play. Accepting the rule of coup plotters or their participation in a power-sharing agreement most certainly violates the provisions of the anti-coup norm. Yet given the limited resources of many ROs and their hesitancy to make demands they ultimately cannot assert, it is not totally surprising that the anti-coup norm is sometimes also subordinated to pragmatic considerations about the domestic power constellation. But the practice of ROs to make concessions to coup plotters with strong positions is not only due to a lack of willingness to confront such powerful actors. Apart from constituting a violation of democratic principles, a coup is also a form of violent civil conflict. In search of timely, stable solutions to such conflicts, ROs are often forced to talk to all powerful actors in the field and to accommodate their preferences.

To summarize, the results of the four case studies imply that an interplay of democracy-related concerns and stability-based considerations about the domestic power constellation determines the role of ROs in the aftermath of coups. ROs sometimes do renege the anti-coup norm when deciding on which post-coup solution to pursue in the aftermath of a coup, contingent on the particular circumstances. The decision-making process of ROs after coups is characterized by the weighing of different considerations and interests. In the final chapter of the book, we uncover the implications of this result, as well as of the findings from the two previous parts of the analysis, for the final evaluation of the role of ROs in the context of coups.

Conclusion

The firm establishment of the African anti-coup norm cannot be disputed. (Souaré, 2018)

[O]n the whole the practice of the AU has been neither consistent in the condemnation of coup regimes nor keen to support popular movements that oppose authoritarian rule… (Wet, 2019)

As the two quotes above show, the question of which role ROs play in the context of coups is an inherently contested one. In recent years, scholarship on the role of ROs in protecting democratic standards and solving violent conflicts within their member states has considerably expanded (McMahon & Baker, 2006; Donno, 2010; Kirchner & Dominguez, 2011; Söderbaum & Tavares, 2011; Suarez, Duarte Villa & Weiffen, 2017; Bamidele & Ayodele, 2018; Closa & Palestini, 2018; Witt, 2020). The study of coups and the regional responses to them forms an integral part of this strand of research. Yet as the two quotes indicate, scholarly opinions on how effective ROs actually are in deterring, combatting and resolving coups vary remarkably. This book sought to contribute to the current debate by providing a balanced and nuanced overview of the role of ROs in the context of coups. It did so through examining three distinct, yet interrelated research questions in a mixed-methods design.

1. First, what measures do ROs use to respond to coups?
2. Second, which factors influence the choice of stronger or weaker responses?
3. Third, which post-coup solutions do ROs pursue through their responses and why?

In sum, the findings on these questions show that ROs play a tremendously important role after coups. Yet their role is complex, which requires a nuanced perspective on the issue. The attitude of ROs towards coups has been strongly shaped by the emergence of a global anti-coup norm in the 1990s. Since the emergence of this norm, the responses of ROs to coups have become dominantly critical and hostile. This tendency can be interpreted as a growing consensus among regional communities all over the world that coups are no longer tolerated as a viable and acceptable means of leader change. However, the analysis also revealed that the anti-coup norm is better perceived as a broad guiding principle than a precise and non-negotiable instruction manual on how to respond to a coup. In general, ROs do follow the spirit of the anti-coup norm, but they adapt the norm to the circumstances and conditions of the respective coup and adjust their responses to the incident accordingly. Democracy- as well as stability-related considerations shape the assessment of coups by ROs. As a consequence, RO responses to coups vary – between organizations as well as across different coups.

In this final chapter of the book, the findings of the analysis are summarized, their relevance for our understanding of the role of ROs in the realms of democracy promotion and conflict resolution is reflected upon and their practical and academic implications are discussed. The chapter is structured in the following way: first, the most important insights from the three parts of the analysis are summarized. Subsequently, their relevance for the role of ROs after coups is reflected on and a final assessment on this issue is drawn. As a final step, the implications of the results for policy-making in the context of coups as well as academic research are sketched and avenues for future research are pointed out.

Findings of the analysis

The role of ROs in the context of coups is complex and multi-dimensional. In order to account for this complexity and to provide an encompassing and accurate picture of the role of ROs in the context of coups, three research questions were formulated (see Chapter 2) and empirically examined. The first research question concerned the global pattern of RO responses to coups (*What measures do ROs use to respond to coups?*), the second focused on the reasons for responses of different strength by ROs (*Which factors influence the choice of stronger or weaker responses?*) and the third addressed the issue of different post-coup scenarios preferred by ROs (*Which post-coup solutions do ROs pursue through their responses and why?*). The findings for each of the research questions are summarized and discussed in detail in the following.

Research question 1: What measures do ROs use to respond to coups?

The first research question was descriptive in nature and concerned the question of what measures ROs apply to respond to coups. To assess this question, data on the prevalence of coups and the respective responses to them in the time period from 1990 to 2019 was collected and presented in Chapter 3. The data presented clearly show that ROs have become noticeably more active after coups and that also strong and decisive measures like suspensions from RO decision-making bodies, economic sanctions or military measures are used by ROs after coups. Importantly, the responses of ROs to coups are overwhelmingly negative; open signs of approval of coups are the absolute exception. While this development indicates that ROs have started to play a stronger role in the context of coups, there is still a long way to go. Despite the progress of some front-runners such as the AU and the OAS, by far not all ROs around the world have become active defendants of the anti-coup norm, sanctioning and fighting coups. Many ROs are still comparatively passive after coups. These organizations often do not respond to coups at all and if they do so they limit their responses to weak responses, such as rhetorical condemnations or concern statements.

Another central insight from the first part of the analysis is the large inter- and intra-organizational diversity of post-coup responses. Even the more active and vocal ROs do not universally address all coups in their sphere of influence and when they do so, they apply instruments of diverging strength. The strong diversity in the strength of responses, ranging from concern statements to military intervention, is very conspicuous and concerns basically all ROs. Taking a temporal perspective does not help to illuminate this issue. There is no clear trend for stronger RO responses to coups over time. While the use of some stronger instruments, for example the suspension of affected states from regional bodies, has become more frequent, for other instruments like economic sanctions this is not the case.

In conclusion, since the emergence of the anti-coup norm after the end of the Cold War, the number of coups has decreased considerably, whereas the number of responses by ROs to the remaining coups has increased noticeably. The strength of the measures taken by ROs after coups varies tremendously and has not clearly increased over time. The broad diversity in the strength of responses raises the question of why ROs apparently penalize some coups more strongly than others.

Research question 2: Which factors influence the choice of stronger or weaker responses?

The question why ROs address some coups but not others and why they show responses of diverging strength touches upon a vital, yet sensitive aspect of the role of ROs after coups. Repeatedly, ROs have been accused of selectively sanctioning takeovers in some states, while turning a blind eye to others (Ikome, 2007). Such allegations of inconsequence and arbitrariness bear the risk of not only undermining the strength of the anti-coup norm, but also of damaging the reputation of ROs as credible supporters of democratic standards and providers of regional stability. Therefore, the second part of the analysis addressed the question of which factors determine the choice of stronger or weaker RO responses to coups.

In a first step, several potential explanatory factors were described and the respective data collected, including characteristics of the RO, democracy-related factors, such as for instance the regime type in the affected country, but also stability-based factors, including security and economic aspects. This information was compiled with the data on coups and RO responses from the first part of the analysis in one dataset. Subsequently, the effects of the potential explanatory factors on the strength of RO responses to coups were tested in a quantitative analysis using zero-inflated ordered probit models. The analysis proceeded in two steps: first, examining the likelihood that a certain RO responds to a particular coup in the first place, and second, focusing on the strength of the response.

The results from this analysis indicate that ROs are particularly likely to respond to coups which take place in their own member states and to successful coups and that the presence of formal democracy provisions within the RO increase the chance of a response to a coup. In itself, these findings do not indicate that ROs apply the anti-coup norm in an utterly inconsistent manner. Instead, they suggest that a sort of 'division of labour' with regard to responses to coups exists. If a coup takes place, not all ROs around the world are likely to respond to it, but a set of ROs with democratic standards from the respective geographical area are identified as the most suitable candidates to address the issue. The fact that ROs are more likely to respond to successful than to failed coups is equally intuitive, given the fact that the consequences of successful coups are much more far-reaching and alarming for ROs.

Yet the allegations of inconsistent RO responses to coups do not only concern the question whether ROs respond in the first place, but also the strength of the responses. Therefore, in a second step of the analysis, the strength of RO responses to coups was analysed. This revealed that the apparent diversity of RO responses to coups is not arbitrary, but follows certain patterns: on the one hand, ROs tend to take normative concerns about democratic standards into account. For instance, they are more likely to show strong responses after coups against democratic governments or after coups which have been orchestrated exclusively by the military without civilian involvement. On the other hand, the results also indicate that ROs are guided by concerns about regional stability in their assessment of coups. For example, they are less likely to use strong instruments against economically and military powerful states or against coups with a low level of violence, which are unlikely to spread instability to the region. Further analyses reveal that while there are common patterns, the weighing of security- and democracy-related aspects also differs between world regions.

Democracy-related factors seem to play a more important role after coups in Latin America and generally for the EU, whereas after coups in Asia and Oceania and Africa security-related aspects exert a stronger effect.

These results suggest that while ROs uphold the consensus that coups should be criticized and sanctioned, the decision about the strength of responses in a particular case firmly depends on the circumstances. In that sense, one can conclude that ROs are not completely uniform in their responses to coups and prefer a more flexible approach in handling takeovers. Given the tremendous diversity of the reasons, motives and ways of conducting coups, the question arises of whether a uniform treatment of all incidences of coups is even feasible and desirable. To conclude, with regard to the factors influencing the presence and strength of RO responses to coups a complex pattern emerges, as a mixture of RO characteristics, democracy-related concerns as well as stability-based considerations shapes the decision-making processes of ROs.

Research question 3: Which post-coup solutions do ROs pursue through their responses and why?

The third and final part of the analysis focused on the question of why ROs choose differential post-coup solutions. Some critics claim that while many ROs condemn and sanction coups immediately after the event, they tend to compromise the anti-coup norm in the aftermath of coups and pursue solutions which are not compatible with the norm (Omorogbe, 2011). For instance, ROs have repeatedly endorsed coup plotters as legitimate new rulers after they had won questionable post-coup elections (Banjo, 2008; Beardsworth et al, 2019). In order to evaluate this aspect of the role of ROs, the present study examined which post-coup solutions ROs pursue and which circumstances influence their decisions in this regard.

Chapter 2 illustrated that ROs can pursue four different solutions in the aftermath of a coup. They can push for the reinstatement of the ousted government, they can strive for the formation of a new government via elections, they can accept the continued rule of the coup plotters or pursue a power-sharing deal between the coup plotters and the ousted government. Subsequently, it was argued that in theory the anti-coup norm would request ROs to push for the reinstatement of the ousted government or the formation of a new government, but that the actual decision of ROs depends on several factors. Not only does the unequivocal applicability of the anti-coup norm matter, but also considerations about the democratic legitimacy of the incumbent, the prospects of democratization under a new leadership and the domestic power constellation.

In Chapter 5, four case studies were conducted to explore the plausibility of these explanations. The analysis of the coups in Madagascar (2009), Niger

(2010), Burkina Faso (2015) and Zimbabwe (2017) revealed that the anti-coup norm is actually sometimes compromised by ROs in the aftermath of coups. Although all four cases clearly fulfil the formal criteria of a coup, only in the case of Burkina Faso did the respective ROs pursue the reinstatement of the government, while in Niger, they called for new elections. In contrast, in Madagascar, the relevant ROs sought a power-sharing deal between the former government and the coup plotters, and in Zimbabwe they endorsed the rule of the coup plotters. Hence, as claimed by critics, the anti-coup is not always enforced in the aftermath of coups.

In the following, the reasons ROs have for pursuing different post-coup solutions were examined. The results indicate that the degree to which ROs are willing to bound the anti-coup norm depends on the unequivocal applicability of the norm to the particular case. If a takeover clearly qualifies as a coup, ROs have less leeway and are less prepared to accommodate the position of the coup plotters than in more ambiguous cases. In addition, in their decision over which position to take after a coup, ROs are influenced by two sets of considerations: on the one hand, ROs take the democratic record of the incumbent as well as the prospects of democratization under the leadership of the coup plotters into account. Democratic state leaders are more likely to be reinstated or to become part of a power-sharing agreement than autocratic incumbents. In turn, if the coup plotters present a credible democratization agenda, the chances of the incumbent to be reinstated or to become part of a power-sharing agreement decline. On the other hand, the case studies also indicate that ROs are driven by stability-related concerns and acknowledge the domestic power constellation. When coup plotters hold a firm position and can count on public, political and military support, they are less likely to be completely excluded from a political post-coup situation compared to coup plotters with a volatile power base.

In a nutshell, ROs are actually sometimes willing to compromise the anti-coup norm in the aftermath of coups. The reasons for doing so are, on the one hand, normatively guided. If the anti-coup norm collides with the more general goal of promoting democracy in a RO member state, the latter tend to trump the former. On the other hand, stability-related considerations about the domestic strength of the coup plotters also shape the decision. Notwithstanding the reasons, the fact that ROs willingly accept or even actively pursue post-coup solutions which blatantly violate the provisions of the anti-coup norm bears the risk of seriously impairing the picture of ROs as credible enforcers of the anti-coup norm.

Summary

To summarize, the analysis of the present book sought to evaluate the role of ROs in the context of coups along three research questions. For doing so quantitative and qualitative methods were combined, including descriptive statistics, large-N explanatory statistics and comparative case study analysis. The results of the three different parts of the analysis provided a differentiated and complex picture of the role of ROs. In the first part of the analysis, the data on the prevalence of coups and the respective responses by ROs to them in the last 30 years indicate that since the emergence of the anti-coup norm the role of ROs as enforcers of the anti-coup norm has been strengthened. ROs use a wide spectrum of rhetorical, diplomatic, economic and military measures to respond to coups and have become more active after coups, although not necessarily through stronger instruments.

Regarding the second research question, the results are more complex. The findings of the quantitative analysis in the second part suggest that ROs with binding democratic commitments are relatively consistent in responding to (successful) coups in their member states. Yet the strength of these responses firmly depends on concerns about democratic standards, yet also on stability-oriented considerations, as well as RO characteristics. As such, ROs do not apply the anti-coup norm in a completely consistent manner. When responding to coups, ROs do not act arbitrarily, yet they follow a selective pattern, seeking to reconcile the principles of the anti-coup norm with other democracy- and stability-related norms and interests of their member states.

Finally, the insights from the last part of the analysis cast doubts on the willingness of ROs to unconditionally enforce the principles of the anti-coup norm in the aftermath of coups. The comparative case study of four coups in Madagascar (2009), Niger (2010), Burkina Faso (2015) and Zimbabwe (2017) shows that ROs are under certain conditions willing to compromise the anti-coup norm and work towards post-coup solutions which are not compatible with the anti-coup norm. The reasons for doing so lie within contradictions of the anti-coup norm with alternative concerns about the democratic situation in particular countries, yet also in stability-based considerations about the domestic power constellation. Regardless of the motivations of ROs for doing so, they have repeatedly favoured and pushed towards post-coup solutions in which coup plotters played an ongoing and influential role. This indicates that the anti-coup norm is not the only criterion guiding RO behaviour in the aftermath of coups. Instead, the desire to reach a stable and ideally also democratic post-coup solution seems to be at least equally important.

The role of ROs in the context of coups – current state and challenges ahead

What do these findings imply for the role of ROs after coups? The answer to this question is not easy. Most certainly, ROs have initiated a remarkable change in the international attitude towards coups. From the 1990s onwards,

ROs promoted an anti-coup norm, which rose remarkably fast and proved far-reaching. Using the momentum of hope about a further global wave of democratization, the anti-coup norm became a prominent and central element in the democracy regimes of a series of ROs, most notably the AU and the OAS (Legler & Tieku, 2010). Since then, the anti-coup norm constitutes a prominent norm, which is frequently referred to in the case of coups. As the mapping in Chapter 3 shows, ROs have emerged as the key actors to promote, protect and enforce this norm. Put differently, they have become the guardians against unconstitutional leader changes in their member states. Importantly, the opposition to coups is not exclusively limited to ROs with a strong democratic commitment. As the analysis has illustrated, stability-related considerations are also important reasons for ROs to address coups and many ROs with a semi-democratic membership and fewer strict democracy provisions have taken measures against coups.

Notwithstanding, ROs continue to face challenges when confronted with coups. The questionable and inconsequential handling of recent coups in Zimbabwe (2017) and Sudan (2019) by ROs painfully illustrates that the anti-coup norm is far from undisputedly determining how ROs should handle undemocratic and unconstitutional leader changes. Although most ROs agree in their general disapproval of coups, the question of how to translate this disapproval into practical consequences is often challenging and disputed. Expressed positively, the anti-coup norm has reached an established, secure status within the normative framework of a series of ROs on different continents. Yet for giving the norm a more decisive status and for strengthening the role of ROs as credible norm enforcers, three essential challenges must be addressed: the strong degree of inter-organizational diversity, the ambiguity of the content of the anti-coup norm and the blend of different motivations of ROs to condemn and sanction coups.

Inter-organizational diversity

First, the diverging extent of acceptance and internalization of the anti-coup norm in different world regions and their respective ROs constitutes a challenge. In a sense, the anti-coup norm can be described as a global norm, because ROs from all over the world have adopted anti-coup provisions and/or condemned coups in the past (see Chapter 2). Hence, the anti-coup norm is not limited to a particular geographic area but enjoys global validity and applicability and shapes the responses of ROs to coups across the globe. Nevertheless, the responses of ROs to coups are characterized by strong regional diversity. The institutionalization of the anti-coup norm on the RO level instead of the development of global binding anti-coup provisions has allowed for regional flexibility in finding suitable ways to deal with coups. The differences between the predominantly diplomatic approach of the

OAS in contrast to the more legalistic and rule-based approach of the AU illustrate that ROs can find different, yet at the same time effective ways to respond to coups (Legler & Tieku, 2010).

However, the institutionalization of the anti-coup norm on the regional level also carries with it problems with regard to the consistent application of the norm by different ROs. An obvious challenge is the uneven distribution of ROs with a strong commitment to the anti-coup norm across the globe. Africa and Latin America have often been described as the regions in which the strongest anti-coup regimes and most active ROs exist (Tansey, 2017). In Europe, the demanding democratic standards of the EU likewise grant a highly sceptical stance towards coups. In Oceania, the PIF as most influential RO has sought to take respective steps (Firth, 2013). Yet Asia and the Middle East constitute the notable and large white spots on the global anti-coup map. In Asia, some influential ROs like the Shanghai Cooperation Organization (SCO) or ASEAN have showed noticeably meagre interest in establishing democratic standards, protecting instead the autocratic status quo of their member states (Ambrosio, 2008; Jones, 2008). In others, like SAARC, the weak institutionalization of ROs impedes strong action against coups (Michael, 2013). The recent stronger engagement of ASEAN after the coup in Myanmar is an important step, yet in comparison with other world regions there is still a long way to go.

In sum, despite the emergence of an increasingly powerful anti-coup norm, not all ROs have taken a strong and decisive role after coups. Whereas many ROs have made noticeable progress in this regard, a considerable number of ROs still only act very passively after coups or even completely ignore them. As a result, some authors deny that ROs as such play an important role after coups. Instead, they argue that only selected ROs are active promoters of a respective regional anti-coup norm (Souaré, 2018). The author does not share this view. The partly subsequent and partly parallel development of anti-coup provisions in a large number of ROs from different regions within the last 30 years clearly indicates that ROs as a group play an important role after coups. Notwithstanding, the diversity of anti-coup provisions, measures and responses in different ROs makes it difficult to talk about one role of ROs after coups. A stronger anti-coup framework on the UN level might be one potential solution within which the approaches of different ROs to coups could be coordinated and aligned. Until then, it is important to keep in mind that the role of ROs after coups is composed of the interplay of the very diverse positions, strategies and actions of different organizations.

Ambiguity of the anti-coup norm

Second, a strong role of ROs in the context of coups is partly impaired by the vagueness and ambiguity of the anti-coup norm itself. Due to the lack of internationally binding law against coups, the anti-coup norm lacks in precision and allows for a large degree of freedom of interpretation. As a result, discussions within ROs regularly emerge about which situations actually constitute a coup, what measures should be taken following a coup and which post-coup solution is suitable to restore constitutional order. Even the AU and the OAS, the ROs with the most explicit and detailed anti-coup provisions, do not specify which criteria a leader change has to fulfil to be considered as a coup. This may seem trivial, but it is not. As the general validity of the anti-coup norm is hardly ever contested, denying the applicability of the anti-coup norm in a particular case is a key strategy for ROs incapable or unable of taking action against coup plotters. Referring to coups in more general terms as 'political crises' or inventing creative neologisms like 'military-assisted transition' allows ROs to circumvent the provisions of the anti-coup norm and to take a more conciliatory stance towards coup plotters.

In addition to the definition of coups, the range of applicable instruments would benefit from a higher degree of precision and clarity. Some ROs avoid mentioning specific instruments to be used against coup plotters altogether, while others list some instruments which could potentially be used (see Chapter 2). While such provisions provide ROs with a general mandate to use the respective measures, they fell far short of establishing standardized and mandatory procedures to be taken in the case of a coup. As a result, RO responses are often diverse in terms of their strength, evoking the impression of arbitrariness and selectivity. Some ROs have sought to streamline their procedures in this regard. Most notably, the AU's approach to unconditionally suspend all states in which a successful coup has taken place has resulted in a strong deterrent effect (Souaré, 2014). Then again, the flexible definition of what is actually considered as coup by the AU allows circumvention of this provision, as for instance in the case of Zimbabwe in 2017 (Asuelime, 2018).

Furthermore, a clearer definition of which post-coup solutions are deemed acceptable and compatible with the anti-coup norm would be of great help to reduce the impression that ROs are readily willing to compromise the anti-coup norm and quickly come to terms with coup plotters. In the past, coup plotters who had first been fiercely criticized and sanctioned were finally accepted as new rulers after minimal concessions (Banjo, 2008). This does not only cast doubts on the seriousness of punitive measures immediately following a coup, but also calls for the development of more coherent and thoughtful post-coup strategies. Again, the AU takes a pioneering role, by stipulating in the Lomé Declaration that coup plotters are not to be accepted as new heads of states and are not allowed to stand in future elections (Lomé Declaration, 2000). However, the inconsistent application of this principle in the past has undermined its credibility.

To sum up, a more precise definition of what constitutes a coup, which steps ROs are required to take in such a case and what needs to be done to restore constitutional order would help tremendously to reduce the ambiguities and inconsistencies accompanying the anti-coup norm. At present, ROs are bound by a vague consensus that they should do something about coups. Yet clearer instructions on what to do exactly would clearly help to sharpen and strengthen the role of ROs in the context of coups.

Mixed motives to respond to coups

Third, the different motivations of ROs to adopt and implement the anti-coup norm and to respond to coups also constitute a challenge. Like a thread throughout the book, the theoretical expectations and empirical results indicate that the role of ROs after coups is characterized by a duality of the aims of promoting democracy and granting stability. On the one hand, ROs seek to guard and promote democratic standards via the anti-coup norm, while on the other they try to protect incumbents from losing power and prevent political instability spillovers into the wider region. As such, ROs and their member states have a dual motivation for following the anti-coup norm: concerns about democracy as well as about stability in the region.

As a result, reasons to adopt the anti-coup norm can differ between organizations, with some ROs putting greater emphasis on promoting democratic standards, while others are more driven by stability concerns (Leininger, 2014). For some ROs, one might conclude with reasonable certainty whether protecting democracy or protecting regional stability is the driving force behind the adoption of the anti-coup norm. For instance, it is unlikely that a RO with a predominantly autocratic membership like the GCC is unduly concerned about violations of democratic standards in its member states when responding to coups. In contrast, the anti-coup policies of the EU are hardly driven by concerns about the destabilizing effect of the practically non-existent risk of a coup in one of its member states. However, for many ROs, both aspects of the anti-coup norm play an essential role.

The duality of these goals is not only mirrored in the wide spectrum of RO instruments to respond to coups (see Chapter 3) and the decision-making process leading to stronger and weaker responses (see Chapter 4). It also becomes apparent in the choice of different post-coup solutions to be pursued by ROs (see Chapter 5). The duality of stability- and democracy-based reasons to adopt, promote and follow the anti-coup norm is not necessarily a problem. International actors often have mixed motives for complying with and exerting norms (Checkel, 1997; Shannon, 2000). Nevertheless, the goals of promoting democracy and ensuring stability do not always go hand in hand. This is most apparent when coups lead to the fall of autocratic state leaders. In such situations, ROs face the thorny dilemma of whether to come to the help of the unconstitutionally ousted leader or to put their bet on democratization under a new leadership. While the former may nourish claims that the anti-coup norm benefits autocratic leaders, the latter can fuel criticisms of inconsistent application of the norm. In the end, the question of the motives of ROs to respond to coups concerns their legitimacy and acceptance to do so. Critics claim that the ultimate goal of ROs in adopting and following the anti-coup norm is not so much to promote democracy, but rather to protect incumbents from losing power by violent means (Ikome, 2007; Omorogbe, 2011). Such allegations can have a severe impact on the credibility of the norm and the reputation of ROs as norm enforcers. As such, the tension between the principles of democracy and stability constitutes a key obstacle for a further strengthening of the role of ROs.

The tension between stability and democracy inherent in the anti-coup norm is not easily resolved by ROs. Denouncing the aim of preserving regional stability as the selfish aim of state leaders to stay in power falls short of adequately describing the complexity of the issue. Instead, both preserving regional stability and protecting democratic standards are valid and important aims pursued by ROs within the normative framework of the anti-coup norm. Notwithstanding, a deliberate and conscious debate about the tension between the two guiding principles is urgently needed for strengthening the position of ROs. Without denying the importance of regional stability, ROs can establish a stronger and more credible democratic mandate for the anti-coup norm if they tie the norm closer to other central democratic principles. ROs could strengthen their position in the context of coups by not only reacting once a coup has happened, but by tackling some of the common root causes of coups – autocratic leadership, electoral fraud, corruption, repression and the manipulation of constitutional provisions – earlier and in a more decisive manner.

To summarize, in the present section, a final evaluation of the role of ROs in the context of coups was made. Although ROs already constitute remarkably influential and important actors in this realm, three central challenges for a stronger and more credible role of ROs were identified. These comprise the varying influence of the anti-coup norm in different organizations, the norm's lack of preciseness and clarity, leading to ambiguities in the application of the norm by ROs, as well as the inherent tension between democracy and stability as guiding motives of ROs to respond to coups.

Implications for research and practice

These insights and the findings of the analysis of the present book have important academic and practical implications. In the subsequent section, these implications are discussed, seeking to illustrate the contribution of the book to the academic knowledge of the role of ROs in the context of democracy and security challenges.

Academic implications

In examining the role of ROs in the context of coups, this book sought to make a contribution to the academic literature on coups and democracy promotion by regional actors. The findings of the study have important implications for our understanding of international (democracy) norms and the role of regional actors in conflicts over democracy and security.

First, by examining the anti-coup norm, the study adds to the impressive body of literature on the decisive role of norms in international politics. The study of norms has been an essential field in the area of International Relations for a long time (Adler, 2002). In recent years, academic research has taken an increasingly critical and reflective stance towards norms, focusing on the contestation and challenges of norms (Bloomfield, 2016; Sandholtz, 2019; Simmons & Jo, 2019). The present study resonates well with this trend. The analysis impressively shows how the anti-coup norm as an international norm can constrain, shape and guide the behaviour of regional actors. The anti-coup norm constitutes a remarkable example of how a democratic norm has emerged, spread and gained influence against all odds (Leininger, 2015). However, the study also indicates that norms cannot be understood as distant, uncontested and sacrosanct rules. Instead, the anti-coup norm constitutes a complex principle, whose application is shaped by a diverse set of considerations.

As such, this book refines the academic understanding of the relevance of the anti-coup norm for ROs. Many existing studies have taken the anti-coup norm as a given and focused on the question whether this norm is successfully put into practice (Ikome, 2007; Omorogbe, 2011; Souaré, 2014; Tansey, 2017). In the author's opinion, this is not the most insightful question. The anti-coup norm is not just complied with or violated in specific cases. Instead, this book focuses on the question of how the anti-coup norm affects the role of ROs in the context of coups. This study provides new insights on the nature of the anti-coup norm, its underlying aims and inherent tensions. Through examining the interplay of the anti-coup norm with other relevant considerations of ROs, it is illustrated that the anti-coup norm is actually an important guiding principle for ROs. Yet the relevance and significance of the norm can only be thoroughly understood in connection with the more encompassing decision-making processes of ROs after coups.

This approach can serve as an example of how to gain a better understanding of the potential, yet also limitations of international norms. Due to the complex nature of norms, such future research must stand on theoretically and methodologically sound foundations. The findings of the present book, in line with other recent research (Deitelhoff & Zimmermann, 2019), suggest that a multidimensional approach, combining different aspects of norms, is a potentially favourable starting point. Furthermore, the present study provides an example of how quantitative and qualitative methods can be fruitfully combined to reach a comprehensive and multifaceted analysis of international norms. A promising avenue for further research is the interplay of democratic norms with other essential norms and principles. A central insight from the analysis of the role of ROs after coups is that democratic norms do not exist in a vacuum, but coexist, overlap and run counter with other norms and interests, such as stability and security, mediation guidelines, yet also state sovereignty and non-interference (Coe, 2015; Nathan, 2016a; Mills & Bloomfield, 2018). The interplay of these factors lies at the heart of decision-making processes of states, as well as ROs and IOs. While the present study allows for first insights on how the anti-coup norm interacts with such aspects, further studies – especially on the weighing of different norms in ROs – constitute an important way forward to picture the general normative framework of ROs.

Second, apart from the specific insights on the anti-coup norm, the book has important implications for the broader academic understanding of democratic standards and principles. In the first place, the findings of the book underline that democratic norms do matter. In this regard, the study adds to the body of literature on the effects of democratic norms for regional and international actors (Boniface, 2002; Manners, 2002; Pevehouse, 2002a, 2002b; McMahon & Baker, 2006; Freyburg et al, 2009; Donno, 2013; Leininger, 2014; Mangu, 2014; Bamidele & Ayodele, 2018). While the findings of the analysis show that the anti-coup norm still faces considerable challenges with regard to consistent application as well as enforcement of the norm in the aftermath of coups, the sincerity of ROs in their attempts to impede unconstitutional and illegal interruptions in democratic processes cannot be denied.

Yet the anti-coup norm in ROs also aptly illustrates some of the challenges democratic norms face at the regional level. The anti-coup norm is an impressive example of the fact that basic democratic principles and norms are anchored in many ROs around the world. But the analysis of the norm also indicates that the content and shape of such norms is tremendously diverse. ROs do not only differ with regard to the extent of commitment to democratic norms, their strategies in how they seek to enforce such norms, but also with respect to what they actually understand by the term 'democratic'. Many existing studies build upon the notion that there is a fixed set of democratic standards, departing from which responses to violations of these standards can be examined in a comparative manner (Donno, 2010; van der Vleuten & Ribeiro Hoffmann, 2010; von Soest & Wahman, 2015).

Particularly the qualitative part of the analysis shows that this notion bears some problems. ROs differ tremendously regarding which political processes in their member states they assess as (un)democratic. This does not only concern coups in themselves, but also pre-coup developments as well as post-coup elections. In sum, the book illustrates that for advancing our understanding of the significance of democratic norms in ROs, it is essential to take a more nuanced view on the differential localization of such norms (Acharya, 2004). Undeniably, democratic norms exist on a global level. Yet for thoroughly understanding their significance, one has to account for the differential extents of internalization of these norms in different regions and particularly their varying specifications and interpretations.

Third, the present study also reveals important insights on the role of regional actors in international politics. Studies on regionalism, once a niche area in political science, have seen a considerable rise in recent years (Hettne & Söderbaum, 2006; Lombaerde & Schulz, 2009; Söderbaum & Tavares, 2011; Börzel et al, 2012; Jetschke & Lenz, 2013; Trithart, 2013; Börzel & van Hüllen, 2015; Suarez, Villa & Weiffen, 2017; Panke & Stapel, 2018). By now, most scholars agree that not only the EU, but also many other ROs play a powerful and decisive role in international politics. In examining the anti-coup norm in ROs, the book has put a particular focus on the role of regional actors in upholding and promoting democratic standards, yet also in upholding stability in their member states and the whole region. The results of the study clearly suggest that ROs are decisive players in this regard. ROs have emerged as the key norm entrepreneurs and enforcers of the anti-coup norm and their engagement exceeds that of IOs and single states.

As such, the book complements the emerging literature on the role of ROs in the context of coups (Boniface, 2002; Cooper & Legler, 2005; Arceneaux & Pion-Berli, 2007; Ikome, 2007; Omorogbe, 2011; Collins & Fraenkel, 2012; Striebinger, 2012; Leininger, 2015; Okafor & Okafor, 2015; Nathan, 2016c; Powell et al, 2016; Souaré, 2018; Wilén & Williams, 2018). However, the findings of this analysis also qualify existing perspectives. While the anti-coup norm is an important guiding motive for ROs, it is far from being the only factor determining their role. This book illustrated that the role of ROs in the context of coups is an inherently complex and challenging one. ROs balance and are often torn between their differential motivations of guarding democratic principles, stabilizing affected countries and protecting the governments of their member states. While on some occasions, these intentions go hand in hand, in others they do not. Hence, for reaching a sound and thorough understanding of the role of regional actors in the context of coups, it is essential to take an encompassing view on the different motives guiding them.

This has wider implications for the study of ROs in the realms of democracy and security governance. The present study indicates that the attempts of ROs to grant peace and stability on the one hand and to protect democratic norms and standards on the other hand cannot always be neatly distinguished. Instead, the realms of democracy and security governance of ROs often overlap. This overlap can lead to conflicting objectives and can complicate RO decision-making procedures. To gain a better understanding of the rationales of ROs to address domestic conflicts in their member states, it would be worth taking a more encompassing perspective, accounting for security- as well as democracy-related aspects.

In this context, it is also essential to pay attention to the intra-organizational dynamics of ROs. The democracy norms as well as security interests of ROs are not homogeneous, but a composition of the normative understandings and interests of the ROs' member states. Undeniably, ROs have become the central institutions to respond to coups and they have gained an increasing extent of actorness and agency in this regard since the 1990s. Yet still, when ROs decide on measures to implement after a coup and post-coup solutions to pursue, they need to take the positions of their member states into account. The methods by which the member states of ROs discuss, negotiate and agree on potential responses to coups are key in this regard and should be examined more extensively in future studies.

Finally, given the tremendous diversity of regional actors, more comparative research on the diverse democracy norms and provisions, as well as on security competencies of different ROs, is urgently needed. The body of literature concerned with this topic has increased tremendously in recent years. A large number of cases studies have allowed for deep insights in the democracy and security politics of particular ROs (Cooper & Legler, 2005; Arceneaux & Pion-Berli, 2007; Schimmelfennig & Scholtz, 2008; Legler & Tieku, 2010; Wetzel & Orbie, 2011; Dandashly, 2015; Hartmann & Striebinger, 2015). In addition, cross-organizational comparative approaches have provided a global picture of the normative standards and competencies of ROs (McMahon & Baker, 2006; Closa, 2013; Panke & Starkmann, 2018).

Cross-regional and cross-organizational research is still to a large extent descriptive in nature and focused on official competencies. Yet official legal competencies do not automatically translate into action. More systematic comparative research, both with qualitative and quantitative methods, on the practices of different ROs in the realms of democracy and security would enhance our knowledge of the increasingly important role of ROs in international politics. Systematic comparison of the practices of different actors in this regard allows us to identify common patterns, drivers and challenges, resulting in the emergence of conclusions on general patterns of regional democracy and security governance. As argued in the quantitative analysis, particularly the interplay and interdependence of the actions of different actors in this regard are mostly unexplored and would definitely deserve future research.

Importantly, the vast majority of existing studies on the democracy and security governance of ROs is focused on the largest and most influential

ROs, such as the OAS, the EU or the AU. Notwithstanding the appeal of these organizations as a choice for a case study, the book has illustrated that a large series of smaller, sub-regional organizations, such as, for instance ANDEAN, CARICOM, SADC or the PIF, are also actively engaged in the realms of democracy and security politics. While these organizations are smaller in size, have fewer resources at their disposal and usually become involved after coups or other democracy and security challenges less frequently, they still make up an important part of regional democracy and security governance that cannot be neglected. Therefore, these examples, as well as many other smaller ROs, are worth studying in future research.

Practical implications

Apart from interesting insights for the academic study of the topic, the findings of the book also have important practical implications. The most central insight from this study is that ROs do matter and that they do play an important role after coups. Against the background of daunting authoritarian tendencies in many states, this is an encouraging message. Against all resistance, democratic norms have spread and developed noticeably. The anti-coup norm in ROs constitutes an impressive example of this trend. Notwithstanding, for strengthening the role of ROs and overcoming existing obstacles, decisive action is needed.

First, the book has illustrated that ROs are promising arenas to anchor the anti-coup norm. While stronger institutionalization on a global level within the UN framework would be desirable, the highly diverse interests, internal blockades and power struggles have impeded real progress in the past and are unlikely to disappear in the near future (Tansey, 2018). Against this background, ROs emerge as an attractive alternative to enable multilaterally coordinated action against coups. Admittedly, in their endeavour to bolster democratic norms ROs face difficulties on their own. Most notably in this regard are the internal resistance of autocratic and semi-democratic member states, weakly institutionalized and professionalized structures and a constant shortage of financial and military resources (Tavares, 2010; Davies, 2018).

However, these issues are not unalterable. Peer pressure among member states can reduce the influence of autocratic states and alleviate their resistance against reforms. A central step towards advancing ROs' capacity to act is to increase their available resources and to create intra-organizational bodies which allow for swift decision-making in the face of crises. The establishment of the Peace and Security Council of the AU serves as a pioneering example in this regard.

Second, as the record of the UN in handling coups is mixed, a strong global power to enforce the anti-coup norm is missing. Therefore, not only the capacity to act of single ROs, but also cooperation, exchange and alignment between ROs should be strengthened. In their desire to impede violent and unconstitutional leader changes, ROs around the world share a common interest. Furthering an exchange of experiences, best practices and remaining challenges between different organizations can facilitate mutual learning and support.

Perhaps even more important than sharing experiences is the coordination of action of different ROs to one and the same coup. Due to the phenomenon of overlapping regionalism, most countries are members of more than one RO. Hence, coups often tend to alarm several organizations at the same time. Past experiences have shown that ROs have been most successful in responding to coups when they managed to meaningfully coordinate and align their responses. In turn, in cases where ROs pursued divergent goals and strategies, this has often led to confusion, power struggles and failure to exert pressure on the respective state (Tansey, 2016b; Witt, 2017). Consequently, the coordination between organizations is a challenging, yet essential prerequisite for a successful enforcement of the anti-coup norm by ROs. Two viable options for such coordination, which have gained support in the past, are joint mediation missions including interlocutors from different organizations, as well as international contact groups, which can constitute a valuable discussion forum for a broader set of actors with interests in a particular state (Henneberg, 2021).

Third, for sharpening the role of ROs in the context of coups, it is crucial to specify the nature of coups and the instruments and procedures to be taken after them in a clear and uncontestable manner. Currently, the comparatively vague status of the anti-coup norm entails numerous loopholes to circumvent the norm. Clear criteria to determine which instances constitute coups can help to avoid coup plotters succeeding in circumventing an application of the anti-coup norm by referring to creative and euphemistic neologisms, like 'military-assisted transition'. Likewise, explicit and mandatory procedures to be taken after coups, such as those which already exist in some pioneering ROs, provide organizations with a clear mandate and a broader scope of action.

In addition, the question of what constitutes an acceptable post-coup solution is seriously underspecified. This point is often deplored as the Achilles heel of the anti-coup norm, as ROs initially condemn coups, but finally turn out to be willing to accept questionable compromises (Omorogbe, 2011). For tackling this issue, unequivocal and demanding criteria for post-coup trajectories must be set by ROs: the reinstatement of the ousted government or timely elections which meet democratic standards, the independence and impartiality of interim governments and the non-participation of coup plotters in post-coup elections or political functions. Yet setting such requests is not sufficient. ROs must be willing and prepared to exert pressure on post-coup regimes when they violate or ignore given promises. A strengthening of RO competencies and capacities as outlined is key in this regard, yet the political will is also necessary.

Fourth, a further challenge for ROs is finding a balance between consistent procedures and consideration for the particularities of specific coups. As previous research has shown, coups have divergent causes and no uniform effect emerges as a result (Marinov & Goemans, 2014; Thyne & Powell, 2016; Powell et al, 2019). With regard to coups against democratically elected governments which uphold democratic standards, ROs should take a clear position which rejects the coup and backs the incumbent against his or her challengers. However, only very few coups happen in model democracies. When coups oust leaders, who have once themselves taken power by undemocratic means, who violate constitutional provisions, who manipulate elections or engage in repression, corruption and violence, unconditional support for such leaders is out of place. In such cases, international actors are best advised to push for a timely democratic transition under the leadership of a newly elected government.

Finally, it is essential that ROs do their best to support the future trajectories of countries in which coups have taken place. Some researchers have described coups against autocratic leaders as windows of opportunity for democratization (Marinov & Goemans, 2014; Powell, 2014a). However, for democratic progress to actually materialize, it is essential that international actors closely follow and support the post-coup trajectory. Free and fair post-coup elections constitute the starting point, but not the finish line for a successful democratization process. In order to avoid autocratic backsliding and future coups, ROs and other international actors have to engage in the time- and resource-intensive process of strengthening civil society and building up independent and strong democratic institutions. In the end, the phenomenon of coups will only disappear if ROs succeed in establishing a political culture in their member states in which democratic and fair political competition supersedes the power of violence.

Appendix

Table A1: Coups between 1990 and 2019

Country	Month	Day	Year
Papua New Guinea	3	14	1990
Afghanistan	3		1990
Nigeria	4	22	1990
Madagascar	5	13	1990
Zambia	6	30	1990
Trinidad & Tobago	7	27	1990
Philippines	10	4	1990
Suriname	12	24	1990
Haiti	1	7	1991
Thailand	2	23	1991
Mali	3	26	1991
Lesotho	4	30	1991
Mali	7	14	1991
Comoros	8	3	1991
Soviet Union	8	21	1991
Togo	8	26	1991
Haiti	9	30	1991
Togo	10	1	1991
Togo	10	7	1991
Chad	10	13	1991
Togo	11	28	1991
Togo	12	3	1991
Algeria	1	11	1992
Venezuela	2	4	1992

(continued)

Table A1: Coups between 1990 and 2019 (continued)

Country	Month	Day	Year
Afghanistan	4	15	1992
Sierra Leone	4	30	1992
Madagascar	7	29	1992
Comoros	9	26	1992
Peru	11	13	1992
Venezuela	11	27	1992
Sierra Leone	12	28	1992
Guatemala	5	25	1993
Burundi	7	3	1993
Burundi	10	21	1993
Libya	10		1993
Nigeria	11	17	1993
Gambia	7	23	1994
Lesotho	8	17	1994
Liberia	9	7	1994
Liberia	9	15	1994
Azerbaijan	10		1994
Gambia	11	10	1994
Azerbaijan	3	13	1995
Qatar	6	27	1995
São Tomé and Príncipe Principe	8	15	1995
Comoros	9	27	1995
Sierra Leone	10	2	1995
Sierra Leone	1	16	1996
Niger	1	27	1996
Guinea	2	2	1996
Qatar	2	20	1996
Paraguay	4	22	1996
Bangladesh	5	20	1996
Burundi	7	25	1996
Sierra Leone	5	25	1997
Cambodia	7	5	1997
Zambia	10	28	1997
Guinea-Bissau	6	7	1998

Table A1: Coups between 1990 and 2019 (continued)

Country	Month	Day	Year
Niger	4	9	1999
Comoros	4	30	1999
Guinea-Bissau	5	7	1999
Honduras	7	30	1999
Pakistan	10	12	1999
Armenia	10		1999
Côte d'Ivoire	12	24	1999
Ecuador	1	21	2000
Comoros	3	21	2000
Paraguay	5	18	2000
Fiji	5	19	2000
Côte d'Ivoire	9	19	2000
Peru	10	30	2000
Fiji	11		2000
Guinea-Bissau	11		2000
Djibouti	12	7	2000
Côte d'Ivoire	1	7	2001
Burundi	4	18	2001
Central African Rep.	5	28	2001
Burundi	7	22	2001
Venezuela	4	12	2002
Côte d'Ivoire	9	19	2002
Nepal	10	4	2002
Central African Rep.	3	15	2003
Mauritania	6	8	2003
São Tomé and Príncipe Principe	7	16	2003
Guinea-Bissau	9	14	2003
D.R. Congo	3	28	2004
D.R. Congo	6	11	2004
Togo	2	5	2005
Mauritania	8	3	2005
Guinea	4	4	2006
Chad	4	13	2006

(continued)

Table A1: Coups between 1990 and 2019 (continued)

Country	Month	Day	Year
Thailand	9	19	2006
Fiji	12	5	2006
Bangladesh	1	11	2007
Philippines	11	29	2007
Chad	2	2	2008
East Timor	2	11	2008
Sudan	5	10	2008
Mauritania	8	6	2008
Guinea-Bissau	8	8	2008
Guinea-Bissau	11	23	2008
Guinea	12	23	2008
Equatorial Guinea	2	11	2009
Madagascar	3	17	2009
Lesotho	4	23	2009
Georgia	5	5	2009
Guinea-Bissau	6	4	2009
Honduras	6	28	2009
Niger	2	18	2010
Guinea-Bissau	4	1	2010
Ecuador	9	30	2010
Madagascar	11	17	2010
D.R. Congo	2	27	2011
Guinea	7	19	2011
Guinea-Bissau	12	26	2011
Papua New Guinea	1	26	2012
Maldives	2	7	2012
Mali	3	21	2012
Guinea-Bissau	4	12	2012
Mali	4	30	2012
Guinea-Bissau	10	21	2012
Sudan	11	22	2012
Eritrea	1	21	2013
Egypt	7	3	2013
South Sudan	12	15	2013

Table A1: Coups between 1990 and 2019 (continued)

Country	Month	Day	Year
Thailand	5	22	2014
Lesotho	8	30	2014
Burkina Faso	10	30	2014
Gambia	12	30	2014
Burundi	5	13	2015
Burkina Faso	9	16	2015
Turkey	7	15	2016
Zimbabwe	11	15	2017
Gabon	1	7	2019
Sudan	4	11	2019

Table A2: Regional organizations

	RO abbreviation	RO name	Founded in	Dissolved in	N founding states	N 2019
1	AC	Arctic Council	1996		8	8
2	ACC	Arab Cooperation Council	1989	1990	4	
3	ACD	Asia Cooperation Dialogue	2001		18	34
4	ACS	Association of Caribbean States	1994		25	25
5	ACTO	Amazon Cooperation Treaty Organization	2003		8	8
6	AL	Arab League	1945		7	22
7	ALADI	Latin American Integration Association	1980		11	13
8	ALBA	Bolivarian Alliance for the Peoples of Our Americas	2004		2	10
9	AMU	Arab Maghreb Union	1989		5	5
10	ANDEAN	Andean Community	1969		5	4
11	APEC	Asia-Pacific Economic Cooperation	1989		12	21
12	ASEAN	Association of Southeast Asian Nations	1967		5	10
13	AU	African Union	2002		53	55
14	BEU	Benelux Economic Union	1960		3	3
15	BIMSTEC	Bay of Bengal Initiative for Multi-Sectoral Technical and Economic Cooperation	1997		4	7
16	BSEC	Black Sea Economic Cooperation	1992		11	12

Table A2: Regional organizations (continued)

	RO abbreviation	RO name	Founded in	Dissolved in	N founding states	N 2019
17	CACM	Central American Common Market	1960		4	5
18	CAEU	Council of Arab Economic Unity	1964		13	18
19	CALC	Cumbre de América Latina y el Caribe sobre Integración y Desarollo	2008	2010	35	35
20	CAREC	Central Asia Regional Economic Cooperation	1997		11	11
21	CARICOM	Caribbean Community	1973		4	15
22	CBSS	Council of Baltic Sea States	1992		11	12
23	CCTS	Cooperation Council of Turkic Speaking States	2009		4	5
24	CE	Conseil de l'Entente	1959		4	5
25	CEEAC	Economic Community of Central African States	1983		10	11
26	CEFTA	Central European Free Trade Association	1992		3	7
27	CELAC	Community of Latin American and Caribbean States	2011		33	33
28	CEMAC	Communauté économique et monétaire de l'Afrique centrale	1994		6	6
29	CENSAD	Community of Sahel-Saharan States	1998		6	29
30	CEPGL	Economic Community of the Great Lakes Countries	1976		3	3
31	CIS	Commonwealth of Independent States	1991		6	9

(continued)

Table A2: Regional organizations (continued)

	RO abbreviation	RO name	Founded in	Dissolved in	N founding states	N 2019
32	CoE	Council of Europe	1949		10	47
33	COMESA	Common Market for Eastern and Southern Africa	1994		16	21
34	Commonwealth	Commonwealth	1931		5	53
35	CPLP	Community of Portuguese Language Countries	1996		7	9
36	CSTO	Collective Security Treaty (Organization)	1992		6	6
37	EAC	East African Community	1999		3	6
38	EAEU	Eurasian Economic Union	2000		3	5
39	ECO	Economic Cooperation Organization	1984		3	10
40	ECOWAS	Economic Community of West African States	1975		12	15
41	EEA	European Economic Area	1992		19	31
42	EFTA	European Free Trade Association	1960		7	4
43	EU	European Union	1950		6	28
44	G5S	G5 du Sahel	2014		4	4
45	GCC	Gulf Cooperation Council	1981		6	6
46	GGC	Gulf of Guinea Commission	2001		5	8
47	GUAM	Organization for Democracy and Economic Development	1997		4	4
48	ICGLR	International Conference on the Great Lakes Region	2004		11	12

Table A2: Regional organizations (continued)

	RO abbreviation	RO name	Founded in	Dissolved in	N founding states	N 2019
49	IGAD	Intergovernmental Authority on Development	1996		6	8
50	IOC	Indian Ocean Commission	1982		5	5
51	IORA	Indian Ocean Rim Association	1997		11	22
52	LCBC	Lake Chad Basin Commission	1964		4	8
53	Mercosur	Mercado Commun del Sur	1994		4	5, Venezuela is suspended permanently
54	MGC	Mekong–Garga Cooperation	2000		6	6
55	MRC	Mekong River Commission	1995		4	4
56	MRU	Manu River Union	1973		2	4
57	MSG	Melanesian Spearhead Group	2007		5	5
58	NAFTA	North American Free Trade Agreement	1992		3	3
59	NATO	North Atlantic Treaty Organization	1949		12	29
60	NC	Nordic Council	1952		3	5
61	OAS	Organization of American States	1948		21	35
62	OECS	Organization of Eastern Caribbean States	1981		7	7
63	OIC	Organization of Islamic Cooperation	1969		24	57

(continued)

Table A2: Regional organizations (continued)

	RO abbreviation	RO name	Founded in	Dissolved in	N founding states	N 2019
64	OIF	Organisation Internationale de la Francophonie	1970		21	54
65	OSCE	Organization for Security and Cooperation in Europe	1975		35	57
66	PA	Pacific Alliance	2012		4	4
67	PIF	Pacific Islands Forum	1971		7	18
68	SAARC	South Asian Association for Regional Cooperation	1985		7	8
69	SACU	Southern African Customs Union	1910		4	5
70	SADC	Southern African Development Community	1992		9	16
71	SCO	Shanghai Cooperation Organization	2001		6	8
72	SELA	Latin American Economic System	1975		25	28
73	SICA	Central American Integration System	1991		6	8
74	SPC	Pacific Community	1947		6	26
75	SPECA	Special Programme for the Economies of Central Asia	1998		7	7
76	UEMOA	West African Economic and Monetary Union	1994		7	8
77	UNASUR	Union of South American Nations	2008		8	5
78	WTO	Warsaw Treaty Organization	1955	1991	8	

Table A3: RO statutes containing democratic provisions

RO	Statutes
ANDEAN	Protocolo Adicional al Acuerdo de Cartagena 'Compromiso de la Comunidad Andina por la Democracia', 1998
ASEAN	Charter of the Association of Southeast Asian Nations, 2007
AU	Lomé Declaration on the Framework for an OAU Response to Unconstitutional Changes of Government, 2000
	African Charter on Democracy, Elections and Governance, 2007
CALC	Declaración de Salvador, Bahía, 2008
CARICOM	Charter of Civil Society for the Caribbean Community, 1997
CBSS	Copenhagen Declaration, 1992
CE	Treaty of the Conseil de l'Entente, 2011
CEEAC	Bata Declaration for the Promotion of Lasting Democracy, Peace and Development in Central Africa, 1998
CELAC	Declaración de Salvador, Bahía, 2008
CENSAD	Traite Revise de la Communaute des Etats Sahelo-Sahariens (CEN-SAD), 2013
COMESA	COMESA Treaty, 1993
CPLP	Estatutos da Comunidade dos Países de Língua Portuguesa, 1996
CoE	European Convention on Human Rights, 1953
Commonwealth	Singapore Declaration of Commonwealth Principles, 1971
	The Harare Commonwealth Declaration, 1991
EAC	The Treaty for the Establishment of the East African Community, 1999
ECOWAS	Treaty of the Economic Community of West African States, 1975
	Declaration of Political Principles of the ECOWAS, 1991
	Protocol on Democracy and Good Governance, 2001
EU	Treaty establishing the European Coal and Steel Community (ECSC), 1951
	Treaty on the Functioning of the European Union, 2000
	Cotonou Agreement, 2000
ICGLR	Dar-es-salaam Declaration on Peace, Security, Democracy, and Development in the Great Lakes Region, 2004
Mercosur	Declaracion Presidencial Sobre Compromiso Democratico en el Mercosur, 1996
	Protocolo de Ushuaia Sobre Compromiso Democrático en el Mercosur, la Republica de Bolivia y la Republica de Chile, 1998
	Protocolo de Montevideo sobre Compromiso con la Democracia en el Mercosur (Ushuaia II), 2011

(continued)

Table A3: RO statutes containing democratic provisions (continued)

RO	Statutes
MSG	Agreement Establishing the Melanesian Spearhead Group, 2007
OAS	Santiago Resolution 1080, 1991
	Protocol of Washington, 1992
	Inter-American Democratic Charter
OIF	Déclaration de Bamako, 2000
	Charte de la Francophonie, 2005
OSCE	Charter of Paris for a New Europe, 1990
	Istanbul Document, 1999
PA	Acuerdo Marco de la Alianza del Pacífico, 2012
PIF	Biketawa Declaration, 2000
SADC	Treaty of the Southern African Development Community, 1992
SICA	Tegucigalpa Protocol, 1991
UNASUR	Tratado Constitutivo de la Unión de Naciones Suramericanas, 2008
	Protocolo Adicional al Tratado Constitutivo de UNASUR sobre Compromiso con la Democracia, 2010

Figure A1: Timeline Madagascar

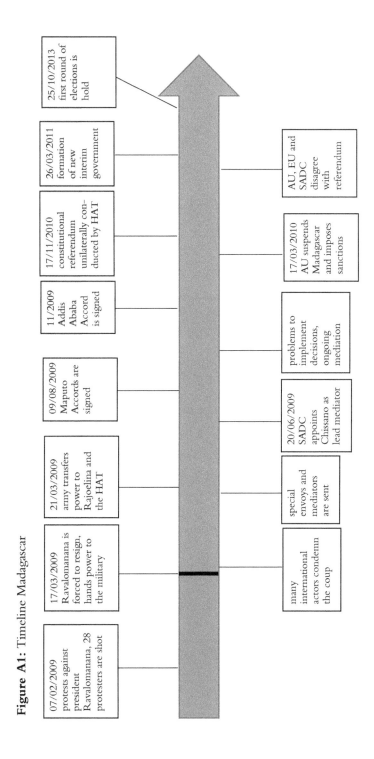

Figure A2: Timeline Niger

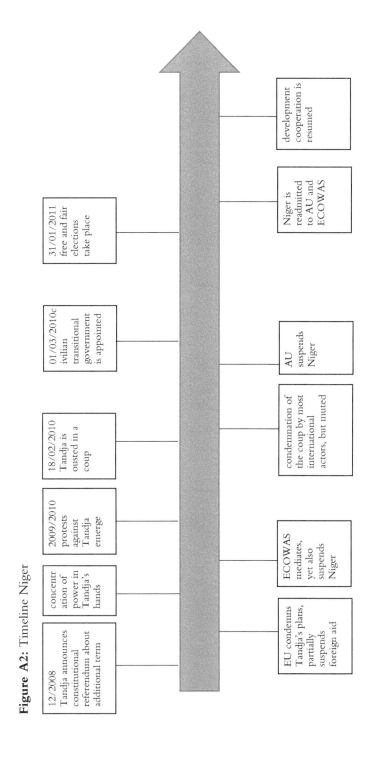

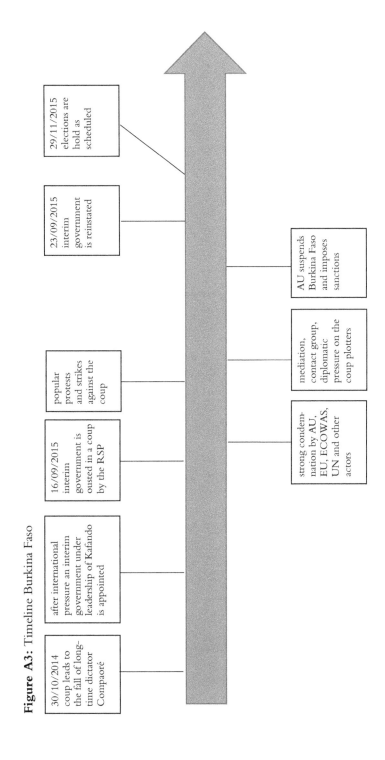

Figure A3: Timeline Burkina Faso

30/10/2014 coup leads to the fall of long-time dictator Compaoré

after international pressure an interim government under leadership of Kafando is appointed

16/09/2015 interim government is ousted in a coup by the RSP

popular protests and strikes against the coup

23/09/2015 interim government is reinstated

29/11/2015 elections are hold as scheduled

strong condemnation by AU, EU, ECOWAS, UN and other actors

mediation, contact group, diplomatic pressure on the coup plotters

AU suspends Burkina Faso and imposes sanctions

Figure A4: Timeline Zimbabwe

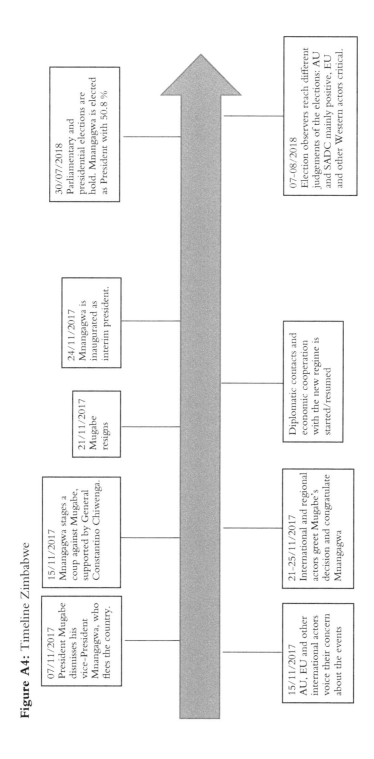

07/11/2017
President Mugabe dismisses his vice-President Mnangagwa, who flees the country.

15/11/2017
Mnangagwa stages a coup against Mugabe, supported by General Constantino Chiwenga.

21/11/2017
Mugabe resigns

24/11/2017
Mnangagwa is inaugurated as interim president.

30/07/2018
Parliamentary and presidential elections are hold. Mnangagwa is elected as President with 50.8 %

07-08/2018
Election observers reach different judgements of the elections: AU and SADC mainly positive, EU and other Western actors critical.

15/11/2017
AU, EU and other international actors voice their concern about the events

21-25/11/2017
International and regional actors greet Mugabe's decision and congratulate Mnangagwa

Diplomatic contacts and economic cooperation with the new regime is started/resumed

Notes

Chapter 1

[1] Categorization based on AU membership and the Polity IV data from Marshall et al (2018). Following common practice, countries scoring 6 or higher on the index qualify as democracies.

[2] The author is aware that many definitions of ROs rely exclusively on criteria of geographic proximity, thereby excluding organizations with linguistic or cultural membership criteria, as for instance the Commonwealth, the Community of Portuguese Language Countries (CPLP) or the Organization of Islamic Cooperation (OIC). The reason for adopting a broader definition of ROs including such organizations is that many of them have developed far-reaching anti-coup policies and play a decisive role after coups. The mechanisms and patterns of responses strongly resemble those of geographically based ROs. Therefore, excluding them from the analysis would have distorted the picture of RO responses after coups.

Chapter 2

[1] In the following, the terms will be used interchangeably.

[2] For instance, the most widely used datasets by Marshall and Marshall (2019) and Powell and Thyne (2019) agree in only 60.16 per cent of the cases in their categorization of leader changes as coups.

Chapter 3

[1] For a complete list of all ROs included in the analysis see Appendix Table A2.

[2] For an overview of the search terms see the online appendix: https://bristoluniversitypr ess.co.uk/regional-organizations-and-their-responses-to-coups.

[3] For an overview of the sources used see the online appendix: https://bristoluniversitypr ess.co.uk/regional-organizations-and-their-responses-to-coups.

[4] For a list with the acronyms and full names of the ROs see Appendix, Table A2.

[5] For a detailed discussion of the instruments, their intensity and the continuum, see Chapter 2.

Chapter 4

[1] For ROs which were founded after the beginning of the observation period in 1990 or resolved before 2019, the respective years were excluded from the analysis.

[2] Unfortunately, it is not possible to cluster the data on the coup level and RO level simultaneously. As the main research interest is on explaining differences in the responses

to different coups, it was decided to cluster on the coup level. In order to test for the robustness of the results, the complete analysis was also run with clustering on the RO level with only very minor differences (see the online appendix: https://bristoluniversi typress.co.uk/regional-organizations-and-their-responses-to-coups).

3   Obviously, the order of the responses is not immune to criticism. For instance, economic sanctions can be of rather symbolic nature and might have in practice less consequences for a country than a suspension from a RO. Similarly, in some mediation attempts ROs might sound more conciliatory than in rhetorical condemnations. However, the present scale ranging from rhetorical over diplomatic and economic to military means is well suited to illustrate the increasing severity and the rising costs of the instruments for ROs. Besides, it captures the temporal order in which the instruments are usually applied.

4   If a RO shows several responses to a coup, the strongest response was coded.

5   To illustrate, one can say that the threat to impose economic sanctions is a more severe response to a coup than an offer to mediate, but one cannot quantify the difference, for example one cannot say that the former is twice as severe as the latter.

6   In the mapping of RO responses in Chapter 3, 15 instances of positive responses to coups are also depicted. These observations are not included in the present statistical analysis. Positive responses to coups are an interesting phenomenon, which definitely deserve further study. However, positive responses are often expressed secretly by the respective international senders and therefore difficult to capture in a quantitative analysis. The issue of approving signals from ROs towards coup plotters is more extensively discussed in Chapter 5.

7   For a list of documents containing binding democratic commitments see Appendix Table A3.

8   For a detailed discussion of the success criteria, see Chapter 2.

9   Alternative measurements with longer or shorter time periods led to very similar results in the analysis.

10 For summary statistics of all independent variables, see the online appendix: https://bri stoluniversitypress.co.uk/regional-organizations-and-their-responses-to-coups.

11 For details, see the correlation table in the online appendix: https://bristoluniversitypr ess.co.uk/regional-organizations-and-their-responses-to-coups.

12 The coefficient for the success criterion is positive and significant for four of the models (Models 2, 4, 6, 8). In contrast, in the other four models it is not significant. In the model specifications which include the success variable in both stages of the model, the effect in the inflation step is not significant anymore and turns negative in Models 1, 3, 5 and 7. This dynamic is no source of concern, but a common feature of zero-inflated models which use the same variables in both sets of the equation (Long & Freese, 2006).

13 As not all variables are included in the same model, several different models are taken as the basis for the following illustrations. But as the analysis has revealed, the effects of the variables are remarkably stable across models, indicating that the choice of models has no major impact on the effect sizes.

14 In the following, the terms 'potentially active ROs' and 'relevant ROs' are used to refer to those ROs which are identified in the inflation step of the models as having a non-zero probability of taking action in the first place.

15 First, single models for each of the sets of explanatory factors were calculated. Next, all models were rerun with clustered standard errors on the RO level to account for the potential non-independence of responses by the same RO. Besides, all model specifications except the ones including the success variable were recalculated for a reduced sample which only includes the successful coups. Finally, the models were run again for a reduced sample of ROs, which only included those ROs which only responded at least once to

a coup. The robustness checks are reported in the online appendix: https://bristoluniv
ersitypress.co.uk/regional-organizations-and-their-responses-to-coups.

[16] See the online appendix: https://bristoluniversitypress.co.uk/regional-organizations-and-
their-responses-to-coups.

[17] The small number of only five coups in Oceania allowed no meaningful separate analysis,
therefore coups from Asia and Oceania are analysed in one subset. The single coup in
Europe (the Soviet Union in 1991) was omitted from the analysis.

[18] For detailed results, see the online appendix: https://bristoluniversitypress.co.uk/regio
nal-organizations-and-their-responses-to-coups.

[19] See the online appendix: https://bristoluniversitypress.co.uk/regional-organizations-and-
their-responses-to-coups.

Chapter 5

[1] For an overview of the sequence of events, see Appendix, Figure A1.

[2] The inclusion of the movements of the former presidents Ratsiraka and Zafy was geared
towards dispersing the polarization between the Ravalomanana and the Rajoelina camp.
However, in the end, the inclusion of two additional negotiation partners complicated
and delayed negotiations even further.

[3] For an overview of the sequence of events, see Appendix, Figure A2.

[4] In 1974, Seyni Kountché took over power with the help of the army. After his death,
a civilian government was reinstated in 1987 and democratic reforms were conducted
resulting in relatively free and fair elections in 1992 and 1993, in which Mahamane
Ousmane became president. Just three years later, Colonel Ibrahim Baré Maïnassara
staged a military coup against him. In 1999, Maïnassara was himself assassinated during
another coup. The fall of Tandja in 2010 was, at the time of writing, the last coup, yet
the country continues to suffer political instability.

[5] In 2007, Prime Minister Hama Amadou, who had been perceived as likely successor
of Tandja, was charged with embezzlement and sentenced to 12 months in prison. In
November 2009, the government also issued warrants against Mahamadou Issoufou and
Mahamane Ousmane, two other prominent and popular Nigerien politicians (EIU, 2010a).

[6] For an overview of the sequence of events, see Appendix, Figure A3.

[7] Powell and Thyne (2019) report successful coups in Burkina Faso in 1966, 1974, 1980,
1982, 1983 and 1987 prior to the two more recent ones in 2014 and 2015.

[8] Blaise Compaoré had repeatedly served as a mediator and key player in resolving regional
crises. His external engagement had not only brought Burkina Faso a good international
reputation and had secured the support of neighbour countries and influential Western
partners, but also diverted from democratic, security and social problems within his
own country.

[9] For an overview of the sequence of events, see Appendix, Figure A4.

[10] While different sources report varying numbers of casualties, ranging between 0 and low
single-digit numbers, Tendi (2020) argues that the coup plotters tried to downplay the
coup's level of violence.

[11] In 1987, Mugabe had forced the Zimbabwe African People's Union (ZAPU) under the
leadership of Joshua Nkomo to unite with his own party, finalized in the so-called Unity
Accord (Marx, 2017).

[12] Parliamentary elections were held in 2000 and 2005, while presidential elections took
place in 2002. From 2008 onwards, so-called harmonized elections for presidential office
as well as the parliament were held in a five-year cycle, leading to the next elections
in 2013.

[13] In the 2000 parliamentary elections, but particularly in the 2008 contest, the MDC did very well, raising justified doubts whether Mugabe could have ever stayed in power under fair electoral conditions.

[14] The direct threat by the army not to accept a victory of the opposition candidate even triggered condemnation on the subsequent SADC summit: 'The Summit expressed serious concern on the statement made by the Zimbabwe army on the outcome of the election, and urged the Government of Zimbabwe to ensure that in accordance with the multiparty political dispensation prevalent in SADC, political statements are not made by the military, but by political leaders' (SADC, 2002).

[15] As illustrated by the cases studies, also several other international actors and ROs (CENSAD, COMESA, IOC, OIF, UEMOA) were involved. But as the research focus lies on the AU, EU and ECOWAS/SADC, they are not discussed in more detail here.

References

Acharya, A. (2004) 'How Ideas Spread: Whose Norms Matter? Norm Localization and Institutional Change in Asian Regionalism', *International Organization*, 58(2): 451.

Acharya, A. (2011) 'Norm Subsidiarity and Regional Orders: Sovereignty, Regionalism, and Rule-Making in the Third World', *International Studies Quarterly*, 55(1): 95–123.

Ackermann, A. (2003) 'The Prevention of Armed Conflicts as an Emerging Norm in International Conflict Management: The OSCE and the UN as Norm Leaders', *Peace and Conflict Studies*, 10(1): 1–14.

Adelmann, M. (2004) 'Quiet Diplomacy: The Reasons behind Mbeki's Zimbabwe Policy', *Africa Spectrum*, 39(2): 249–276.

Adler, E. (2002) 'Constructivism and International Relations', in W. Carlsnaes, T. Risse & B.A. Simmons (eds) *Handbook of International Relations*, London: Sage, pp 95–118.

AFP (2010) 'African Union Suspends Niger as Junta Tightens Control', 19 February.

African Charter on Democracy, Elections and Governance (2007) Available from: https://au.int/en/treaties/african-charter-democracy-elections-and-governance [Accessed 7 May 2022].

Afrobarometer (2018) 'Bounded Autonomy. What Limits Zimbabweans' Trust in Their Courts and Electoral Commission?', Afrobarometer Policy Paper: 52 (December), Available from: https://afrobarometer.org/sites/default/files/publications/Policy%20papers/ab_r7_policypaperno52_bounded_autonomy_of_zimbabwes_electoral_commission_and_courts.pdf [Accessed 26 April 2022].

Ahmad, R.W. (2011) 'Ecowas, EU Say Niger Elections Satisfactory', *Daily Trust*, 2 March.

Ahmed, Z.S. (2016) *Regionalism and Regional Security in South Asia. The Role of SAARC.* London: Routledge.

Albrecht, H. (2015) 'The Myth of Coup-proofing: Risk and Instances of Military Coups d'État in the Middle East and North Africa, 1950–2013', *Armed Forces & Society*, 41(4): 659–687.

Ambrosio, T. (2008) 'Catching the "Shanghai Spirit": How the Shanghai Cooperation Organization Promotes Authoritarian Norms in Central Asia', *Europe-Asia Studies*, 60(8): 1321–1344.

Amnesty International, International Bar Association, ARTICLE 19, The Redress Trust & Human Rights Watch (2007) 'Zimbabwe: Human Rights in Crisis. Shadow Report to the African Commission on Human and Peoples' Rights', Available from: https://www.amnesty.org/en/docume nts/afr46/016/2007/en/ [Accessed 7 May 2022].

Andrews, S. & Honig, L. (2019) 'Elite Defection and Grassroots Democracy under Competitive Authoritarianism: Evidence from Burkina Faso', *Democratization*, 26(4): 626–644.

Arbatli, C.E. & Arbatli, E. (2016) 'External Threats and Political Survival: Can Dispute Involvement Deter Coup Attempts?' *Conflict Management and Peace Science*, 33(2): 115–152.

Arceneaux, C. & Pion-Berli, D. (2007) 'Issues, Threats, and Institutions: Explaining OAS Responses to Democratic Dilemmas in Latin America', *Latin American Politics and Society*, 49(2): 1–31.

Ariotti, M. (2016) 'Election Note: Burkina Faso's 2015 Presidential and Legislative Elections', *Electoral Studies*, 44: 445–448.

Asuelime, L.E. (2018) 'A Coup or not a Coup: That is the Question in Zimbabwe', *Journal of African Foreign Affairs*, 5(1): 5–24.

AU (2002) 'Zimbabwe. Report of the Fact-Finding Mission', June, Available from: https://www.achpr.org/states/missionreport?id=51 [Accessed 7 May 2022].

AU (2009a) 'Communiqué of the 180th Meeting of the Peace and Security Council', 17 March, Available from: https://www.peaceau.org/en/article/ communique-of-the-180th-meeting-of-the-peace-and-security-council [Accessed 7 May 2022].

AU (2009b) 'Press Statement of the 169th Meeting of the Peace and Security Council', 2 October, Available from: https://www.peaceau.org/en/resou rce/documents?keywords=&organ=90&theme=&conflict=&location= &txtEndDate=2009-12-31&txtStartDate=2009-01-01&txtDate=yyyy- mm-dd&orderByDate=newest&orderByName=alpha-a-z&searchMet hod=all&fulltextsearch=0&p=4 [Accessed 7 May 2022].

AU (2010a) 'Communiqué of the 216th Meeting of the Peace and Security Council', 19 February, Available from: https://www.peaceau.org/en/arti cle/communique-of-the-216th-meeting-of-the-peace-and-security-coun cil-1 [Accessed 7 May 2022].

AU (2010b) 'Press Statement of the 232nd Meeting of the Peace and Security Council', 17 June, Available from: https://www.peaceau.org/en/article/ press-statement-of-the-232nd-meeting-of-the-peace-and-security-coun cil [Accessed 7 May 2022].

AU (2011) 'Communiqué of the 266th Meeting of the Peace and Security Council', 16 March, Available from: https://www.peaceau.org/en/arti cle/communique-of-the-266th-meeting-of-the-peace-and-security-coun cil [Accessed 7 May 2022].

AU (2014) 'Press Release: The African Union Welcomes the Steps Taken towards a Civilian-Led Transition in Burkina Faso', 17 November, Available from: https://au.int/en/newsevents/20141117/african-union-welco mes-steps-taken-towards-civilian-led-transition-burkina-faso [Accessed 7 May 2022].

AU (2015a) 'Communiqué of the 544th Meeting of the Peace and Security Council', 18 September, Available from: https://www.peaceau.org/en/ article/communique-of-the-544th-psc-meeting-on-the-situation-in-burk ina-faso [Accessed 7 May 2022].

AU (2015b) 'Communiqué of the 547th Meeting of the Peace and Security Council at the level of Heads of State and Government', 26 September, Available from: https://reliefweb.int/report/burkina-faso/communiqu-547th-meeting-psc-level-heads-state-and-government-situation-burkina [Accessed 7 May 2022].

AU (2015c) 'Press Release: The African Union Concerned by the Situation in Burkina Faso', 4 February, Available from: https://reliefweb.int/report/ burkina-faso/african-union-concerned-situation-burkina-faso [Accessed 7 May 2022].

AU (2015d) 'Press Release: The African Union Reiterates Its Full Support to the Transition in Burkina Faso and to its Successful Conclusion within the Agreed Timeframe', 7 December, Available from: https://archives. au.int/handle/123456789/6145?show=full [Accessed 7 May 2022].

AU (2017a) 'Statement by the Chairperson of the African Union Commission on the Situation in Zimbabwe', Available from: https://au.int/en/pressr eleases/20171115/statement-chairperson-african-union-commission-situat ion-zimbabwe [Accessed 7 May 2022].

AU (2017b) 'Statement of the Chairperson of the Commission of the African Union on the Situation in Zimbabwe', Available from: https:// au.int/en/pressreleases/20171121/statement-chairperson-commission-afri can-union-situation-zimbabwe [Accessed 7 May 2022].

AU (2018) 'African Union Election Observation Mission to the 30 July and 8 September 2018 Harmonised Elections in Zimbabwe', Available from: https://au.int/en/documents/20190514/report-african-union-election-observation-mission-30-july-and-8-september-2018 [Accessed 7 May 2022].

AU, ECOWAS & UN (2015) 'Joint Press Release of ECOWAS, the African Union and the United Nations on the Situation in Burkina Faso', 17 September, Available from: https://www.peaceau.org/en/article/160 [Accessed 7 May 2022].

Aydin, A. (2010) 'Where Do States Go? Strategy in Civil War Intervention', *Conflict Management and Peace Science*, 27(1): 47–66.

Bader, J., Grävingholt, J. & Kästner, A. (2010) 'Would Autocracies Promote Autocracy? A Political Economy Perspective on Regime-Type Export in Regional Neighbourhoods', *Contemporary Politics*, 16(1): 81–100.

Bagozzi, B.E., Hill, D.W., Moore, W.H. & Mukherjee, B. (2015) 'Modeling Two Types of Peace: The Zero-inflated Ordered Probit (ZiOP) Model in Conflict Research', *Journal of Conflict Resolution*, 59(4): 728–752.

Balch-Lindsay, D. & Enterline, A.J. (2000) 'Killing Time: The World Politics of Civil War Duration, 1820–1992', *International Studies Quarterly*, 44: 615–642.

Bamidele, O. & Ayodele, B. (2018) 'In the Service of Democratic Governance: The African Union Normative Framework on Unconstitutional Change of Government and ECOWAS Protocol on Good Governance and Democracy in the Post-Arab Spring', *Journal of Asian and African Studies*, 53(1): 132–146.

Banjo, A. (2008) 'The Politics of Succession Crisis in West Africa: The Case of Togo', *International Journal on World Peace*, 25(2): 33–55.

Bapat, N.A., Heinrich, T., Kobayashi, Y. & Morgan, T.C. (2013) 'Determinants of Sanctions Effectiveness: Sensitivity Analysis Using New Data', *International Interactions*, 39(1): 79–98.

Bapat, N.A. & Kwon, B.R. (2015) 'When Are Sanctions Effective? A Bargaining and Enforcement Framework', *International Organization*, 69(1): 131–162.

Barbarinde, O. (2011) 'The African Union and the Quest for Security Governance in Africa', in E.J. Kirchner & R. Dominguez (eds) *The Security Governance of Regional Organizations*, Abingdon: Routledge, pp 273–299.

Barclay, P. (2010) *Zimbabwe: Years of Hope and Despair*, London: Bloomsbury.

Barqueiro, C., Seaman, K. & Towey, K.T. (2016) 'Regional Organizations and Responsibility to Protect: Normative Reframing or Normative Change?' *Politics and Governance*, 4(3): 37–49.

Barracca, S. (2007) 'Military Coups in the Post-Cold War Era: Pakistan, Ecuador and Venezuela', *Third World Quarterly*, 28(1): 137–154.

Baudais, V. & Chauzal, G. (2011) 'Briefing: The 2010 Coup d'État in Niger: A Prateorian Regulation of Politics?' *African Affairs*, 110(439): 295–304.

BBC (2015) 'Burkina Faso Coup Crisis: Key Players', 26 September, Available from: https://www.bbc.co.uk/news/world-africa-34318822 [Accessed 26 April 2022].

BBC (2017) 'Zimbabwe Latest: Mugabe in Crunch Talks over His Future', 16 November, Available from: https://www.bbc.co.uk/news/world-afr ica-42006777 [Accessed 26 April 2022].

Beardsley, K. & Schmidt, H. (2012) 'Following the Flag or Following the Charter? Examining the Determinants of UN Involvement in International Crises, 1945–2002', *International Studies Quarterly*, 56(1): 33–49.

Beardsworth, N., Cheeseman, N. & Tinhu, S. (2019) 'Zimbabwe: The Coup that Never Was, and the Election that Could Have Been', *African Affairs*, 118(472): 580–596.

Belkin, A. & Schofer, E. (2003) 'Toward a Structural Understanding of Coup Risk', *Journal of Conflict Resolution*, 47(5): 594–620.

Bell, C. & Sudduth, J.K. (2017) 'The Causes and Outcomes of Coup during Civil War', *Journal of Conflict Resolution*, 61(7): 1432–1455.

Bertelsmann Stiftung (2010) Niger Country Report 2010, Available from: https://bti-project.org/en/?&cb=00000 [Accessed 7 May 2022].

Bertelsmann Stiftung (2014) Burkina Faso Country Report 2014, Available from: https://bti-project.org/en/?&cb=00000 [Accessed 7 May 2022].

Biketawa Declaration (2000) Available from: https://pacificsecurity.net/resource/biketawa-declaration/ [Accessed 7 May 2022].

Bjarnesen, J. & Lanzano, C. (2015) 'Burkina Faso's One-Week Coup and Its Implications for Free and Fair Elections'. Nordic Africa Institute Policy Note: 10.

Bjørnskov, C., Freytag, A. & Gutmann, J. (2018) 'Coups, Regime Transition, and the Dynamics of Press Freedom'. CESifo Working Paper No. 719, Available from: https://www.cesifo.org/en/publikationen/2018/working-paper/coups-regime-transition-and-dynamics-press-freedom [Accessed 7 May 2022].

Black, N. (2013) 'When Have Violent Civil Conflicts Spread? Introducing a Dataset of Substate Conflict Contagion', *Journal of Peace Research*, 50(6): 751–759.

Bloomfield, A. (2016) 'Norm Antipreneurs and Theorising Resistance to Normative Change', *Review of International Studies*, 42(2): 310–333.

Böhmelt, T., Escribà-Folch, A. & Pilster, U. (2019) 'Pitfalls of Professionalism? Military Academies and Coup Risk', *Journal of Conflict Resolution*, 63(5): 1111–1139.

Böhmelt, T. & Pilster, U. (2015) 'The Impact of Institutional Coup-Proofing on Coup Attempts and Coup Outcomes', *International Interactions*, 41(1): 158–182.

Boniface, D.S. (2002) 'Is There a Democratic Norm in the Americas – An Analysis of the Organization of American States', *Global Governance*, 8: 365–381.

Börzel, T.A., Goltermann, L., Lohaus, M. & Striebinger, K. (eds) (2012) *Roads to Regionalism: Genesis, Design and Effects of Regional Organizations*, Farnham: Ashgate.

Börzel, T.A. & van Hüllen, V. (eds) (2015) *Governance Transfer by Regional Organizations: Patching Together a Global Script*, New York: Palgrave Macmillan.

Boulden, J. (Ed.) (2013) *Responding to Conflict in Africa: The United Nations and Regional Organizations*, New York: Palgrave Macmillan.

Bove, V., Gleditsch, K.S. & Sekeris, P.G. (2016) '"Oil above Water": Economic Interdependence and Third-party Intervention', *Journal of Conflict Resolution*, 60(7): 1251–1277.

Bove, V. & Rivera, M. (2015) 'Elite Co-optation, Repression, and Coups in Autocracies', *International Interactions*, 41(3): 453–479.

Bratton, M. & Penar, P. (2018) 'Dropping the Democracy Ball in Southern Africa', *Taiwan Journal of Democracy*, 14(1): 41–65.

Brown, C.S., Fariss, C.J. & McMahon, R.B. (2015) 'Recouping after Coup-Proofing: Compromised Military Effectiveness and Strategic Substitution', *International Interactions*, 42(1): 1–30.

Byron, J. (2011) 'The Caribbean Community's "Fourth Pillar": The Evolution of Regional Security Governance', in E.J. Kirchner and R. Dominguez (eds) *The Security Governance of Regional Organizations*, Abingdon: Routledge, pp 136–162.

Cardenas, S. (2004) 'Norm Collision: Explaining the Effects of International Human Rights Pressure on State Behavior', *International Studies Review*, 6(2): 213–231.

Casper, B.A. & Tyson, S.A. (2014) 'Popular Protest and Elite Coordination in a Coup d'État', *The Journal of Politics*, 76(2): 548–564.

Cederman, L.-E., Gleditsch, K.S., Salehyan, I. & Wucherpfennig, J. (2013) 'Transborder Ethnic Kin and Civil War', *International Organization*, 67(2): 389–410.

Chacha, M. & Powell, J. (2017) 'Economic Interdependence and Post-coup Democratization', *Democratization*, 24(5): 819–838.

Chané, A.-L. & Killander, M. (2018) 'EU Cooperation with Regional Organizations in Africa', KU Leuven, Working Paper No. 197.

Chanona, A. (2011) 'Regional security Governance in the Americas: the OAS', in E.J. Kirchner & R. Dominguez (eds) *The Security Governance of Regional Organizations*, Abingdon: Routledge, pp 107–135.

Charron, A. (2013) 'Sanctions and Africa: United Nations and Regional Responses', in J. Boulden (ed) *Responding to Conflict in Africa. The United Nations and Regional Organizations*, New York: Palgrave Macmillan, pp 77–98.

Charter of the Association of Southeast Asian Nations (2007) Available from: https://treaties.un.org/Pages/showDetails.aspx?objid=080000028 025f1e4 [Accessed 7 May 2022].

Chauprade, A. (2009) 'Sauver Madagascar. Entretien avec Andry Rajoelina', *La Revue*, 21 March.

Checkel, J.T. (1997) 'International Norms and Domestic Politics: Bridging the Rationalist–Constructivist Divide', *European Journal of International Relations*, 3(4): 473–495.

Cheeseman, N. & Klaas, B. (2018) *How to Rig an Election*. New Haven, CT: Yale University Press.

Chimage, A. (2015) 'The Electoral Authoritarian Regimes and election violence: The case of Manicaland Communities in Zimbabwe 2008–2013', PhD thesis, University of Freiburg.

Clark, D.H. & Regan, P.M. (2019) Mass Mobilization Project, Available from: https://massmobilization.github.io/ [Accessed 8 September 2019].

Clifton, M.T., Bapat, N.A. & Kobayashi, Y. (2014) 'The Threat and Imposition of Sanctions: Updating the TIES Dataset', *Conflict Management and Peace Science*, 31(5): 541–558.

Closa, C. (2013) 'Institutional Design of Democratic Conditionality in Regional Organizations', European University Institute, EUI Working Papers: 45, Available from: https://doi.org/10.2139/ssrn.2355307 [Accessed 26 April 2022].

Closa, C. & Palestini, S. (2018) 'Tutelage and Regime Survival in Regional Organizations' Democracy Protection', *World Politics*, 70(3): 443–476.

Clottey, P. (2010) 'ECOWAS Abhors Coup D'états, Says President Chambas', *Voice of America*, 17 February.

Coe, B. (2015) 'Sovereignty Regimes and the Norm of Noninterference in the Global South: Regional and Temporal Variation', *Global Governance*, 21: 275–298.

Collier, P. & Hoeffler, A. (2005) 'Coup Traps: Why Does Africa Have so Many Coups d'Etat?', Working Paper, University of Oxford: Centre for the Study of African Economies.

Collins, C. & Fraenkel, J. (2012) 'Conflict Prevention in the Commonwealth: The 2000 Fiji Coup', *International Negotiation*, 17(3): 449–484.

Collins, K. (2009) 'Economic and Security Regionalism among Patrimonial Authoritarian Regimes: The Case of Central Asia', *Europe-Asia Studies*, 61(2): 249–281.

Connolly, L. (2013) 'The Troubled Road to Peace: Reflections on the Complexities of Resolving the Political Impasse in Madagascar', Policy & Practice Brief, African Centre for the Constructive Resolution of Disputes, 18 February.

Cooper, A.F. & Legler, T. (2001) 'The OAS Democratic Solidarity Paradigm: Questions of Collective and National Leadership', *Latin American Politics and Society*, 43(1): 103–126.

Cooper, A.F. & Legler, T. (2005) 'A Tale of Two Mesas: The OAS Defense of Democracy in Peru and Venezuela', *Global Governance*, 11(4): 425–444.

Coppedge, M. (2012) *Democratization and Research Methods*, New York: Cambridge University Press.

Cortell, A.P. & Davis, J.W. (2005) 'When Norms Clash: International Norms, Domestic Practices, and Japan's Internalisation of the GATT/WTO', *Review of International Studies*, 31(1): 3–25.

Croissant, A. (2004) 'Riding the Tiger: Civilian Control and the Military in Democratizing Korea', *Armed Forces & Society*, 30(3): 357–381.

Croissant, A., Kuehn, D., Chambers, P. & Wolf, S.O. (2010) 'Beyond the Fallacy of Coup-ism: Conceptualizing Civilian Control of the Military in Emerging Democracies', *Democratization*, 17(5): 950–975.

Crush, J. & Tevera, D. (eds) (2010) *Zimbabwe's Exodus. Crisis, Migration, Survival*, Kingston: Southern African Migration Programme.

Cunningham, D.E., Skrede Gleditsch, K. & Salehyan, I. (2009) 'It Takes Two: A Dyadic Analysis of Civil War Duration and Outcome', *Journal of Conflict Resolution*, 53(4): 570–597.

Curtice, T.B. & Arnon, D. (2020) 'Deterring Threats and Settling Scores: How Coups Influence Respect for Physical Integrity Rights', *Conflict Management and Peace Science*, 37(6): 655–673.

Daily Independent (2010) 'Nigeria; ECOWAS Leader Demands Fresh Polls in Niger', 25 February.

Dandashly, A. (2015) 'The EU Response to Regime Change in the Wake of the Arab Revolt: Differential Implementation', *Journal of European Integration*, 37(1): 37–56.

d'Aspremont, J. (2010) 'Responsibility for Coups d'Etat in International Law', *Tulane Journal of International & Comparative Law*, 18(2): 451–475.

David, S.R. (1987) *Third World Coups d'Etat and International Security*, Baltimore, MD: Johns Hopkins University Press.

Davies, M. (2018) 'Regional Organisations and Enduring Defective Democratic Members', *Review of International Studies*, 44(1): 174–191.

de Bruin, E. (2018) 'Preventing Coups d'Etat: How Counterbalancing Works', *Journal of Conflict Resolution*, 7(3): 1–26.

de Bruin, E. (2019) 'Will There Be Blood? Explaining Violence during Coups d'Etat', *Journal of Peace Research*, 56(6): 797–811.

de Bruin, E. (2020) *How to Prevent Coups d'État: Counterbalancing and Regime Survival*, Ithaca, NY: Cornell University Press.

Deitelhoff, N. & Zimmermann, L. (2019) 'Norms under Challenge: Unpacking the Dynamics of Norm Robustness', *Journal of Global Security Studies*, 4(1): 2–17.

Derman, B. & Kaarhus, R. (eds) (2013) *In the Shadow of a Conflict: Crisis in Zimbabwe and Its Effects in Mozambique, South Africa and Zambia*. Harare: Weaver Press.

Derpanopoulos, G., Frantz, E., Geddes, B. & Wright, J. (2016) 'Are Coups Good for Democracy?' *Research & Politics*, 3(1): 1–7.

Dersso, S.A. (2017) 'Defending Constitutional Rule as a Peacemaking Enterprise: The Case of the AU's Ban of Unconstitutional Changes of Government', *International Peacekeeping*, 24(4): 639–660.

Dimitrova, A. & Dragneva, R. (2009) 'Constraining External Governance: Interdependence with Russia and the CIS as Limits to the EU's Rule Transfer in the Ukraine', *Journal of European Public Policy*, 16(6): 853–872.

Donno, D. (2010) 'Who Is Punished? Regional Intergovernmental Organizations and the Enforcement of Democratic Norms', *International Organization*, 64(4): 593–625.

Donno, D. (2013) *Defending Democratic Norms: International Actors and the Politics of Electoral Misconduct*, Oxford: Oxford University Press.

DPA (2010) 'Roundup: African Union Suspends Niger after Coup, 20 February.

Dwyer, M. (2017) 'Situating Soldiers' Demands: Mutinies and Protests in Burkina Faso', *Third World Quarterly*, 38(1): 219–234.

Dzimiri, P. (2017) 'African Multilateral Responses to the Crisis in Zimbabwe: A Responsibility to Protect Perspective', *Strategic Review for Southern Africa*, 39(2): 50–77.

Easton, M.R. & Siverson, R.M. (2018) 'Leader Survival and Purges after a Failed Coup d'État', *Journal of Peace Research*, 55(5): 596–608.

ECOWAS (2001) 'Protocol on Democracy and Good Governance', Available from: https://www2.ohchr.org/english/law/compilation_democracy/ecowasprot.htm [Accessed 7 May 2022].

ECOWAS (2009a) 'Final Communiqué Extraordinary Summit of ECOWAS Heads of State and Government', 17 October, Available from: https://ecowas.int/ecowas-law/application-of-ecowas-law/ [Accessed 7 May 2022].

ECOWAS (2009b) 'Final Communiqué Thirty-Eighth Ordinary Session of the Authority of ECOWAS Heads of State and Government', 22 June, Available from: https://ecowas.int/ecowas-law/application-of-ecowas-law/ [Accessed 7 May 2022].

ECOWAS (2014) 'Press Release: ECOWAS welcomes the solemn signing of the charter of the transition and the appointment of H.E. MICHEL KAFANDO as Transitional President in BURKINA FASO', 26 November, Available from: https://ecowas.int/ecowas-welcomes-the-solemn-signing-of-the-charter-of-the-transition-and-the-appointment-of-h-e-michel-kafando-as-transitional-president-in-burkina-faso/ [Accessed 7 May 2022].

ECOWAS (2015) 'Final Communiqué: Extraordinary Session of the Authority of Heads of State and Government on the Political Crisis in Burkina Faso', 22 September, Available from: https://ecowas.int/ecowas-law/application-of-ecowas-law/ [Accessed 7 May 2022].

EIU (2005) 'Country Report Mauritania October 2005', Available from: https://store.eiu.com/product/country-report/mauritania [Accessed 7 May 2022].

EIU (2009a) 'Country Report Madagascar June 2009', Available from: https://store.eiu.com/product/country-report/madagascar [Accessed 7 May 2022].

EIU (2009b) 'Country Report Madagascar March 2009', Available from: https://store.eiu.com/product/country-report/madagascar [Accessed 7 May 2022].

EIU (2009c) 'Country Report Niger May 2009', Available from: https://store.eiu.com/product/country-report/niger [Accessed 7 May 2022].

EIU (2009d) 'Country Report Niger November 2009', Available from: https://store.eiu.com/product/country-report/niger [Accessed 7 May 2022].

EIU (2010a) 'Country Report Niger February 2010', Available from: https://store.eiu.com/product/country-report/niger [Accessed 7 May 2022].

EIU (2010b) 'Country Report Niger May 2010', Available from: https://store.eiu.com/product/country-report/niger [Accessed 7 May 2022].

EIU (2013) 'Country Report Egypt November 2013', Available from: https://store.eiu.com/product/country-report/egypt [Accessed 7 May 2022].

EIU (2014) 'Country Report Guinea-Bissau 2nd Quarter 2014', Available from: https://store.eiu.com/product/country-report/guinea-bissau [Accessed 7 May 2022].

EIU (2015a) 'Country Report Burkina Faso 1st Quarter 2015', Available from: https://store.eiu.com/product/country-report/burkina-faso [Accessed 7 May 2022].

EIU (2015b) 'Country Report Burkina Faso 4th Quarter 2015', Available from: https://store.eiu.com/product/country-report/ burkina-faso [Accessed 7 May 2022].

EIU (2016a) 'Country Report Burkina Faso 1st Quarter 2016', Available from: https://store.eiu.com/product/country-report/ burkina-faso [Accessed 7 May 2022].

EIU (2016b) 'Country Report Burkina Faso 4th Quarter 2015', Available from: https://store.eiu.com/product/country-report/ burkina-faso [Accessed 7 May 2022].

EIU (2018) 'Country Report Zimbabwe 1st Quarter 2018', Available from: https://store.eiu.com/product/country-report/zimbabwe [Accessed 7 May 2022].

Elischer, S. (2013) 'Contingent Democrats in Action: Organized Labor and Regime Change in the Republic of Niger', GIGA Working Papers: 231.

Elischer, S. & Mueller, L. (2019) 'Niger Falls Back off Track', *African Affairs*, 118(471): 392–406.

Engel, U. (2010) 'Unconstitutional Changes of Government – New AU Policies in Defense of Democracy', Working Paper Series: 9.

Engel, U. & Mattheis, F. (eds) (2020) *The Finances of Regional Organisations in the Global South*, Abingdon: Routledge.

Engels, B. (2015) 'Political Transition in Burkina Faso: The Fall of Blaise Compaoré', *Governance in Africa*, 2(1): 1–6.

Esarey, J. & DeMeritt, J.H.R. (2017) 'Political Context and the Consequences of Naming and Shaming for Human Rights Abuse', *International Interactions*, 43(4): 589–618.

Escribà-Folch, A. (2013) 'Accountable for What? Regime Types, Performance, and the Fate of Outgoing Dictators, 1946–2004', *Democratization*, 20(1): 160–185.

Escribà-Folch, A., Böhmelt, T. & Pilster, U. (2020) 'Authoritarian Regimes and Civil–Military Relations: Explaining Counterbalancing in Autocracies', *Conflict Management and Peace Science*, 37(5): 559–579.

Esen, B. & Gumuscu, S. (2017) 'Turkey: How the Coup Failed', *Journal of Democracy*, 28(1): 59–73.

EU (2009a) 'Declaration by the Presidency on behalf of the European Union on Madagascar', 6 February, Available from: https://ec.europa.eu/commiss ion/presscorner/detail/en/PESC_09_18 [Accessed 7 May 2022].

EU (2009b) 'Declaration by the Presidency on behalf of the European Union on recent developments in Madagascar', 20 March, Available from: https:// ec.europa.eu/commission/presscorner/detail/en/pesc_09_35 [Accessed 7 May 2022].

EU (2010a) 'Press Release: Council sets out roadmap for resuming development cooperation with Niger', 27 September, Available from: https://ec.europa. eu/commission/presscorner/detail/en/pres_10_251 [Accessed 7 May 2022].

EU (2010b) 'Statement by the spokesperson of HR of the European Union Catherine Ashton on Niger', 19 February, Available from: https://www. globaldefence.net/archiv/defence-news/euniger [Accessed 7 May 2022].

EU (2011a) 'Niger. Final Report of the Election Observation Mission of the European Union', Available from: https://ec.europa.eu/info/strategy/relati ons-non-eu-countries/types-relations-and-partnerships/election-observation/ mission-recommendations-repository/missions/182 [Accessed 7 May 2022].

EU (2011b) 'Press Release: Niger: EU to Observe the Presidential and Legislative Elections', 19 January, Available from: https://ec.europa.eu/ commission/presscorner/detail/en/ip_11_51 [Accessed 7 May 2022].

EU (2011c) 'Press Statement by Mrs Catherine Ashton, High Representative for External Affairs and Security Politics of the European Union and Vice-President of the European Commission and Mr Andris Piebalgs, Commissioner responsible for Development', 3 March, Available from: https://ec.europa.eu/commission/presscorner/detail/en/MEMO_ 11_69 [Accessed 7 May 2022].

EU (2011d) 'Statement by EU High representative Catherine Ashton and Commissioner for Development Andris Piebalgs on presidential elections in Niger', 15 March, Available from: https://ec.europa.eu/commission/presscorner/detail/en/MEMO_11_165 [Accessed 7 May 2022].

EU (2014) 'Statement by HR/VP Federica Mogherini on the signing of the Charter for the Transition and the appointment of a President of the Transition in Burkina Faso', 17 November, Available from: https://eeas.eur opa.eu/headquarters/headquarters-homepage/390/statement-hrvp-feder ica-mogherini-signing-charter-transition-and-appointment-president_en [Accessed 16 March 2020].

EU (2015a) 'Press Release: The European Union Increases its Support for the Transition in Burkina Faso', 11 June, Available from https://ec.europa.eu/commission/presscorner/detail/en/ip_15_5158 [Accessed 7 May 2022].

EU (2015b) 'Statement by High Representative/Vice-President Federica Mogherini on the Coup d'État in Burkina Faso', 17 September, Available from: http://eueuropaeeas.fpfis.slb.ec.europa.eu:8084/generic-warning-sys tem-taxonomy/404/3164/statem [Accessed 16 March 2020].

EU (2015c) 'Statement by the Spokesperson on the Reinstatement of President Kafando as Leader of the Transitional Government in Burkina Faso', 23 September, Available from: http://eueuropaeeas.fpfis.slb.ec.eur opa.eu:8084/generic-warning-system-taxonomy/404/4766/statem ent-spokesperson-reinstatement-president-kafando-leader-transitional-government-burkina_en [Accessed 16 March 2020].

EU (2017) 'Statement by the High Representative/Vice-President Federica Mogherini on the Situation in Zimbabwe', 21 November, Available from: http://eueuropaeeas.fpfis.slb.ec.europa.eu:8084/headquarters/headq uarters-homepage/35984/statem [Accessed 16 March 2020].

EU (2018) 'Final Report Republic of Zimbabwe Harmonised Elections 2018', Available from: https://ec.europa.eu/info/strategy/relations-non-eu-countries/types-relations-and-partnerships/election-observation/miss ion-recommendations-repository/missions/14 [Accessed 7 May 2022].

Ezrow, N. & Frantz, E. (2011) *Dictators and Dictatorships: Understanding Authoritarian Regimes and Their Leaders*, New York: Continuum.

Farrelly, N. (2013) 'Why Democracy Struggles: Thailand's Elite Coup Culture', *Australian Journal of International Affairs*, 67(3): 281–296.

Fehl, C. (2018) 'Navigating Norm Complexity: A Shared Research Agenda for Diverse Constructivist Perspectives', Hessische Stiftung Friedens- und Konfliktforschung, PRIF Working Papers: 41.

Findley, M.G. & Marineau, J.F. (2015) 'Lootable Resources and Third-Party Intervention into Civil Wars', *Conflict Management and Peace Science*, 32(5): 465–486.

Finer, S.E. (1962) *The Man on Horseback: The Role of the Military in Politics*, London: Pall Mall Press.

Finnemore, M. (1996) 'Constructing Norms of Humanitarian Intervention', in P.J. Katzenstein (ed) *The Culture of National Security*, New York: Columbia University Press, pp 153–185.

Finnemore, M. & Sikkink, K. (1998) 'International Norm Dynamics and Political Change', *International Organization*, 52(4): 887–917.

Firth, S. (2013) 'Australia's Policy towards Coup-Prone and Military Regimes in the Asia-Pacific: Thailand, Fiji and Burma', *Australian Journal of International Affairs*, 67(3): 357–372.

Foot, R. (2012) 'Asia's Cooperation and Governance: The Role of East Asian Regional Organizations in Regional Governance: Constraints and Contributions', *Japanese Journal of Political Science*, 13(1): 133–142.

Foster, G.D. (2005) 'Civil–Military Relations: The Postmodern Democratic Challenge', *World Affairs*, 167(3): 91–100.

Fosu, A.K. (2002) 'Political Instability and Economic Growth: Implications of Coup Events in Sub-Saharan Africa', *American Journal of Economics and Sociology*, 61(1): 329–348.

Francis, D.J. (2010) 'Peacekeeping in a Bad Neighbourhood: The Economic Community of West African States (ECOWAS) in Peace and Security in West Africa', *African Journal on Conflict Resolution*, 9(3): 87–116.

Franck, T.M. (1992) 'The Emerging Right to Democratic Governance', *The American Journal of International Law*, 86(1): 46–91.

Freedom House (2008) 'Country Report Madagascar', Available from: https://freedomhouse.org/reports/publication-archives [Accessed 7 May 2022].

Freyburg, T., Lavenex, S., Schimmelfennig, F., Skripka, T. & Wetzel, A. (2009) 'EU Promotion of Democratic Governance in the Neighbourhood', *Journal of European Public Policy*, 16(6): 916–934.

Galetovic, A. & Sanhueza, R. (2000) 'Citizens, Autocrats, and Plotters: A Model and New Evidence on Coups d'État', *Economics and Politics*, 12(2): 183–204.

Gassebner, M., Gutmann, J. & Voigt, S. (2016) 'When to Expect a Coup d'État? An Extreme Bounds Analysis of Coup Determinants', *Public Choice*, 169(3–4): 293–313.

Gerling, L. (2017) 'Urban Protests, Coups d'état and Post-Coup Regime Change', *Peace Economics, Peace Science and Public Policy*, 23(4): 1–8.

Gerring, J. & Thomas, C.W. (2005) 'Comparability. A Key Issue in Research Design', Committee on Concepts and Methods, Working Paper: 4.

Ghobarah, H.A., Huth, P. & Russett, B. (2003) 'Civil Wars Kill and Maim People – Long after the Shooting Stops', *American Political Science Review*, 97(2): 189–202.

GISAT-BF (2015a) 'Conclusions of the Inaugural Meeting of International Follow-Up and Support Group for the Transition in Burkina Faso', 13 January, Available from: http://archives.au.int/handle/123456789/2764 [Accessed 7 May 2022].

GISAT-BF (2015b) 'Conclusions of the Second Meeting of the International Follow-Up and Support Group for the Transition in Burkina Faso', 30 March, Available from: https://archives.au.int/handle/123456789/2766 [Accessed 7 May 2022].

GISAT-BF (2015c) 'Joint Press Release of the International Follow-up and Support Group for the Transition in Burkina Faso (GISAT-BF)', 18 September, Available from: https://reliefweb.int/report/burkina-faso/joint-press-release-international-support-group-and-transition-support-burkina [Accessed 7 May 2022].

Giumelli, F. (2013) *The Success of Sanctions: Lessons Learned from the EU Experience*, Farnham: Ashgate.

Gong, X. & Rao, M. (2016) 'The Economic Impact of Prolonged Political Instability: A Case Study of Fiji', *Policy Studies*, 37(4): 370–386.

Grauvogel, J. (2015) 'Regional Sanctions against Burundi: The Regime's Argumentative Self-entrapment', *The Journal of Modern African Studies*, 53(2): 169–191.

Grebe, J. (2010) 'And They Are Still Targeting: Assessing the Effectiveness of Targeted Sanctions against Zimbabwe', *Africa Spectrum*, 45(1): 3–29.

Grewal, S. & Kureshi, Y. (2019) 'How to Sell a Coup: Elections as Coup Legitimation', *Journal of Conflict Resolution*, 63(4): 1001–1031.

Grugel, J.B. (2004) 'New Regionalism and Modes of Governance – Comparing US and EU Strategies in Latin America', *European Journal of International Relations*, 10(4): 603–626.

Hagberg, S. (2015) '"Thousands of New Sankaras": Resistance and Struggle in Burkina Faso', *Africa Spectrum*, 50(3): 109–121.

Hammerstad, A. (2005) 'Domestic Threats, Regional Solutions? The Challenge of Security Integration in Southern Africa', *Review of International Studies*, 31(1): 69–87.

Hartmann, C. (2017) 'ECOWAS and the Restoration of Democracy in The Gambia', *Africa Spectrum*, 52(1): 85–99.

Hartmann, C. & Striebinger, K. (2015) 'Writing the Script? ECOWAS's Military Intervention Mechanism', in T.A. Börzel & V. van Hüllen (eds) *Governance Transfer by Regional Organizations: Patching Together a Global Script*, New York: Palgrave Macmillan, pp 68–83.

Hauge, W. (2010) 'When Peace Prevails: The Management of Political Crisis in Ecuador, Madagascar, Tunisia, and Venezuela', *Alternatives: Global, Local, Political*, 35(4): 469–493.

Hawkins, D. & Shaw, C. (2008) 'Legalising Norms of Democracy in the Americas', *Review of International Studies*, 34(3): 459–480.

Hegre, H. & Sambanis, N. (2006) 'Sensitivity Analysis of Empirical Results on Civil War Onset', *Journal of Conflict Resolution*, 50(4): 508–535.

Heiduk, F. (2011) 'From Guardians to Democrats? Attempts to Explain Change and Continuity in the Civil–Military Relations of Post-authoritarian Indonesia, Thailand and the Philippines', *The Pacific Review*, 24(2): 249–271.

Henneberg, I. (2021) 'International Contact Groups: Ad Hoc Coordination in International Conflict Management', *South African Journal of International Affairs*, 27(4): 445–472.

Hentz, J.J., Söderbaum, F. & Tavares, R. (2009) 'Regional Organizations and African Security: Moving the Debate Forward', *African Security*, 2(2–3): 206–217.

Herz, M., Siman, M. & Telles, A.C. (2017) 'Regional Organizations, Conflict Resolution and Mediation in South America', in M.A. Suarez, R.D. Villa & B. Weiffen (eds) *Power Dynamics and Regional Security in Latin America*, London: Palgrave Macmillan, pp 123–148.

Hettne, B. & Söderbaum, F. (2006) 'The UN and Regional Organizations in Global Security: Competing or Complementary Logics?', *Global Governance*, 12: 227–232.

Hinthorne, L.L. (2011) 'Democratic Crisis or Crisis of Confidence? What Local Perceptual Lenses Tell Us about Madagascar's 2009 Political Crisis', *Democratization*, 18(2): 535–561.

Hiroi, T. & Omori, S. (2013) 'Causes and Triggers of Coups d'État: An Event History Analysis', *Politics & Policy*, 41(1): 39–64.

Hiroi, T. & Omori, S. (2015) 'Policy Change and Coups: The Role of Income Inequality and Asset Specificity', *International Political Science Review*, 36(4): 441–456.

Horning, N.R. (2008) 'Strong Support for Weak Performance: Donor Competition in Madagascar', *African Affairs*, 107(428): 405–431.

Houle, C. (2016) 'Why Class Inequality Breeds Coups but not Civil Wars', *Journal of Peace Research*, 53(5): 680–695.

Houle, C. & Bodea, C. (2017) 'Ethnic Inequality and Coups in Sub-Saharan Africa', *Journal of Peace Research*, 54(3): 382–396.

Hovi, J., Huseby, R. & Sprinz, D.F. (2005) 'When Do (Imposed) Economic Sanctions Work?', *World Politics*, 57(4): 479–499.

Hoyle, J.A. (2019) 'To Govern, or Not to Govern? Opportunity and Post-Coup Military Behaviour in Egypt 2011–2014', *Democratization*, 26(6): 993–1010.

Hufbauer, G.C., Schott, J.J. & Elliott, K.A. (1990) *Economic Sanctions Reconsidered*, New York: Institute for International Economics.

Humphreys, M. & Weinstein, J.M. (2006) 'Handling and Manhandling Civilians in Civil War', *American Political Science Review*, 100(3): 429–447.

ICG (2002) 'All Bark and No Bite? The International Response to Zimbabwe's Crisis', Africa Report: 40, Available from: https://www.crisisgroup.org/africa/southern-africa/zimbabwe/all-bark-and-no-bite-international-response-zimbabwes-crisis [Accessed 8 May 2022].

ICG (2008) 'Zimbabwe: Prospects from a Flawed Election', Africa Report: 138, Available from: https://www.crisisgroup.org/africa/southern-africa/zimbabwe/zimbabwe-prospects-flawed-election [Accessed 8 May 2022].

ICG (2010a) 'Madagascar: Crisis Heating Up', Africa Report: 166, Available from: https://www.crisisgroup.org/africa/southern-africa/madagascar/madagascar-crisis-heating [Accessed 8 May 2022].

ICG (2010b) 'Madagascar: sortir du cycle de crises', Africa Report: 156, Available from: https://www.crisisgroup.org/fr/africa/southern-africa/madagascar/madagascar-ending-crisis [Accessed 8 May 2022].

ICG (2013) 'Burkina Faso: With or Without Compaoré, Times of Uncertainty', Africa Report: 205, Available from: https://www.crisisgroup.org/africa/west-africa/burkina-faso/burkina-faso-or-without-compaore-times-uncertainty [Accessed 8 May 2022].

ICG (2014) 'A Cosmetic End to Madagascar's Crisis?', Africa Report: 218, Available from: https://www.crisisgroup.org/africa/southern-africa/madagascar/cosmetic-end-madagascar-s-crisis [Accessed 8 May 2022].

ICG (2015a) 'Burkina Faso: cap sur octobre', Africa Briefing: 112, Available from: https://www.crisisgroup.org/fr/africa/west-africa/burkina-faso/burkina-faso-meeting-october-target [Accessed 8 May 2022].

ICG (2015b) 'Burkina Faso: neuf mois pour achever la transition', Africa Report: 222, Available from: https://www.crisisgroup.org/fr/africa/west-africa/burkina-faso/burkina-faso-nine-months-complete-transition [Accessed 8 May 2022].

ICG (2016) 'Zimbabwe: Stranded in Stasis', Africa Briefing: 118, Available from: https://www.crisisgroup.org/africa/southern-africa/zimbabwe/zimbabwe-stranded-stasis [Accessed 8 May 2022].

ICG (2017) 'Zimbabwe's "Military-assisted Transition" and Prospects for Recovery', Africa Briefing: 134, Available from: https://www.crisisgroup.org/africa/southern-africa/zimbabwe/b134-zimbabwes-military-assisted-transition-and-prospects-recovery [Accessed 8 May 2022].

ICG (2021) 'After the Coup, Restoring Sudan's Transition', Q&A / Africa, Available from: https://www.crisisgroup.org/africa/horn-africa/sudan/after-coup-restoring-sudans-transition [Accessed 8 May 2022].

ICG (2022) 'One Year On from the Myanmar Coup', Q&A / Asia, Available from: https://www.crisisgroup.org/asia/south-east-asia/myanmar/one-year-myanmar-coup [Accessed 8 May 2022].

ICG-M (2009) '1st Consultative Meeting of the International Contact Group on Madagascar', Available from: https://malagasyaho.blogspot.com/2009/05/madagascar-communique-of-consultative.html [Accessed 12 May 2022].

Ikome, F.N. (2007) 'Good Coups and Bad Coups. The Limits of the African Union's Injunction on Unconstitutional Changes of Power in Africa', Institute for Global Dialogue, Occasional Paper: 55.

IMF (2019) Direction of Trade Statistics, Available from: https://data.imf.org/?sk=9D6028D4-F14A-464C-A2F2-59B2CD424B85 [Accessed 8 September 2019].

Janowitz, M. (1977) *Military Institutions and Coercion in the Developing Countries*, Chicago: University of Chicago Press.

Jetschke, A. & Lenz, T. (2013) 'Does Regionalism Diffuse? A New Research Agenda for the Study of Regional Organizations', *Journal of European Public Policy*, 20(4): 626–637.

Johnson, J. & Thyne, C.L. (2016) 'Squeaky Wheels and Troop Loyalty: How Domestic Protests Influence Coups d'État, 1951–2005', *Journal of Conflict Resolution*, 62(3): 597–625.

Jones, D.M. (2008) 'Security and Democracy: The ASEAN Charter and the Dilemmas of Regionalism in South-East Asia', *International Affairs*, 84(4): 735–756.

Kamrava, M. (2009) 'Royal Factionalism and Political Liberalization in Qatar', *Middle East Journal*, 63(3): 401–420.

Kang, S. & Meernik, J. (2005) 'Civil War Destruction and the Prospects for Economic Growth', *The Journal of Politics*, 67(1): 88–109.

Kim, N.K. (2016) 'Revisiting Economic Shocks and Coups', *Journal of Conflict Resolution*, 60(1): 3–31.

Kinney, D.H. (2019) 'Politicians at Arms: Civilian Recruitment of Soldiers for Middle East Coups', *Armed Forces & Society*, 45(4): 681–701.

Kirchner, E.J. & Dominguez, R. (eds) (2011) *The Security Governance of Regional Organizations*, Abingdon: Routledge.

Koga, K. (2016) *Reinventing Regional Security Institutions in Asia and Africa: Power Shifts, Ideas, and Institutional Change*, London: Routledge.

Kotzian, P., Knodt, M. & Urdze, S. (2011) 'Instruments of the EU's External Democracy Promotion', *Journal of Common Market Studies*, 49(5): 995–1018.

Krcmaric, D. (2018) 'Varieties of Civil War and Mass Killing: Reassessing the Relationship between Guerrilla Warfare and Civilian Victimization', *Journal of Peace Research*, 55(1): 18–31.

Kuehn, D. (2017) 'Midwives or Gravediggers of Democracy? The Military's Impact on Democratic Development', *Democratization*, 24(5): 783–800.

Lachapelle, J. (2020) 'No Easy Way Out: The Effect of Military Coups on State Repression', *The Journal of Politics*, 82(4): 1354–1372.

Lantis, J.S. & Wunderlich, C. (2018) 'Resiliency Dynamics of Norm Clusters: Norm Contestation and International Cooperation', *Review of International Studies*, 44(3): 570–593.

Lanz, D. & Gasser, R. (2013) 'A Crowded Field: Competition and Coordination in International Peace Mediation', Working Paper, Mediation Arguments, Centre for Mediation in Africa 2, Available from: https://www.swisspeace.ch/publications/reports/a-crowded-field-competition-and-coordination-in-international-peace-mediation [Accessed 12 May 2022].

Leech, N.L. & Onwuegbuzie, A.J. (2009) 'A Typology of Mixed Methods Research Designs', *Quality & Quantity*, 43(2): 265–275.

Legler, T. & Tieku, T.K. (2010) 'What Difference Can a Path Make? Regional Democracy Promotion Regimes in the Americas and Africa', *Democratization*, 17(3): 465–491.

Lehoucq, F. & Pérez-Liñán, A. (2014) 'Breaking Out of the Coup Trap: Political Competition and Military Coups in Latin America', *Comparative Political Studies*, 47(8): 1105–1129.

Leininger, J. (2014) 'A Strong Norm for Democratic Governance in Africa', Working Paper, International Institute for Democracy and Electoral Assistance, Available from: https://www.die-gdi.de/en/others-publi cations/article/a-strong-norm-for-democratic-governance-in-africa/ [Accessed 12 May 2022].

Leininger, J. (2015) 'Against All Odds: Strong Democratic Norms in the African Union', in T.A. Börzel and V. van Hüllen (eds) *Governance Transfer by Regional Organizations: Patching Together a Global Script*, New York: Palgrave Macmillan, pp 51–67.

Le Monde (2017) 'Alpha Condé: "la lutte contre le terrorisme en Afrique ne peut être faite que par des Africains"', 17 November.

Levitt, B.S. (2006) 'A Desultory Defense of Democracy: OAS Resolution 1080 and the Inter-American Democratic Charter', *Latin American Politics and Society*, 48(3): 93–123.

Lindberg, S.I. & Clark, J.F. (2008) 'Does Democratization Reduce the Risk of Military Interventions in Politics in Africa?' *Democratization*, 15(1): 86–105.

Lombaerde, P. de & Schulz, M. (eds) (2009) *The EU and World Regionalism: The Makability of Regions in the 21st Century*, Farnham: Ashgate.

Lombaerde, P. de, Söderbaum, F., van Langenhove, L. & Baert, F. (2010) 'The Problem of Comparison in Comparative Regionalism', *Review of International Studies*, 36(3): 731–753.

Lomé Declaration (2000) Available from: https://archives.au.int/handle/123456789/571 [Accessed 8 May 2022].

Long, J.S. & Freese, J. (2006) *Regression Models for Categorical Dependent Variables Using Stata*, College Station, TX: Stata Press.

Magaisa, A. (2019) 'Zimbabwe: An Opportunity Lost', *Journal of Democracy*, 30(1): 143–157.

Magnani, V. (2018) L'armée entre en scène au Zimbabwe Coup de théâtre ou théâtre sans fin?, Centre Afrique subsaharienne, Working Paper, Available from: https://www.ifri.org/fr/publications/notes-de-lifri/larmee-entre-scene-zimbabwe-coup-de-theatre-theatre-fin [Accessed 12 May 2022].

Mangu, A.M. (2014) 'The African Union and the Promotion of Democracy and Good Political Governance under the African Peer-Review Mechanism: 10 Years on', *Africa Review*, 6(1): 59–72.

Manirakiza, P. (2016) 'Insecurity Implications of Unconstitutional Changes of Government in Africa: From Military to Constitutional Coups', *Journal of Military and Strategic Studies*, 17(2): 86–106.

Manners, I. (2002) 'Normative Power Europe: A Contradiction in Terms?' *Journal of Common Market Studies*, 40(2): 235–258.

Marcum, A.S. & Brown, J.N. (2016) 'Overthrowing the "Loyalty Norm": The Prevalence and Success of Coups in Small-coalition Systems, 1950 to 1999', *Journal of Conflict Resolution*, 60(2): 256–282.

Maringira, G. (2017) 'Politics, Privileges, and Loyalty in the Zimbabwe National Army', *African Studies Review*, 60(2): 93–113.

Marinov, N. & Goemans, H. (2014) 'Coups and Democracy', *British Journal of Political Science*, 44(4): 799–825.

Marshall, M.G., Gurr, T.R. & Jaggers, K. (2018) Polity IV Project: Political Regime Characteristics and Transitions, 1800–2017, Available from: http://www.systemicpeace.org/polityproject.html [Accessed 20 December 2018].

Marshall, M.G. & Marshall, D.R. (2019) Coups d'État Events, 1946–2017, Available from: https://www.systemicpeace.org/inscrdata.html [Accessed 7 October 2019].

Marsteintredet, L. & Malamud, A. (2019) 'Coup with Adjectives: Conceptual Stretching or Innovation in Comparative Research?', *Political Studies*, 64(4): 1014–1035.

Marx, C. (2017) *Mugabe: Ein afrikanischer Tyrann*, Munich: Beck.

Masaki, T. (2016) 'Coups d'État and Foreign Aid', *World Development*, 79: 51–68.

Maunganidze, O. (2009) 'Madagascar: Anatomy of a Recurrent Crisis', Institute for Security Studies (ISS), Situation Report.

May, R.J. (2013) 'Papua New Guinea: From Coup to Reconciliation', *Journal of Democracy*, 24(1): 165–171.

McCoy, J.L. (2006) 'International Response to Democratic Crisis in the Americas, 1990–2005', *Democratization*, 13(5): 756–775.

McGowan, P.J. (2003) 'African Military Coups d'État, 1956–2001: Frequency, Trends and Distribution', *The Journal of Modern African Studies*, 41(3): 339–370.

McMahon, E. & Baker, S. (2006) *Piecing a Democratic Quilt? Regional Organizations and Universal Norms*, Bloomfield, CT: Kumarian Press.

Melnykovska, I., Plamper, H. & Schweickert, R. (2012) 'Do Russia and China Promote Autocracy in Central Asia?', *Asia Europe Journal*, 10(1): 75–89.

Meyer, A. (2011) 'Regional Conflict Management in Central Africa: From FOMUC to MICOPAX', in F. Söderbaum & R. Tavares (eds) *Regional Organizations in African Security*, Abingdon: Routledge, pp 90–106.

Mhango, G.A. (2012) 'Is Quiet Diplomacy in Consonance with Meaningful Peacemaking in SADC? Lessons from Zimbabwe', *Southern African Peace and Security Studies*, 1(1): 14–25.

Michael, A. (2013) 'Sovereignty vs. Security: SAARC and Its Role in the Regional Security Architecture in South East Asia', *Harvard Asia Quarterly*, 15(2): 37–45.

Miller, A.C. (2011) 'Debunking the Myth of the "Good" Coup d'État in Africa', *African Studies Quarterly*, 12(2): 45–70.

Miller, M.K. (2012) 'Economic Development, Violent Leader Removal, and Democratization', *American Journal of Political Science*, 56(4): 1002–1020.

Miller, M.K., Joseph, M. & Ohl, D. (2018) 'Are Coups Really Contagious? An Extreme Bounds Analysis of Political Diffusion', *Journal of Conflict Resolution*, 62(2): 410–441.

Mills, K. & Bloomfield, A. (2018) 'African Resistance to the International Criminal Court: Halting the Advance of the Anti-impunity Norm', *Review of International Studies*, 44(1): 101–127.

Mnangagwa, E. (2017) President Mnangagwa's inauguration speech in full, 30 November, Available from: https://www.chronicle.co.zw/president-mnangagwas-inauguration-speech-in-full/ [Accessed 8 May 2022].

Molenaers, N., Dellepiane, S. & Faust, J. (2015) 'Political Conditionality and Foreign Aid', *World Development*, 75: 2–12.

Mueller, L. (2013) 'Democratic Revolutionaries or Pocketbook Protesters? The Roots of the 2009–2010 Uprisings in Niger', *African Affairs*, 112(448): 398–420.

Mueller, L. (2018) *Political Protest in Contemporary Africa*, Cambridge: Cambridge University Press.

Müller, M. (2019) *Simbabwe nach Mugabe – Akteure, Reformen, Konfliktfelder*, Stiftung Wissenschaft und Politik, SWP-Studie 7.

Murithi, T. (2011) 'Inter-governmental Authority on Development on the Ground: Comparing Interventions in Sudan and Somalia', in F. Söderbaum & R. Tavares (eds) *Regional Organizations in African Security*, Abingdon: Routledge, pp 68–89.

Nathan, L. (2013) 'A Clash of Norms and Strategies in Madagascar: Mediation and the AU Policy on Unconstitutional Change of Government', Center for Mediation in Africa, Mediation Arguments: 4.

Nathan, L. (2016a) 'How and Why African Mediators Compromise Democracy', Working Paper prepared for the International Conference on Mediation, University of Base, 21–23 June.

Nathan, L. (2016b) 'Situational Incompability of Good Norms: How and Why African Mediators Compromise Democracy', Working Paper Prepared for the Conference on the Ethics of Negotiation in Armed Conflicts, Centre for Ethics and the Rule of Law, University of Pennsylvania, 14–16 April.

Nathan, L. (2016c) 'Trends in Mediating in Africa Coups, 2000–2015', Working Paper presented at the International Studies Association 2016 Annual Convention, Atlanta, 16–19 March 2016.

Newman, E. & Rich, R. (2004) *The UN Role in Promoting Democracy: Between Ideals and Reality*, Tokyo and New York: United Nations University Press.

Nguyen, T.H.Y. (2002) 'Beyond Good Offices? The Role of Regional Organizations in Conflict Resolution', *Journal of International Affairs*, 55(2): 463–484.

Nolte, D. (2018) 'Costs and Benefits of Overlapping Regional Organizations in Latin America: The Case of the OAS and UNASUR', *Latin American Politics and Society*, 60(1): 128–153.

Nooruddin, I. (2002) 'Modeling Selection Bias in Studies of Sanction Efficacy', *International Interactions*, 28: 59–75.

Nordlinger, E.A. (1977) *Soldiers in Politics: Military Coups and Governments*, Englewood Cliffs, NJ: Prentice-Hall.

Nossiter, A. (2010) 'Palace in Niger Is Attacked by Soldiers', *New York Times*, 18 February.

Nugraha, I.Y. (2018) 'Human Rights Derogation during Coup Situations', *The International Journal of Human Rights*, 22(2): 194–206.

OAU (1997) 'Decisions Adopted by the Sixty-Sixth Ordinary Session of the Council of Ministers', 31 May, Available from: https://www.google.com/url?sa=t&rct=j&q=&esrc=s&source=web&cd=&cad=rja&uact=8&ved=2ahUKEwjfmczqltD3AhVV8LsIHV10AkAQFnoECAUQAQ&url=https%3A%2F%2Fau.int%2Fsites%2Fdefault%2Ffiles%2Fdecisions%2F9622-council_en_28_31_may_1997_council_ministers_sixty_sixth_ordinary_session.pdf&usg=AOvVaw3MoxBgfSXBfgCnDHN9_4S9 [Accessed 8 May 2022].

Obydenkova, A.V. & Libman, A. (2019) *Authoritarian Regionalism in the World of International Organizations: Global Perspective and the Eurasian Enigma*, Oxford: Oxford University Press.

Odinius, D. & Kuntz, P. (2015) 'The Limits of Authoritarian Solidarity: The Gulf Monarchies and Preserving Authoritarian Rule during the Arab Spring', *European Journal of Political Research*, 54(4): 639–654.

Okafor, J.C. & Okafor, U. (2015) 'ECOWAS and Democratic Reversal in West Africa: Re-visiting Military Incursion on the State Leadership', *International Affairs and Global Strategies*, 37: 120–128.

O'Kane, R. (1987) *The Likelihood of Coups*, Aldershot: Avebury.

Omede, J., Ngwube, A. & Okoroafor, C. (2018) 'The Internationalization of the Coup in Burkina Faso', *Journal of African-Centered Solutions in Peace and Security*, 2(1): 65–79.

Omorogbe, E.Y. (2011) 'A Club of Incumbents? The African Union and Coups d'État', *Vanderbilt Journal of Transnational Law*, 44: 123–154.

Onwuegbuzie, A.J. & Leech, N.L. (2010) 'Generalization Practices in Qualitative Research: A Mixed Methods Case Study', *Quality & Quantity*, 44(5): 881–892.

Panke, D. & Stapel, S. (2018) 'Exploring Overlapping Regionalism', *Journal of International Relations and Development*, 21(3): 635–662.

Panke, D. & Starkmann, A. (2018) 'Responding to Problem Pressure: When do Regional Organizations Change?', Working Paper, University of Freiburg.

Pape, R.A. (1997) 'Why Economic Sanctions Do Not Work', *International Security*, 22(2): 90–136.

Pawlitzky, C. (2009) 'Krise im Niger: Demontage der Demokratie im Namen des Volkes?', German Institute of Global and Area Studies, GIGA Focus Afrika: 6.

Percy, S.V. (2007) 'Mercenaries: Strong Norm, Weak Law', *International Organization*, 61(2): 367–397.

Pérez-Liñán, A. & Polga-Hecimovich, J. (2017) 'Explaining Military Coups and Impeachments in Latin America', *Democratization*, 24(5): 839–858.

Perry, A. (2010) 'A Coup in Niger Adds to West Africa's Instability', *Time*, 19 February.

Pevehouse, J. (2002a) 'Democracy from the Outside-In? International Organizations and Democratization', *International Organization*, 56(3): 515–549.

Pevehouse, J. (2002b) 'With a Little Help from My Friends? Regional Organizations and the Consolidation of Democracy', *American Journal of Political Science*, 46(3): 611–626.

Pevehouse, J. (2005) *Democracy from Above: Regional Organizations and Democratization*, Cambridge: Cambridge University Press.

Pilster, U. & Böhmelt, T. (2012) 'Do Democracies Engage Less in Coup-Proofing? On the Relationship between Regime Type and Civil–Military Relations', *Foreign Policy Analysis*, 8(4): 355–372.

Piplani, V. & Talmadge, C. (2016) 'When War Helps Civil–Military Relations: Prolonged Interstate Conflict and the Reduced Risk of Coups', *Journal of Conflict Resolution*, 60(8): 1368–1394.

Pirzer, C. (2012) 'MERCOSUR's Contribution to Democratic Consolidation', in T.A. Börzel, L. Goltermann, M. Lohaus and K. Striebinger (eds) *Roads to Regionalism: Genesis, Design and Effects of Regional Organizations*, Farnham: Ashgate, pp 199–214.

Poast, P. & Urpelainen, J. (2015) 'How International Organizations Support Democratization: Preventing Authoritarian Reversals or Promoting Consolidation?' *World Politics*, 67(1): 72–113.

Powell, J. (2019) 'Leader Survival Strategies and the Onset of Civil Conflict: A Coup-Proofing Paradox', *Armed Forces & Society*, 45(1): 27–44.

Powell, J. & Chacha, M. (2016) 'Investing in Stability: Economic Interdependence, Coups d'État, and the Capitalist Peace', *Journal of Peace Research*, 53(4): 525–538.

Powell, J. & Chacha, M. (2019) 'Closing the Book on Africa's First Generation Coups', *African Studies Quarterly*, 18(2): 87–94.

Powell, J., Chacha, M. & Smith, G.E. (2019) 'Failed Coups, Democratization, and Authoritarian Entrenchment: Opening Up or Digging In?' *African Affairs*, 118(471): 238–258.

Powell, J., Faulkner, C., Dean, W. & Romano, K. (2018) 'Give Them Toys? Military Allocations and Regime Stability in Transitional Democracies', *Democratization*, 25(7): 1153–1172.

Powell, J., Lasley, T. & Schiel, R. (2016) 'Combating Coups d'État in Africa, 1950–2014', *Studies in Comparative International Development*, 51(4): 482–502.

Powell, J.M. (2014a) 'An Assessment of the "Democratic" Coup Theory', *African Security Review*, 23(3): 213–224.

Powell, J.M. (2014b) 'Trading Coups for Civil War', *African Security Review*, 23(4): 329–338.

Powell, J.M. & Thyne, C.L. (2011) 'Global Instances of Coups from 1950 to 2009: A New Dataset', *Journal of Peace Research*, 48(2): 249–259.

Powell, J.M. & Thyne, C.L. (2019) Coups in the World, 1950–Present, Available from: https://www.jonathanmpowell.com/coup-detat-dataset.html [Accessed 7 October 2019].

Protocolo de Montevideo sobre Compromiso con la Democracia en el Mercosur (Ushuaia II) (2011) Available from: https://www.mercosur.int/documento/protocolo-ushuaia-compromiso-democratico-mercosur-bolivia-chile/ [Accessed 9 May 2022].

Rabinowitz, B. & Jargowsky, P. (2018) 'Rethinking Coup Risk', *Armed Forces & Society*, 44(2): 322–346.

Rajoelina, A. (2009) Phone Interview, 15 March.

Ratsimbaharison, A.M. (2016) 'The Obstacles and Challenges to Democratic Consolidation in Madagascar (1992–2009)', *International Journal of Political Science*, 2(2): 1–17.

Ratsimbaharison, A.M. (2017) 'The Politics of Labeling in International Relations: The Case of the So-Called "Coup d'Etat of March 2009" in Madagascar', *Global Journal of Human-Social Science*, 17(1): n.p.

Ratuva, S. (2011) 'The Military Coups in Fiji: Reactive and Transformative Tendencies', *Asian Journal of Political Science*, 19(1): 96–120.

Regan, P.M. (1996) 'Conditions of Successful Third-Party Intervention in Intrastate Conflicts', *The Journal of Conflict Resolution*, 40(2): 336–359.

Reiter, D. (2020) 'Avoiding the Coup-Proofing Dilemma: Consolidating Political Control while Maximizing Military Power', *Foreign Policy Analysis*, 16(3): 312–331.

Reuters (2009) 'COMESA Says Military Option for Madagascar Possible', 6 August, Available from: https://www.reuters.com/article/idINIndia-401 65720090608 [Accessed 9 May 2022].

Reuters (2010) 'Army to Run Niger until Election: ECOWAS', 22 February, Available from: https://www.reuters.com/article/uk-niger-coup-idUKTR E61K1VW20100221 [Accessed 9 May 2022].

Reyes, J., Wooster, R. & Shirrell, S. (2014) 'Regional Trade Agreements and the Pattern of Trade: A Networks Approach', *The World Economy*, 37(8): 1128–1151.

RFI (2010) 'Niger Junta Leader to Hand over Power by Next March', 6 January, Available from: https://www.rfi.fr/en/africa/20100601-niger-junta-leader-hand-over-power-next-march [Accessed 9 May 2022].

Roessler, P. (2011) 'The Enemy within: Personal Rule, Coups, and Civil War in Africa', *World Politics*, 63(2): 300–346.

Rozenas, A. & Zeigler, S.M. (2019) 'From Ballot-Boxes to Barracks: Votes, Institutions, and Post-Election Coups', *Journal of Peace Research*, 56(2): 175–189.

RTT News (2010) 'AU, ECOWAS Condemn Niger Military Coup', 19 February.

Ruggeri, A. & Burgoon, B. (2012) 'Human Rights "Naming & Shaming" and Civil War Violence', *Peace Economics, Peace Science and Public Policy*, 18(3): 1–12.

Rushton, S. (2006) 'The UN Secretary-General and Norm Entrepreneurship: Boutros Boutros-Ghali and Democracy Promotion', *Global Governance*, 14(1): 95–110.

SADC (2002) 'SADC Extra-Ordinary Summit Communiqué', Blantyre, Malawi, 14 January, Available from: https://www.sadc.int/documents-publi cations/show/7813 [Accessed 9 May 2022].

SADC (2003) 'Summit Communiqué', Dar Es Salaam, Tanzania, 25–26 August, Available from: https://www.sadc.int/documents-publications/ show/7813 [Accessed 9 May 2022].

SADC (2009) 'Communiqué Extraordinary Summit of SADC Heads of State and Government', 20 June, Available from: https://www.sadc.int/ documents-publications/show/7813 [Accessed 9 May 2022].

SADC (2017a) 'Press Release: SADC Congratulates His Excellency Emmerson Dambudzo Mnangagwa, President of the Republic of Zimbabwe', 24 November, Available from: https://www.sadc.int/news-events/news/sadc-congratulates-his-excellency-emmerson-dambudzo-mnangagwa-president-republic-zimbabwe/ [Accessed 9 May 2022].

SADC (2017b) 'SADC Statement on the Unfolding Events in the Republic of Zimbabwe by H.E. Jacob Zuma, President of the Republic of South Africa and Chairperson of the Southern African Development Community (SADC)', 15 November, Available from: https://www.sadc.int/news-eve nts/news/sadc-statement-unfolding-events-republic-zimbabwe-he-jacob-zuma-president-republic-south-africa-and-chairperson-southern-african/ [Accessed 9 May 2022].

SADC (2017c) 'Statement by the Executive Secretary of SADC Following the Resignation of President Robert Mugabe', 24 November, Available from: https://www.sadc.int/news-events/news/statement-executive-secret ary-sadc-following-resignation-president-robert-mugabe/ [Accessed 9 May 2022].

SADC (2018) 'SADC Electoral Observation Mission (SEOM) to the Republic of Zimbabwe. Preliminary Statement by His Excellency Manuel Domingos Augusto Minister of External Relations of the Republic of Angola and Head of the SEOM to the 2018 Harmonised Elections in the Republic of Zimbabwe', Available from: https://www.sadc.int/news-eve nts/news/sadc-election-observation-mission-releases-its-preliminary-statement-2018-harmonized-elections-republic-zimbabwe1/ [Accessed 9 May 2022].

Salehyan, I. & Gleditsch, K.S. (2006) 'Refugees and the Spread of Civil War', *International Organization*, 60(2): 335–366.

Sandholtz, W. (2019) 'Norm Contestation, Robustness, and Replacement', *Journal of Global Security Studies*, 4(1): 139–146.

Santiso, C. (2002) 'Promoting Democracy by Conditioning Aid? Towards a More Effective EU Development Assistance', *Internationale Politik und Gesellschaft*, 3: 107–133.

Santiso, C. (2003) 'Sisyphus in the Castle: Improving European Union Strategies for Democracy Promotion and Governance Conditionality', *The European Journal of Development Research*, 15(1): 1–28.

Saunderson-Meyer, W. (2017) 'Commentary: Africa's Deft Handling of Zimbabwe's "Coup"', *Reuters*, 21 November.

Schiel, R., Powell, J. & Daxecker, U. (2020) 'Peacekeeping Deployments and Mutinies in African Sending States', *Foreign Policy Analysis*, 16(3): 251–271.

Schiel, R.E. (2019) 'An Assessment of Democratic Vulnerability: Regime Type, Economic Development, and Coups d'État', *Democratization*, 42(10): 1–19.

Schimmelfennig, F. & Scholtz, H. (2008) 'EU Democracy Promotion in the European Neighbourhood: Political Conditionality, Economic Development and Transnational Exchange', *European Union Politics*, 9(2): 187–215.

Schoeman, M. & Muller, M. (2011) 'Southern African Development Community as Regional Peacekeeper: Myth or Reality', in F. Söderbaum & R. Tavares (eds) *Regional Organizations in African Security*, Abingdon: Routledge, pp 107–124.

Seawright, J. & Gerring, J. (2008) 'Case Selection Techniques in Case Study Research', *Political Research Quarterly*, 61(2): 294–308.

Seibert, G. (2003) 'Coup d'État in São Tomé e Príncipe. Domestic Causes, the Role of Oil and Former "Buffalo" Battalion soldiers'. ISS Paper: 81.

Shannon, M., Thyne, C., Hayden, S. & Dugan, A. (2015) 'The International Community's Reaction to Coups', *Foreign Policy Analysis*, 11(4): 363–376.

Shannon, V.P. (2000) 'Norms Are What States Make of Them: The Political Psychology of Norm Violation', *International Studies Quarterly*, 44: 293–316.

Simmons, B.A. & Jo, H. (2019) 'Measuring Norms and Normative Contestation: The Case of International Criminal Law', *Journal of Global Security Studies*, 4(1): 18–36.

Singh, N. (2014) *The Strategic Logic of Military Coups*, Baltimore, MD: Johns Hopkins University Press.

Smith, M. (2005) 'An Island among Islands: Haiti's Strange Relationship with the Caribbean Community', *Social and Economic Studies*, 54(3): 176–195.

Söderbaum, F. & Tavares, R. (eds) (2011) *Regional Organizations in African Security*, Abingdon: Routledge.

Söderbaum, F. & van Langenhove, L. (2005) 'Introduction: The EU as a Global Actor and the Role of Interregionalism', *Journal of European Integration*, 27(3): 249–262.

Souaré, I.K. (2014) 'The African Union as a Norm Entrepreneur on Military Coups d'État in Africa (1952–2012): An Empirical Assessment', *The Journal of Modern African Studies*, 52(1): 69–94.

Souaré, I.K. (2018) 'The Anti-Coup Norm', in K.P. Coleman & T.K. Tieku (eds) *African Actors in International Security*, Boulder, CO: Lynne Rienner Publishers, pp 117–136.

Sousa Santos, B. de (2005) *Democratizing Democracy: Beyond the Liberal Democratic Canon*, London: Verso.

Southall, R. (2013) 'How and Why ZANU-PF Won the 2013 Zimbabwe Elections', *Strategic Review for Southern Africa*, 35(2): 135–151.

Stapel, S. & Söderbaum, F. (2020) 'Mapping and Problematising External Funding to the African Union and the Regional Economic Communities', in U. Engel & F. Mattheis (eds) *The Finances of Regional Organisations in the Global South*, Abingdon: Routledge, pp 112–125.

Stojek, S.M. & Chacha, M. (2015) 'Adding Trade to the Equation: Multilevel Modeling of Biased Civil War Interventions', *Journal of Peace Research*, 52(2): 228–242.

Striebinger, K. (2012) 'When Pigs Fly: ECOWAS and the Protection of Constitutional Order in Events of Coups d'État', in T.A. Börzel, L. Goltermann, M. Lohaus & K. Striebinger (eds) *Roads to Regionalism: Genesis, Design and Effects of Regional Organizations*, Farnham: Ashgate, pp 179–198.

Striebinger, K. (2015) *Should I Stay or Should I Go? The Influence of International Actors on the Degree of Military Involvement after Coups d'Etat in West Africa*, Berlin: Freie Universität Berlin.

Suarez, M.A., Villa, R.D. & Weiffen, B. (eds) (2017) *Power Dynamics and Regional Security in Latin America*, London: Palgrave Macmillan.

Sudduth, J.K. & Bell, C. (2018) 'The Rise Predicts the Fall: How the Method of Leader Entry Affects the Method of Leader Removal in Dictatorships', *International Studies Quarterly*, 62(1): 145–159.

Tansey, O. (2016a) *The International Politics of Authoritarian Rule*, Oxford: Oxford University Press.

Tansey, O. (2016b) 'The Limits of the "Democratic Coup" Thesis: International Politics and Post-Coup Authoritarianism', *Journal of Global Security Studies*, 1(3): 220–234.

Tansey, O. (2017) 'The Fading of the Anti-Coup Norm', *Journal of Democracy*, 28(1): 144–156.

Tansey, O. (2018) 'Lowest Common Denominator Norm Institutionalization: The Anti-Coup Norm at the United Nations', *Global Governance*, 24: 287–305.

Tavares, R. (2010) *Regional Security: The Capacity of International Organizations*, London: Routledge.

Tavares, R. (2011) 'The Participation of SADC and ECOWAS in Military Operations: The Weight of National Interests in Decision-Making', *African Studies Review*, 54(2): 145–176.

Taylor, A. (2017) 'Zimbabwe: When a Coup Is not a Coup', *Washington Post*, 15 November.

Tendi, B.-M. (2020) 'The Motivations and Dynamics of Zimbabwe's 2017 Military Coup', *African Affairs*, 119(1): 39–67.

Terechshenko, Z., Crabtree, C., Eck, K. & Fariss, C.J. (2019) 'Evaluating the Influence of International Norms and Shaming on State Respect for Rights: An Audit Experiment with Foreign Embassies', *International Interactions*, 45(4): 720–735.

Thompson, W.R. (1974) *Grievances of Military Coup-Makers*, Beverly Hills, CA: Sage.

Thyne, C. (2017) 'The Impact of Coups d'État on Civil War Duration', *Conflict Management and Peace Science*, 34(3): 287–307.

Thyne, C. & Hitch, K. (2020) 'Democratic versus Authoritarian Coups: The Influence of External Actors on States' Postcoup Political Trajectories', *Journal of Conflict Resolution*, 64(10): 1857–1884.

Thyne, C., Powell, J., Hayden, S. & VanMeter, E. (2018) 'Even Generals Need Friends: How Domestic and International Reactions to Coups Influence Regime Survival', *Journal of Conflict Resolution*, 62(7): 1406–1432.

Thyne, C.L. (2010) 'Supporter of Stability or Agent of Agitation? The Effect of US Foreign Policy on Coups in Latin America, 1960–99', *Journal of Peace Research*, 47(4): 449–461.

Thyne, C.L. & Powell, J.M. (2016) 'Coup d'État or Coup d'Autocracy? How Coups Impact Democratization, 1950–2008', *Foreign Policy Analysis*, 26(5): 192–213.

Timans, R., Wouters, P. & Heilbron, J. (2019) 'Mixed Methods Research: What It Is and What It Could Be', *Theory and Society*, 48(2): 193–216.

Transitional Charter of Burkina Faso (2014) Available from: https://cons titutionnet.org/vl/item/transitional-charter-burkina-faso-november-2014 [Accessed 9 May 2022].

Trithart, A. (2013) 'Democratic Coups? Regional Responses to the Constitutional Crises in Honduras and Niger', *Journal of Public & International Affairs*, 24: 112–133.

Tusalem, R.F. (2010) 'Determinants of Coup d'État Events 1970–90: The Role of Property Rights Protection', *International Political Science Review*, 31(3): 346–365.

van der Vleuten, A. & Ribeiro Hoffmann, A. (2010) 'Explaining the Enforcement of Democracy by Regional Organizations: Comparing EU, Mercosur and SADC', *Journal of Common Market Studies*, 48(3): 737–758.

van Sickle, A. & Sandholtz, W. (2009) 'The Emerging Right to Democracy', in W. Sandholtz & K. Stiles (eds) *International Norms and Cycles of Change*, New York: Oxford University Press, pp 289–321.

van Wyk, J.-A. (2018) 'Sanctions and Summits: Sanctioned African Leaders and EU–Africa Summits', *South African Journal of International Affairs*, 25(4): 497–515.

Varol, O.O. (2012) 'The Democratic Coup d'État', *Harvard International Law Journal*, 53(2): 292–356.

Varol, O.O. (2017) *The Democratic Coup d'État*, New York: Oxford University Press.

von Soest, C. & Wahman, M. (2015) 'Not all Dictators Are Equal: Coups, Fraudulent Elections, and the Selective Targeting of Democratic Sanctions', *Journal of Peace Research*, 52(1): 17–31.

Webber, J.R. & Gordon, T. (2013) 'Post-Coup Honduras: Latin America's Corridor of Reaction', *Historical Materialism*, 21(3): 16–56.

Weiffen, B. (2017) 'Institutional Overlap and Responses to Political Crises in South America', in M.A. Suarez, R.D. Villa & B. Weiffen (eds) *Power Dynamics and Regional Security in Latin America*, London: Palgrave Macmillan, pp 173–197.

Weiffen, B., Wehner, L. & Nolte, D. (2013) 'Overlapping Regional Security Institutions in South America: The Case of OAS and UNASUR', *International Area Studies Review*, 16(4): 370–389.

Welsh, J.M. (2019) 'Norm Robustness and the Responsibility to Protect', *Journal of Global Security Studies*, 4(1): 53–72.

Wet, E. de (2019) 'The Role of Democratic Legitimacy in the Recognition of Governments in Africa since the End of the Cold War', *International Journal of Constitutional Law*, 17(2): 470–478.

Wetzel, A. & Orbie, J. (2011) 'With Map and Compass on Narrow Paths and through Shallow Waters: Discovering the Substance of EU Democracy Promotion', *European Foreign Affairs Review*, 16: 705–725.

Wig, T. & Rød, E.G. (2016) 'Cues to Coup Plotters: Election as Coup Triggers in Dictatorships', *Journal of Conflict Resolution*, 60(5): 787–812.

Wilén, N. & Williams, P.D. (2018) 'The African Union and Coercive Diplomacy: The Case of Burundi', *The Journal of Modern African Studies*, 56(4): 673–696.

Witt, A. (2013) 'Convergence on Whose Terms? Reacting to Coups d'État in Guinea and Madagascar', *African Security*, 6(3–4): 257–275.

Witt, A. (2017) 'Mandate Impossible: Mediation and the Return to Constitutional Order in Madagascar (2009–2013)', *African Security*, 10(3–4): 205–222.

Witt, A. (2020) *Undoing Coups: The African Union and Post-Coup Intervention in Madagascar*, London: Zed Books.

Wobig, J. (2015) 'Defending Democracy with International law: Preventing Coup Attempts with Democracy Clauses', *Democratization*, 22(4): 631–654.

Wood, R.M. (2014) 'Opportunities to Kill or Incentives for Restraint? Rebel Capabilities, the Origins of Support, and Civilian Victimization in Civil War', *Conflict Management and Peace Science*, 31(5): 461–480.

World Bank (2019) World Development Indicators, Available from: https://databank.worldbank.org/source/world-development-indicators [Accessed 7 October 2019].

Worrall, J. (2017) *International Institutions of the Middle East: The GCC, Arab League, and Arab Maghreb Union*, London: Routledge.

Xiang, J. (2010) 'Relevance as a Latent Variable in Dyadic Analysis of Conflict', *The Journal of Politics*, 72(2): 484–498.

Yarwood, J. (2016) 'The Power of Protest', *Journal of Democracy*, 27(3): 51–60.

Yukawa, T., Hidaka, K. & Kushima, K. (2020) 'Coups and Framing: How Do Militaries Justify the Illegal Seizure of Power?' *Democratization*, 27(5): 816–835.

Yukawa, T., Kushima, K. & Hidaka, K. (2019) 'Coups, Justification, and Democracy', OSIPP Discussion Paper, Available from: https://ideas.repec.org/p/osp/wpaper/19e003.html [Accessed 9 May 2022]

Zounmenou, D.D. & Loua, R.S. (2011) 'Confronting Complex Political Crises in West Africa: An Analysis of ECOWAS Responses to Niger and Côte d'Ivoire', Institute for Security Studies, ISS Paper: 230.

Index

References to figures appear in *italic* type; those in **bold** type refer to tables. References to endnotes show both the page number and the note number (221n2).